Computer Architecture
and Communications

D1078414

1λʃ

Other titles in this series

Applications in Business Data Processing
Carol Beech and Janice Burn

Business Information Systems
Chris Clare

Information Analysis
Janice Burn and Mike O'Neil

Introduction to Programming
Jeffrey Naylor

Software: Its Design, Implementation and Support
Michael Curtis, David Leigh and Roy Newton

THE COMPUTER STUDIES SERIES

Computer Architecture and Communications

Neil Willis

Series Editor: David Hatter

Paradigm

Paradigm Publishing Ltd
131 Holland Park Avenue
London W11 4UT

First published 1986. Reprinted 1988

British Library Cataloguing in Publication Data

Willis, Neil
     Computer architecture and communications—
     (The computer studies series)
     1. Computer architecture
     I. Title   II. Series
     004.2′1   QA76.9.A73

     ISBN 0–948825–40–5

Printed at The Bath Press, Avon

Contents

About the book

This book has been written to provide a student text that presents, in a logical and straightforward way, the ideas and concepts of computer architecture and the principles of computer communication. It is particularly suitable for students taking BTEC Higher National Certificate and Diploma courses in computer studies, and also for many computer studies and computer science degree courses. It covers the range of computer architecture from the very building blocks that go to make up a computer—the logic gate—to collections of computers linked together—networks.

No prerequisite knowledge of computers is assumed, but many of the concepts will be more easily grasped if they are related to a parallel course in assembler language programming. Indeed, assembler level programming might well form the practical or tutorial part of such a course in computer architecture.

The discussion is not restricted to one particular processor: in illustration of the principles, examples are drawn from a variety of computers. Clearly, however, the principles can equally well be illustrated by reference to the particular facilities available on the computer used for the student's practical work. Most chapters include problems designed to reinforce understanding of the application of the theory.

A general introduction, in Chapter 1, to all the basic concepts of computer systems gives definitions of processors, memory, peripherals, backing store and communications. The following chapters then form three broad sections.

Chapter 2 deals with the basic logic circuits that are the building blocks in the design of a computer.

In Chapters 3 to 10 the structure of a single processor system is explained in detail: peripherals, file store, numbers and character codes, memory, machine codes and addressing techniques, the CPU, interrupt mechanisms and input/output.

The final chapters are concerned with networks of computers. After defining a network and discussing its possible topologies, Chapters 11 introduces the ISO OSI reference model. Chapters 12 to 14 then deal with physical transmission, protocols and network aspects such as routing, finishing with a discussion of local area networks.

About the series

This series of books is the first which presents an integrated approach to the complete range of topics needed by students of Computer Studies who are currently on the Higher National Certificate and Diploma courses or the first two years of a degree course.

Each volume has been so designed through its approach and treatment of a particular subject area to stand alone: at the same time the books in the series together give a comprehensive and integrated view of computing with special attention devoted to applications in business and industry.

The authors are experienced teachers and practitioners of computing and are responsible for the design of computing syllabuses and courses for the Business and Technician Education Council, the British Computer Society and the Council for National Academic Awards. In addition many of them are members of the appropriate boards of studies for the three organisations. Their combined experience in computing practice covers all aspects of the subject.

The series presents a uniform and clear treatment of the subject and will fit well into the syllabuses of the great majority of undergraduate courses.

Acknowledgements

This book is based on lectures that I have given over some years on courses in Computer Studies and Information Technology, and consequently much of the text and many of the problems have been class tested. I am grateful to many students who have provided feedback on the material.

Very useful comments were also provided by the Series Editor, Dave Hatter, during his reading of the entire text. I am also grateful to the Computer Services Department of Sheffield City Polytechnic for their typing of the text into a word processor.

Texas Instruments have kindly given permission for the reproduction of extracts from their Chip manual in Chapter 2.

I am also very grateful to my wife Lynda and to Debra and Andrew for their support during the writing of this text. In particlar, Lynda did a heroic job in helping with the proofreading.

Finally, I would like to acknowledge the patience of my flute teacher, Judith Appleton, who, in the final stages of writing, had to endure some poor flute playing due to lack of practice.

Neil Willis

Basic concepts of computer systems

Computers are constructed from many different component parts and by connecting these parts together in different ways computers with different facilities can be built. However, there is within this variation much that is common. This chapter introduces the basic concepts that are common to all computers.

1.1 Computers and computer systems

The first computers were built in the late 1940s. In comparison with modern computers they were extremely limited as they were designed to solve one particular problem or a small class of problems. Throughout the 1950s and 1960s developments were made which allowed the same computer to be used for many different classes of problem, and during this time technological changes from the valve to the transistor allowed more complex and more reliable computers to be built. It was also during this period that software was developed opening up the computer to the less specialised user. This was achieved by means of programming languages which did not require the user to have intimate knowledge of the construction of the computer. There was also a lot of software developed which made the computers more flexible, and this gave rise to the term 'computer system'.

During the 1970s there were significant developments in the electronics technology industry which brought about a dramatic fall in the price of computers and meant that it was possible to build computer systems which were constructed from more than one computer.

1.1.1 What is a computer?

A computer is a piece of electronic equipment which, when given some data, will process that data in some pre-defined way to produce the required results. It is fundamental to the concept that the operations which take place do so in a finite time. A computer requires some means of accepting data, somewhere to store the sequence of operations to be carried out, some means of performing the calculations required and finally a method of communicating the results. These facilities are common to any computer regardless of the task to which it will be put.

1.1.2 The difference between computers and computer systems

A computer system takes the basic computer and by the addition of software makes the computer more flexible so that it can be used to solve many different types of problem. In the simplest case there is a one-to-one correspondence between a computer and a computer system, i.e. the computer system uses only one computer.

However, the tendency is to develop computer systems that consist of several computers (distributed computer systems). There are two important reasons for this. First, the nature of the environment may best be supported by providing many localised computers, which also provide flexibility by communicating with each other. Secondly, there may be a security aspect which requires certain information held by the computer system to be maintained separate from other parts of the system. Such systems are called computer *networks,* an example of which is a medical information system for a hospital. Each ward requires rapid access to information about patients on that ward, but when a patient is moved within the hospital the information relating to that patient should still be available. Also by distributing patient information it is inherently more secure.

These variations of requirements arise, for example, when many computers form a computer system but where some of the computers are *general purpose* and others are *dedicated* machines.

A general-purpose computer is one which can be used to solve many types of problem. A dedicated computer is one used for one task only, e.g. controlling a process in the manufacturing industry. In a computer system constructed from such components the general-purpose computer could be used to extract information maintained by the dedicated machine.

A dedicated computer is the same as a general-purpose computer in its fundamental construction. It is only dedicated by the connections made between it and the environment in which it operates. An illustration would be a computerised railway system where there will be specialised sensors, some able to detect the presence of a train and others to check that a set of

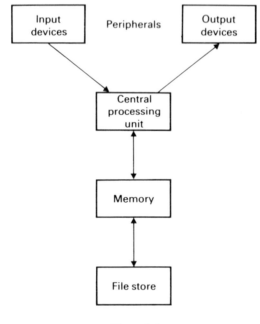

Figure 1.1

points have moved, as well as the electronically controlled equipment which moves the points. The computer which controls such a system will be dedicated to the task of controlling the movement of trains and will not be used for any other task. These specialised sensors and the equipment which causes mechanical operations to take place are called *transducers*.

1.2 Basic components of a computer

Computers, whether dedicated or general purpose, can be represented by the block diagram shown in Figure 1.1. Obviously in particular instances some of the components may assume greater importance.

1.2.1 Central processing unit

The central processing unit (CPU) provides central control of the functions of the whole computer. In order to function correctly a computer requires all necessary data to be made available to the component parts of the machine at exactly the right time. If this is not done the user of the computer would find that the results produced by the computer would be wrong. As well as providing control functions the CPU also provides the arithmetic and logic capability of the computer.

1.2.2 Memory

The memory of a computer is used to hold two distinct types of information: first the data which is to be processed by the computer, and secondly the finite sequence of operations which will process that data to produce the results. The sequence of operations is called an *algorithm*. The algorithm is said to operate upon a *data structure*, the data structure being a description of the *form* of the data rather than the particular data values. The combination of an algorithm and its associated data structure is called a *program*.

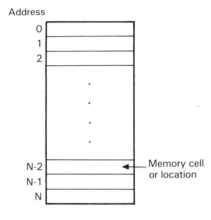

Figure 1.2

The memory of a computer is divided into many similar cells or locations each of which is individually addressable as illustrated in Figure 1.2. To say that a cell is *addressable* means that a CPU can uniquely identify a location within a program so that it can hold a specified data item value. Similarly, the address can be used by the algorithmic part of a program to alter the sequence of execution of operations. Instructions are stored in the memory of the computer in sequence, one location after another. Computers are extremely good at carrying out repetitive sequences of operations because they are fast and accurate.

This situation is very similar to the way in which knitting patterns are described. The knitter is told the sequence of stitches required to produce a desired effect and then told to repeat that sequence until the desired length has been achieved.

In order that repetitions can be generated in algorithms it is necessary for the sequence to be able to go back over itself, thus generating the necessary repetitions. The addresses of the memory locations are utilised by some of the operations within the computer to achieve this effect.

Most memories are unable to distinguish from the contents of a location whether it contains data, algorithm or irrelevant information. It is up to the user of a computer to ensure that appropriate locations of memory are filled with sensible data and an algorithm before commencing any processing.

1.2.3 File store

The file store holds bulk data and its storage capacity is very large. A single unit of file store may contain ten or a hundred times more locations than the memory itself and the whole store may be constructed from many such units. In order that this large amount of storage space can be more easily managed it is logically split into smaller sections called *files*. It is then usual to associate some of the files with a particular program. However, in most computer systems there is nothing to stop any file being processed by any program provided the data is stored in the correct format according to the data structure in the program. It is usual to have a means of identifying users of the computer system so that only those with appropriate authorisation can process specific data files with particular programs.

Memory is one of the more expensive components of a computer and is not an infinite resource. Hence, within one computer it would not take long before the memory was filled by programs which, although required, were not currently being executed. The file store provides a means of keeping copies of these programs available to the computer in a state of readiness. When such a stored program is required it can be brought from the file store and placed in memory so that it can be executed. On completion, the program will be returned to the file store until required again.

Probably a more important use of file store is for the recording of bulk data. The program describes the data structure upon which it will operate but not the actual data values to be manipulated. These data values have to be stored somewhere and presented to the program as required. In the majority of data processing applications there is far too much data to be processed for it all to be in memory at the same time. This bulk data is stored in the file store and then transferred to the program as necessary.

1.2.4 Peripherals

The majority of data processed by a computer together with the programs has to be placed in the computer by some means. A peripheral provides this communication with the outside world. Well known examples of such peripherals are printers and visual display units (VDUs).

Peripherals can be divided into three classes: input devices, output devices and i/o devices which are capable of communicating in both modes.

In a general-purpose computer system there will be many different peripherals, so that the user has a degree of flexibility and the use of peripherals is thus tailored to the needs of the application.

In a dedicated computer system it is often the peripherals which make the system dedicated. Up to this stage the computer could have been used for many different applications. The connection of certain peripherals in the form of specific transducers dedicates the computer system. Such dedication is found in process control.

In this case the computer system has to be able to respond rapidly to the requirements of the process being controlled. It would not be sufficient for this data to be transferred by a human operator. Thus it is necessary for the information collected from the parameter being sensed to be entered directly into the computer.

1.3 Putting it all together

Up to this stage it may have appeared that the only place for variation in computers and computer systems is in the nature of peripherals and in the amount of memory and file store available. This is not the case and it is the role of the computer architect to design a computer so that it will best respond to the environment in which it will be used. To this end, the computer architect has to make a great many decisions about the way in which the basic building blocks will be constructed and then how they will be connected together to form a unified solution to the problem. There is no one correct solution for a single environment because each architect has individual ideas and there is usually a financial compromise to be taken into account. Hence, given the same initial building blocks, it is possible to construct many different computers, some of which will be more appropriate to particular problem areas.

We will discuss briefly some of these design criteria at this stage but they will be expanded upon in later chapters.

1.3.1 Interconnection

The architect or designer has initially many ways in which he can connect the component parts of the computer together. By incorporating a large number of specific connections the computer can be made to process extremely quickly. This approach is, however, costly because it requires a lot of expensive electronic components.

Conversely, the components of the computer can be connected together in a far more generalised way which saves on component costs as not so many are used. In that event the computer system will process information more slowly because it is typical of such systems that the same components are used for many different data transfers. Hence some transfers may have to wait until a previous transfer has been completed. It is thus the job of the architect to choose the right compromise between speed and cost so that the computer system satisfies its design criteria.

1.3.2 Operating systems

Besides producing the computer a computer manufacturer usually provides some means of controlling the complete computer system. In very small systems this may be left to the purchaser. The computer system control mechanism is provided by means of a program called the *operating system*.

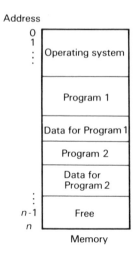

Address

Memory

Figure 1.3

The operating system is a program always available to the computer. It allows the computer to be operated at maximum efficiency within a system related to a particular environment. Figure 1.3 illustrates a possible memory layout.

A computer system provides the user with three basic resources: processing time, memory to store algorithms and data, and the use of peripherals. One measure of operating system efficiency is to see how effectively it manages these resources so as to ensure that each resource is used to the maximum. One way is to keep several programs simultaneously in a partial state of execution within the computer, each being given a share of the machine in turn. Obviously this requires a very complex operating system which will maintain a list of programs waiting to be executed for the first time, and from this list will select that program which allows it to make most effective use of the resources.

An alternative approach is to initiate a program and then let it execute until processing is completed. This will obviously be wasteful of resources, but the operating system will be much simpler and quicker in operation.

The computer architect has to be aware of the sort of operating system to be used with the computer and the design of the computer has to take into account the proposed operating system. It is possibly true to say that there is more cost involved in the analysis, design and implementation of the operating system than there is of the underlying computer. Hence the computer and the operating system are normally designed in parallel.

1.3.3 Distribution

Increasingly the computer architect has had to become more aware of the problems caused by *distributed computer systems.*

As explained earlier, a distributed computer system is one which is constructed from several computers. Each of the computers needs to communicate with its neighbours in the system and so that this may be done in an orderly fashion facilities have to be provided either by programs within the operating system or by the CPUs of the machines. Such facilities are called *protocols.*

If copies of the same data are stored on several different computers then there has to be a mechanism to ensure that all copies have been updated before any user has access to any copy of the data.

Another major problem arises when deciding what facilities of the computer system are to be distributed. The facilities to be considered are processing capability and data storage. The spectrum ranges from a distributed system which has a central file store with many computers connected, to a system which has processing and data storage capabilities uniformly distributed.

The computer architect has to ensure that computers are constructed that can operate in all these modes or a range of computers are constructed each of which is suited to a particular role within the distributed system.

1.4 Summary

This chapter has introduced the underlying concepts of computers and computer systems. These underlying concepts will be enlarged upon in subsequent chapters. Chapters 2 to 10 essentially look at the concepts of a single computer and computer system. Chapters 11 to 14 look at the techniques involved in connecting computers together in distributed systems or networks.

Digital logic circuits and integrated circuits

Digital computers use the binary number system for representing information internally. The binary number system has two digits 0 and 1, a binary digit being called a *bit*. Information is represented by a group of bits. Using suitable coding methods this group of bits can be made to represent not only binary numbers but decimal digits, alphabetic characters or even instructions (see Chapters 5 and 7).

Although digital computers are said to represent information using binary numbers the binary digits themselves are represented by some physical characteristic or quantity which can be manipulated by electronic circuits. For example, a particular system may use different voltages to represent the two digits 0 and 1. Typically this may be 5 volts to represent a binary 1 and 0 volts to represent binary 0. In actual fact there would usually be a tolerance of about 1 volt around these figures, so that binary zero would be represented by a voltage between 4.5 and 5.5 volts and a binary 0 by a voltage between 0 and 1 volt. This chapter is concerned with the basic fundamental circuits that manipulate these voltages and hence their representative binary values.

2.1 Logic gates

In mathematics, the manipulation of binary variables with operations that have a logic meaning is known as binary logic. In digital computer systems this manipulation of binary information (voltage signals) is done by logic

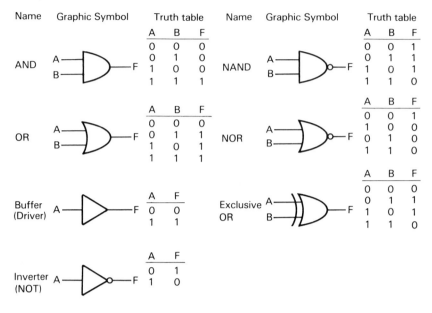

Name	Graphic Symbol	Truth table			Name	Graphic Symbol	Truth table		
		A	B	F			A	B	F
		0	0	0			0	0	1
AND		0	1	0	NAND		0	1	1
		1	0	0			1	0	1
		1	1	1			1	1	0
		A	B	F			A	B	F
		0	0	0			0	0	1
OR		0	1	1	NOR		1	0	0
		1	0	1			0	1	0
		1	1	1			1	1	0
		A	F				A	B	F
		0	0				0	0	0
Buffer		1	1		Exclusive		0	1	1
(Driver)					OR		1	0	1
							1	1	0
		A	F						
		0	1						
Inverter		1	0						
(NOT)									

Figure 2.1

circuits known as *logic gates*. There are a variety of basic logic gates some
of which are listed in Figure 2.1. Each logic gate is represented by a distinct
graphical symbol and its operation can be described by either an algebraic
function or a truth table. A truth table defines what the output of a logic
gate is for all the combinations of inputs.

Referring to Figure 2.1, an AND gate produces an output of logic 1 if
input A *and* input B are both 1, otherwise the output is logic 0. Note that
the logic gates shown in Figure 2.1 having two inputs may in fact have more
than two. In the case of the AND gate the output is 1 only when *all* the
inputs are 1. With the OR gate the output is 1 if any of the inputs are 1,
otherwise it is 0. A buffer or driver gate does not have any particular logic
function since the binary value of the output is the same as the binary value
of the input. However, its use lies in the fact that it will amplify the
incoming signal so that the current produced at its output is much greater
than that supplied at its input. This allows the buffer to drive (supply input)
many other gates which would not be possible with the small current
present on its input.

A small circle on the output of the graphic symbol indicates a logic
complement. Hence, for example, the output of a NOT gate is the inverse
(complement) of its input. The NAND and NOR gates produce an output
which is the inverse or complement of the corresponding AND and OR
gates.

The Exclusive OR gate produces an output binary value of 1 if any of its inputs is 1, but only when only one of its inputs is 1.

Note that on many logic gates an unconnected input behaves as if it were a logic 1. Many logic gates can be constructed by an equivalent circuit using other logic gates. Problems 1, 2 and 3 at the end of this chapter explore these characteristics.

2.2 Combinational circuits

A *combinational* circuit is a circuit made up of a set of connected logic gates, where the output binary values are a function of the binary input values (there are other circuits where this is not the case, described in section 2.3).

Combinational circuits are used for generating binary control functions and for implementing other logic or digital functions required. Any combinational circuit can be described by a truth table showing the relationship between the output values and the input values.

Consider some examples of combinational circuits.

2.2.1 Central heating control function

An electric pump circulates water through the radiators of a central heating system. This pump should operate only when a time switch is on and the room temperature is below a pre-selected level. The logic circuit is shown

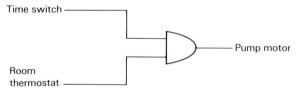

Figure 2.2

in Figure 2.2. If there are two rooms each with its own thermostat and the pump should be on if either of the thermostats is on, the circuit would be as in Figure 2.3.

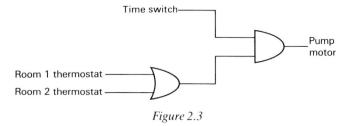

Figure 2.3

Table 2.1

Time switch	Roomstat 1	Roomstat 2	Pump motor
0	0	0	0
0	0	1	0
0	1	0	0
0	1	1	0
1	0	0	0
1	0	1	1
1	1	0	1
1	1	1	1

0 means off
1 means on

A truth table for this combinational circuit can be developed by considering every possible combination of inputs in turn, as shown in Table 2.1. This can then be checked against the truth table developed from the verbal description of the problem, and if the two truth tables agree then the logic circuit is correct.

2.2.2 Half adder

This circuit is one of a number of circuits which serve as basic building blocks for the construction of arithmetic digital functions as implemented in the arithmetic unit of a digital computer (see 8.1.2). A half-adder circuit implements the arithmetic function of the addition of two binary digits. It is called a half adder since, although it will not cater for the addition of a carry digit (from the addition of lower order bits), two such half-adder circuits can be used to implement a full adder which includes the addition of a carry digit (see 2.2.3).

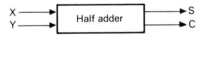

Input		Output	
X	Y	S	C
0	0	0	0
0	1	1	0
1	0	1	0
1	1	0	1

Figure 2.4

First, establish the truth table for such a half-adder device: assume that X and Y represent the two binary digits and S and C represent the sum and carry digits respectively—see Figure 2.4. To design the logic circuit examine the truth table. It can be seen that the output S is simply the

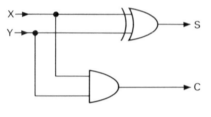

Figure 2.5

exclusive OR function of the two input values and the output C is 1 only when both inputs are 1. Hence this leads to the logic circuit shown in Figure 2.5.

2.2.3 Full adder

When adding two binary numbers together, in any bit position there are three binary digits to sum. Two of them are the significant bits to be added and the third is the carry bit from the sum of the previous lower significant bits. A full adder is a logic circuit that will add these three input bits and produce two output bits, the sum S and the carry C. Two half-adder circuits can be combined as shown in Figure 2.6.

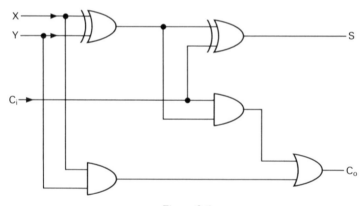

Figure 2.6

This circuit can be perhaps more clearly understood and verified by redrawing it as in Figure 2.7. The truth table, also shown in Figure 2.7, can then be developed and checked.

2.2.4 Decoders

A decoder is a circuit which takes as input a complicated bit pattern (a number coded into binary) and produces as output a signal on only one of several output lines. Hence, it decodes the input value. An example of the

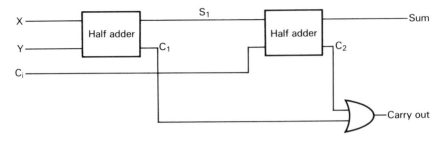

Input			Intermediate			Output	
X	Y	Carry$_{in}$	S$_1$	C$_1$	C$_2$	Sum	Carry$_{out}$
0	0	0	0	0	0	0	0
0	1	0	1	0	0	1	0
1	0	0	1	0	0	1	0
1	1	0	0	1	0	0	1
0	0	1	0	0	0	1	0
0	1	1	1	0	1	0	1
1	0	1	1	0	1	0	1
1	1	1	0	1	0	1	1

Figure 2.7

use of decoding is when a machine code instruction is being executed. A bit pattern of the 'operation code' is decoded to produce a signal activating the necessary hardware for that particular operation (see 8.1.1). Similarly, addresses of memory locations have to be decoded so that only one memory location is read from or written to (see 8.2.2).

As an example, consider a two input decoder. Since there are two inputs these can be 00, 01, 10 or 11, and hence there needs to be four outputs to indicate which one of the input combinations is present. In general, a decoder with N inputs will usually have 2^N outputs. The circuit for such a two input decoder is shown in Figure 2.8.

2.2.5 Multiplexers

The purpose of a multiplexer is to allow signals from several input lines to share fewer output lines (usually 1) by using some special control signals. Typically, a multiplexer would have i data inputs D_1 . . . D_i, one output line and n control inputs C_1 . . . C_n. The function of the circuit is to use the control inputs to select one of the data inputs and to make this signal the multiplexer's output signal.

Consider the two input multiplexer shown in Figure 2.9. The control

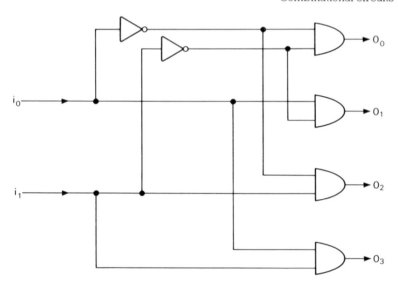

Truth table

Inputs		Outputs			
i_0	i_1	O_0	O_1	O_2	O_3
0	0	1	0	0	0
1	0	0	1	0	0
0	1	0	0	1	0
1	1	0	0	0	1

Figure 2.8

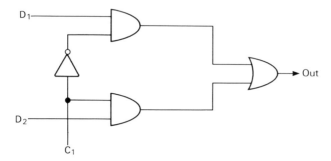

Figure 2.9

Table 2.2(a)			
C_1	D_1	D_2	Out
0	0	0	0
0	0	1	0
0	1	0	1
0	1	1	1
1	0	0	0
1	0	1	1
1	1	0	0
1	1	1	1

Table 2.2(b)	
C_1	Out
0	D_1
1	D_2

signal C_1 is used to control which of the signals D_1 or D_2 is allowed through onto the output line. Its truth table is shown in Table 2.2(a), and on inspection it will be seen that this can be abbreviated to that shown in Table 2.2(b).

2.3 Sequential devices

The logic circuits described in 2.2, combinational circuits, are such that at any time the output of a circuit is a direct function of its inputs. With a sequential device or circuit the output at any time is a function of both its current inputs and its previous inputs (and hence its current state). A sequential circuit therefore involves some sort of memory.

A *flip-flop* or *bistable* is a device that is capable of storing or remembering one bit.

2.3.1 The R-S flip-flop

The R-S flip-flop is a device that has two inputs, conventionally called R and S and two outputs Q and $\bar{Q}$ where $\bar{Q}$ is the complement of Q.

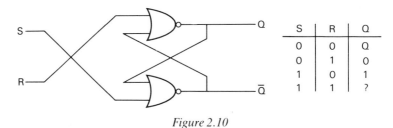

S	R	Q
0	0	Q
0	1	0
1	0	1
1	1	?

Figure 2.10

Such a flip-flop is normally made up of two NOR gates with feed back, as shown in Figure 2.10. To establish the truth table, suppose R=1 and S=0. Then Q=0 (remember it is a NOR gate) and $\bar{Q}=1$. If R is now

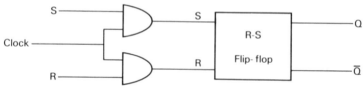

Figure 2.11

changed to 0 the other input at that NOR gate is still 1 and so Q still remains at 0. If S is set to 1 with R=0, then Q and Q̄ become 1 and 0 respectively and continue in the same state even after S is returned to 0. Thus, the output Q can be set to 1 or reset to 0 by signals applied to S and R (even if only very briefly) but while S and R both are zero the output remains at its last state.

One drawback is that with both R and S equal to 1 the circuit cannot satisfy the requirement that Q̄ is the complement of Q and so the output is said to be undefined. Uses of the R-S flip-flop must avoid the situation of both inputs being 1.

2.3.2 Clocked R-S flip-flops

On many occasions it is necessary that the time a flip-flop is set or reset is controlled by an external source such as a clock pulse.

We could add a clock input to the R-S flip-flop as shown in Figure 2.11. The truth table remains the same as for a non-clocked R-S but the set and reset actions can only take place at the instant the clock input is 1.

2.3.3 D flip-flop

Instead of controlling a clocked flip-flop by two separate inputs it is sometimes more convenient to use just a single data input D. Here, the output from the flip-flop is set to the same as the input D when a clock pulse occurs, otherwise the output remains unchanged. Figure 2.12 shows a D flip-flop constructed from an R-S flip-flop, and its usual circuit symbol.

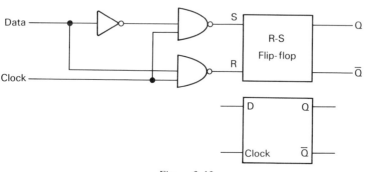

Figure 2.12

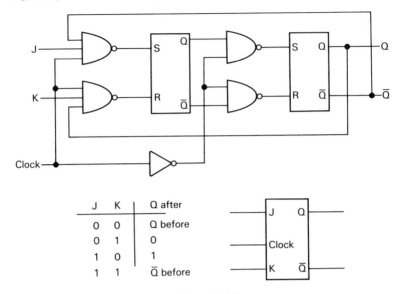

J	K	Q after
0	0	Q before
0	1	0
1	0	1
1	1	$\bar{Q}$ before

Figure 2.13

2.3.4 J-K flip-flop

A further development of the clocked R-S flip-flop removes the undefined state when the inputs are both 1. The J-K flip-flop has the same truth table as the R-S except for when both inputs are equal to 1. In this case when a clock pulse occurs the output is inverted. That is, if it was 0 it will change to 1 and if it was 1 it will change to 0.

Figure 2.13 shows a circuit for the J-K flip-flop based on R-S flip-flops, the truth table where 'Q before ' and 'Q after' represent the output before and after a clock pulse, and the usual circuit symbol.

2.4 Common sequential circuits

Section 2.3 has examined a number of flip-flop or bistable devices, each with different properties, but all having the characteristic ability to store the state of one binary digit or bit. These flip-flops can be used in many practical circuits and this section will examine some of the more common applications.

2.4.1 A parallel register

A single bit can be stored for a time in a flip-flop, hence storing a group of bits in a parallel set of flip-flops will permit a larger number to be stored and will constitute a register (see Chapters 7 and 8).

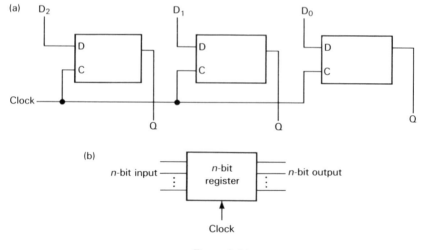

Figure 2.14

Figure 2.14 shows a 3-bit register constructed from three D flip-flops. When the clock line is pulsed, data presented to the input of the register is then transferred, or latched, onto its output. Since all the bits are transferred from input to output at the same time it is said to be a parallel register.

2.4.2 A shift register

A shift register is a register connected so that its contents will shift left one bit or right one bit when a clock pulse is applied to it. Consider the 3-bit right shift register shown in Figure 2.15. If it initially contains 101 then three successive clock pulses will cause the following shifts:

$$101 \ldots 010 \ldots 001 \ldots 000$$

If, synchronised with each clock pulse, a new bit is input to the left-most J-K flip-flop in Figure 2.15, then after three successive clock pulses the register will contain the three successive input bits. Figure 2.16 illustrates the circuit for this.

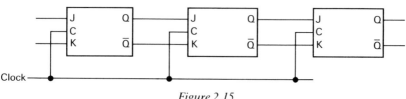

Figure 2.15

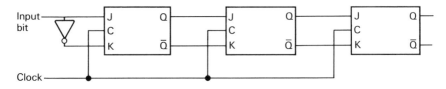

Figure 2.16

Such a register is particularly useful in situations where the bits to be stored in a register are being presented individually in a serial form, for example communication down a serial I/O line (see Chapters 10 and 12). When a key is depressed on a computer terminal, the corresponding character code (see Chapter 5) may be transmitted serially over a single communication line to the computer. Typically, this serially transmitted character may be clocked into a shift register which is located outside the CPU. It would interrupt the operation of the CPU for a much shorter time if the contents of that shift register were then transferred into a register in the CPU in parallel. The shift register would then be performing a *serial-to-parallel conversion*. The reverse operation (parallel-to-serial) is also possible since bits are output from a shift register on each clock pulse as well as being input to it. A general register which can be loaded or output in parallel or serial form is shown in Figure 2.17. In this general register the J-K flip-flops have additional inputs to allow the second R-S flip-flop (see Figure 2.13) to be set or reset (and hence the J-K output) directly. This allows the whole register to be cleared or loaded in parallel.

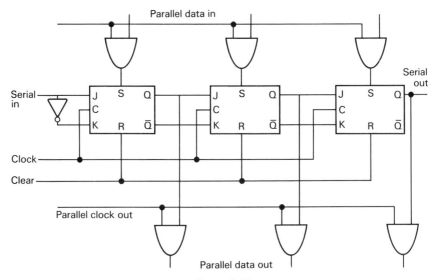

Figure 2.17

2.4.3 Binary ripple counter

If the circuit for a J-K flip-flop is examined (see Figure 2.13) it will be seen that the output for the second R-S flip-flop can only be altered when the inverted clock input goes to a 1. This only occurs when the original clock input goes from 1 back to 0. Thus, a clock pulse must be a change from logic 0 to 1 and back to 0, the output occurring very soon after the change from 1 to 0. This fact can be used in the construction of a *ripple counter* in which the value of the binary output of this counter is incremented by 1 on each clock pulse (see Figure 2.18).

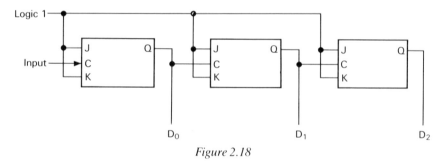

Figure 2.18

Output D_0 changes at each pulse of the input (actually as the input line is undergoing the 1⟶0 phase of its pulse). Output D_1 changes at each 1⟶0 change of D_0, D_2 changes at each 1⟶0 change of D_1, etc. The binary counting is said to ripple through the counter with each clock pulse. Given that an unconnected input behaves as if it were a logic 1 (see 2.1) all the J-K inputs could be left unconnected.

2.5 Integrated circuits

So far there has been no discussion about the implementation of logic gates. Many modern integrated circuit logic implementations use transistors as basic switches (see Figure 2.19). A transistor connects its 'emitter' to its 'collector' by a high resistance if the voltage on its 'base' is low (thus ensuring that the emitter and collector are effectively disconnected). It connects its emitter to its collector by a low resistance if the voltage on its base is high. Figure 2.20 illustrates the use of transistors in the implementation of NOT, NOR, and NAND gates.

An integrated circuit is a small silicon semiconductor crystal called a *chip*. This contains a variety of electrical components, including transistors, interconnected inside the chip to form an electronic circuit. The chip is contained within a metal or plastic package and has connections to external pins. Constructing circuits within such chips has a number of

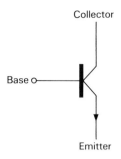

Figure 2.19

advantages over circuits made up from discrete components. There is a substantial reduction in size, a reduction in power requirements, an increase in operating speed, and if volume of production is sufficient a reduction in cost. The actual manufacturing process is complex and highly specialised and a description is beyond the scope of this text.

The number of logic gates contained within one chip is used to classify the complexity of the chip or the 'scale of integration'. Small scale integration (SSI) describes those chips containing only a few gates (10–20 typically). Functions offered include a variety of simple gates, flip-flops, bus drivers and simple counters. Medium scale integrated (MSI) circuits can provide a complete function on a single chip. The number of gates per chip is higher, typically 20–100 gates, and functions provided include decoders, multiplexers and shift registers. Large scale integrated (LSI) circuits, containing more than 100 gates, provide functions such as complete memories, calculator chips, microprocessor CPUs and input/ output chips. Very large scale integrated (VLSI) circuits are chips with typically more than 1000 gates, providing functions such as complete microprocessor systems and very large memory arrays. Some VLSI chips have become very complex, containing as many as 400 000 transistors on a chip, as the technology for their fabrication has developed.

2.5.1 Circuit families

Integrated circuits can be classified not only by their functions and complexity but also by being members of a particular 'family'. Each family is based on a different technology, where the particular characteristics of a family are determined by the electronic components used and their interconnections. The more common families are:

TTL   Transistor transistor logic
ECL   Emitter coupled logic
MOS   Metal-oxide semiconductor

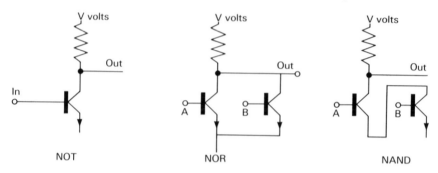

Figure 2.20

The TTL logic family has become very extensive and is based on the use of so-called bipolar transistors as described in 2.5 above (bipolar is the name given to transistors where the working current passes through semiconductor material of both polarities). There are many versions or series of the TTL gate all of which have different characteristics in terms of power requirements and propagation delay (propagation delay is the average delay time for the signal to propagate from input to output when the binary signals change in value). Table 2.3 gives some typical values for these characteristics.

Table 2.3

Series	Name	Propagation delay (ns)	Power requirements (mW)
Standard	TTL	10	10
Low power	LTTL	33	1
High speed	HTTL	6	22
Schottky	STTL	3	19
Low power Schottky	LSTTL	9.5	2

The ECL logic family use a slightly different type of transistor (still, however, bipolar) that achieves very low propagation delay (typically 1–2 ns) and consequently is used in systems requiring very high speed operation.

MOS is a quite different type of transistor—it is unipolar meaning the working current flows through only one type of semiconductor material. Its main advantage is that it allows a much greater packing density so that much more circuitry can be contained in the same area of a semiconductor chip. There are, however, two other advantages. There are simpler processing techniques when fabricated in integrated circuits and it is therefore more economical to manufacture, and its power consumption is less than the bipolar gate making it more economical to operate. Within the MOS family there are different series such as PMOS, NMOS, CMOS, each with different characteristics, just as there are different series of TTL gates.

2.5.2 IC packaging

Digital integrated circuits are most commonly manufactured mounted in a dual-in-line (DIP) package. The IC chip is mounted in a block of plastic or ceramic which serves two functions: one is to simply give some protection to the very tiny chip, but the main reason is to enable the metal leads (or pins), which are necessary for connecting this circuit to others, to be of such a size that they are stiff enough for insertion into printed circuit boards. The term dual-in-line (DIP) refers to the two lines of pins down either side of the plastic package. There are standard size packages and a standard range of pin numbers (typically 14 to 64) depending on the complexity of the connections required to other circuits. Each DIP has a numerical designation number printed on the surface of the chip assigned by the semiconductor manufacturer.

TTL ICs usually have designation numbers of the 5400 or 7400 series (these two series have different operating temperature ranges). One common ECL series is known as the 10000 series. CMOS 4000 series are also common and there are CMOS 54C00 and 74C00 series which are pin compatible with their TTL series counterparts.

2.5.3 Integrated circuit specifications

All semiconductor manufacturers publish handbooks specifying the details of all the integrated circuits that they manufacture. These details include a functional specification, a pin specification and the electrical characteristics of the chip. Whilst this chapter has introduced some of the circuits that are common there are in fact thousands of different chips available. The following details are those of just six typical chips of both SSI and MSI scale. Note that in all the diagrams, pin Vcc represents the pin to which the 5 volt power supply should be connected and pin GND is the ground (earth) pin.

2.6 Summary

The purpose of this chapter has been to introduce the fundamental concepts of logic gates and how, using these basic gates, more complex circuits can be developed which can either be used in control functions or

QUADRUPLE 2-INPUT POSITIVE-NOR GATES

02

positive logic:
$Y = \overline{A+B}$

See page 6-8

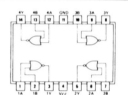

SN5402 (J)   SN7402 (J, N)
SN54LS02 (J, W)   SN74LS02 (J, N)
SN54S02 (J, W)   SN74S02 (J, N)
SN54ALS02 (J)   SN74ALS02 (N)
PLANNED PRODUCT: SN54AS02 (J)   SN74AS02 (N)

HEX INVERTERS

04

positive logic:
$Y = \overline{A}$

See page 6-2

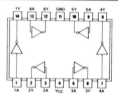

SN5404 (J)   SN7404 (J, N)   SN5404 (W)
SN54H04 (J)   SN74H04 (J, N)   SN54H04 (W)
SN54LS04 (J, W)   SN74LS04 (J, N)
SN54S04 (J, W)   SN74S04 (J, N)
SN54ALS04 (J)   SN74ALS504 (N)

QUADRUPLE 2-INPUT POSITIVE-AND GATES

08

positive logic:
$Y = AB$

See page 6-10

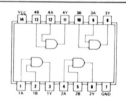

SN5408 (J, W)   SN7408 (J, N)
SN54LS08 (J, W)   SN74LS08 (J, N)
SN54S08 (J, W)   SN74S08 (J, N)
SN54ALS08 (J)   SN74ALS08 (N)
PLANNED PRODUCT: SN54AS08 (J)   SN74AS08 (N)

DUAL J-K FLIP-FLOPS WITH PRESET AND CLEAR

76

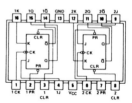

'76, 'H76 FUNCTION TABLE

INPUTS					OUTPUTS	
PRESET	CLEAR	CLOCK	J	K	Q	$\overline{Q}$
L	H	X	X	X	H	L
H	L	X	X	X	L	H
L	L	X	X	X	H*	H*
H	H	⊓	L	L	Q_0	$\overline{Q}_0$
H	H	⊓	H	L	H	L
H	H	⊓	L	H	L	H
H	H	⊓	H	H	TOGGLE	

'LS76A FUNCTION TABLE

INPUTS					OUTPUTS	
PRESET	CLEAR	CLOCK	J	K	Q	$\overline{Q}$
L	H	X	X	X	H	L
H	L	X	X	X	L	H
L	L	X	X	X	H*	H*
H	H	↓	L	L	Q_0	$\overline{Q}_0$
H	H	↓	H	L	H	L
H	H	↓	L	H	L	H
H	H	↓	H	H	TOGGLE	
H	H	H	X	X	Q_0	$\overline{Q}_0$

SN5476 (J, W)   SN7476 (J, N)
SN54H76 (J, W)   SN74H76 (J, N)
SN54LS76A (J, W)   SN74LS76A (J, N)

See pages 6-46, 6-50 and 6-54

TTL
MSI

TYPES SN54154, SN74154,
4-LINE-TO-16-LINE DECODERS/DEMULTIPLEXERS

BULLETIN NO. DL S 7211805, DECEMBER 1972

- '154 is Ideal for High-Performance Memory Decoding

- Decodes 4 Binary-Coded Inputs into One of 16 Mutually Exclusive Outputs

- Performs the Demultiplexing Function by Distributing Data From One Input Line to Any One of 16 Outputs

- Input Clamping Diodes Simplify System Design

- High Fan-Out, Low-Impedance, Totem-Pole Outputs

- Fully Compatible with Most TTL, DTL, and MSI Circuits

SN54154 . . . J OR W PACKAGE
SN74154 . . . J, N OR NT PACKAGE
(TOP VIEW)

positive logic: see function table

TYPE	TYPICAL AVERAGE PROPAGATION DELAY		TYPICAL POWER DISSIPATION
	3 LEVELS OF LOGIC	STROBE	
'154	23 ns	19 ns	170 mW

description

Each of these monolithic, 4-line-to-16-line decoders utilizes TTL circuitry to decode four binary-coded inputs into one of sixteen mutually exclusive outputs when both the strobe inputs, G1 and G2, are low. The demultiplexing function is performed by using the 4 input lines to address the output line, passing data from one of the strobe inputs with the other strobe input low. When either strobe input is high, all outputs are high. These demultiplexers are ideally suited for implementing high-performance memory decoders. For ultra-high-speed systems, SN54S138/SN74S138 and SN54S139/SN74S139 are recommended.

These circuits are fully compatible for use with most other TTL and DTL circuits. All inputs are buffered and input clamping diodes are provided to minimize transmission-line effects and thereby simplify system design.

Series 54 devices are characterized for operation over the full military temperature range of −55°C to 125°C; Series 74 devices are characterized for operation from 0°C to 70°C.

as further building blocks for the construction of more complex digital systems. It is important that the exercises which now follow should not be regarded as just paper exercises, but that some of the circuits should be built on a suitable logic trainer in order to reinforce understanding.

TYPES SN54154, SN74154
4-LINE-TO-16-LINE DECODERS/ DEMULTIPLEXERS

logic

FUNCTION TABLE

INPUTS						OUTPUTS															
G1	G2	D	C	B	A	0	1	2	3	4	5	6	7	8	9	10	11	12	13	14	15
L	L	L	L	L	L	L	H	H	H	H	H	H	H	H	H	H	H	H	H	H	H
L	L	L	L	L	H	H	L	H	H	H	H	H	H	H	H	H	H	H	H	H	H
L	L	L	L	H	L	H	H	L	H	H	H	H	H	H	H	H	H	H	H	H	H
L	L	L	L	H	H	H	H	H	L	H	H	H	H	H	H	H	H	H	H	H	H
L	L	L	H	L	L	H	H	H	H	L	H	H	H	H	H	H	H	H	H	H	H
L	L	L	H	L	H	H	H	H	H	H	L	H	H	H	H	H	H	H	H	H	H
L	L	L	H	H	L	H	H	H	H	H	H	L	H	H	H	H	H	H	H	H	H
L	L	L	H	H	H	H	H	H	H	H	H	H	L	H	H	H	H	H	H	H	H
L	L	H	L	L	L	H	H	H	H	H	H	H	H	L	H	H	H	H	H	H	H
L	L	H	L	L	H	H	H	H	H	H	H	H	H	H	L	H	H	H	H	H	H
L	L	H	L	H	L	H	H	H	H	H	H	H	H	H	H	L	H	H	H	H	H
L	L	H	L	H	H	H	H	H	H	H	H	H	H	H	H	H	L	H	H	H	H
L	L	H	H	L	L	H	H	H	H	H	H	H	H	H	H	H	H	L	H	H	H
L	L	H	H	L	H	H	H	H	H	H	H	H	H	H	H	H	H	H	L	H	H
L	L	H	H	H	L	H	H	H	H	H	H	H	H	H	H	H	H	H	H	L	H
L	L	H	H	H	H	H	H	H	H	H	H	H	H	H	H	H	H	H	H	H	L
L	H	X	X	X	X	H	H	H	H	H	H	H	H	H	H	H	H	H	H	H	H
H	L	X	X	X	X	H	H	H	H	H	H	H	H	H	H	H	H	H	H	H	H
H	H	X	X	X	X	H	H	H	H	H	H	H	H	H	H	H	H	H	H	H	H

H = high level, L = low level, X = irrelevant

functional block diagram and schematics of inputs and outputs

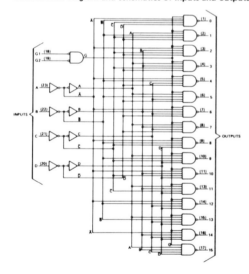

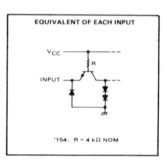

EQUIVALENT OF EACH INPUT

Vcc

R

INPUT

'154: R = 4 kΩ NOM

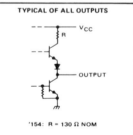

TYPICAL OF ALL OUTPUTS

Vcc

R

OUTPUT

'154: R = 130 Ω NOM

TTL
MSI

TYPES SN54145, SN54LS145, SN74145, SN74LS145
BCD-TO-DECIMAL DECODERS/DRIVERS

BULLETIN NO. DL-S 7611815, MARCH 1974–REVISED OCTOBER 1976

FOR USE AS LAMP, RELAY, OR MOS DRIVERS

- Full Decoding of Input Logic
- SN54145, SN74145, and SN74LS145 Have 80-mA Sink-Current Capability
- All Outputs Are Off for Invalid BCD Input Conditions
- Low Power Dissipation of 'LS145 . . . 35 mW Typical

logic

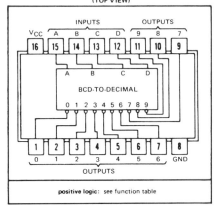

SN54145, SN54LS145 . . . J OR W PACKAGE
SN74145, SN74LS145 . . . J OR N PACKAGE
(TOP VIEW)

positive logic: see function table

FUNCTION TABLE

NO.	INPUTS				OUTPUTS									
	D	C	B	A	0	1	2	3	4	5	6	7	8	9
0	L	L	L	L	L	H	H	H	H	H	H	H	H	H
1	L	L	L	H	H	L	H	H	H	H	H	H	H	H
2	L	L	H	L	H	H	L	H	H	H	H	H	H	H
3	L	L	H	H	H	H	H	L	H	H	H	H	H	H
4	L	H	L	L	H	H	H	H	L	H	H	H	H	H
5	L	H	L	H	H	H	H	H	H	L	H	H	H	H
6	L	H	H	L	H	H	H	H	H	H	L	H	H	H
7	L	H	H	H	H	H	H	H	H	H	H	L	H	H
8	H	L	L	L	H	H	H	H	H	H	H	H	L	H
9	H	L	L	H	H	H	H	H	H	H	H	H	H	L
INVALID	H	L	H	L	H	H	H	H	H	H	H	H	H	H
	H	L	H	H	H	H	H	H	H	H	H	H	H	H
	H	H	L	L	H	H	H	H	H	H	H	H	H	H
	H	H	L	H	H	H	H	H	H	H	H	H	H	H
	H	H	H	L	H	H	H	H	H	H	H	H	H	H
	H	H	H	H	H	H	H	H	H	H	H	H	H	H

H = high level (off), L = low level (on)

description

These monolithic BCD-to-decimal decoder/drivers consist of eight inverters and ten four-input NAND gates. The inverters are connected in pairs to make BCD input data available for decoding by the NAND gates. Full decoding of valid BCD input logic ensures that all outputs remain off for all invalid binary input conditions. These decoders feature high-performance, n-p-n output transistors designed for use as indicator/relay drivers or as open-collector logic-circuit drivers. Each of the high-breakdown output transistors (15 volts) of the SN54145, SN74145, or SN74LS145 will sink up to 80 milliamperes of current. Each input is one Series 54/74 or Series 54LS/74LS standard load, respectively. Inputs and outputs are entirely compatible for use with TTL or DTL logic circuits, and the outputs are compatible for interfacing with most MOS integrated circuits. Power dissipation is typically 215 milliwatts for the '145 and 35 milliwatts for the 'LS145.

functional block diagram

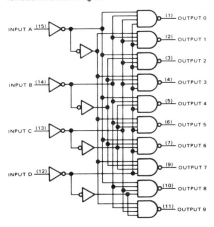

2.7 Problems

Note: Many of these problems require the use of a suitable logic trainer system which allows you to build and test circuits from a range of logic components.

(1) By connecting switches to the inputs and a lamp to the output produce the truth tables for each of the logic gates AND, OR, Exclusive OR, Inverter.

(2) Determine what logic state is assumed by an unconnected input on the above logic gates.

(3) Many of these logic functions can be developed using simply NAND gates. By producing truth tables, show that the following circuits are functionally equal.

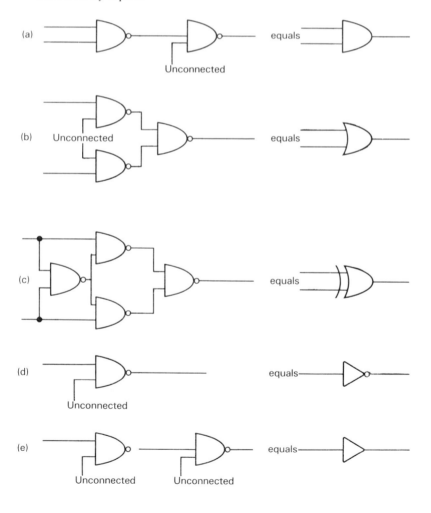

(4) On an automatic plant alarm system the following events occur as a result of fault detection:

    (i)   Fault signal arrives—red lamp on, buzzer on, operator acknowledges that he has received the alarm by operating the acknowledge switch.

    (ii) Acknowledge switch on—red lamp off, buzzer off, yellow lamp on.

When the fault is corrected:

    (iii) Fault signal clears—yellow lamp off, green lamp on, buzzer on.

    (iv) Acknowledge switch returned to normal—buzzer off, green lamp on.

From the above it can be determined that the system will consist of two inputs (*alarm* and *acknowledge*) and four outputs (*red, yellow, green* lamps and *buzzer*). Produce a truth table to describe the system. Implement the system practically and test for correct operation.

(5) Build the circuit below for a half adder and by changing the switches produce its truth table. Check it against Figure 2.4.

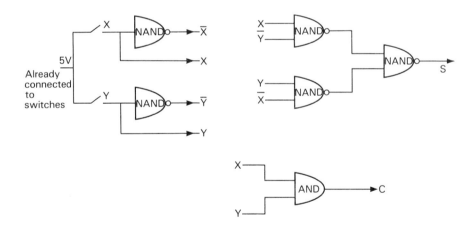

(6) Connect a full adder as shown in Figure 2.7 and verify its truth table.

(7) Build the two-input decoder shown in Figure 2.8 and verify its truth table.

(8) Construct the following circuit and produce the truth table by experiment.

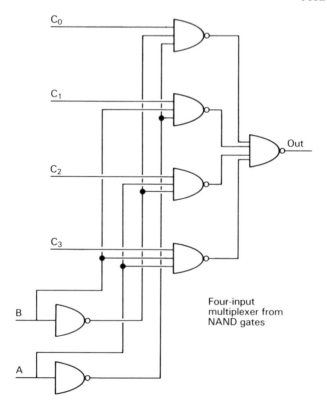

C₀

C₁

C₂

C₃

Out

B

A

Four-input
multiplexer from
NAND gates

(9) Test the truth table for Problem 8 on the following IC package (the three state output of the device may be ignored—if output control is connected to logic 0 then the output is activated).

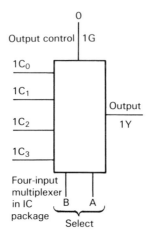

0

Output control   1G

1C₀

1C₁

1C₂

1C₃

Output

1Y

Four-input
multiplexer
in IC   B   A
package
        Select

(10) Sketch a circuit which realises an eight-input multiplexer from two four-input multiplexers available in IC form and NAND gates. Produce its truth table.

(11) Verify the truth tables of the R-S, the J-K and D flip-flops.

(12) The block diagram of a J-K flip-flop is shown in Figure 2.13. Using this device, connect up the shift register circuit shown in Figure 2.17, excluding preset/clear sections. By applying a series of different states to the serial input and clocking the register, show how this series eventually becomes available in parallel from the four flip-flop outputs.

Connect the parallel inputs and clock to the preset/clear inputs as shown. Place a 4-bit parallel data signal on the four parallel inputs.

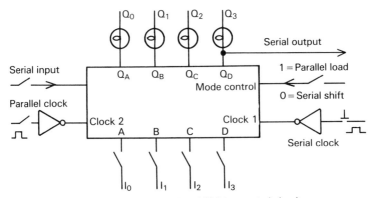

The 4-bit shift register PIPO integrated circuit

Clock this into the register by briefly switching the parallel clock input to 1. Check that the intended 4-bit signal has been successfully entered into the register.

Press the serial clock button 3 times and note the series of four bits presented at the serial output. Satisfy yourself that this series represents the 4-bit signal entered earlier in parallel.

Leave the previous circuit connected, but connect a 4-bit shift register PIPO IC up in the same way, using the same serial clock but a separate set of switches and lamps for the other inputs and outputs as above. Convince yourself by repeating the above operations that this circuit operates in the same way. The mode control input must be set or reset to select parallel or serial operation respectively.

(13) Connect together the serial inputs and outputs of your two registers as shown below. This forms a serial half-duplex synchronous communication link between the two registers, which could be in separate computers several hundred metres apart:

Serial —because the bits of a word are transmitted one after the other.

Half-duplex —because there are separate wires for transmit and receive, but only one may be active at any time.

Synchronous —because the clock signal is transmitted between the two devices.

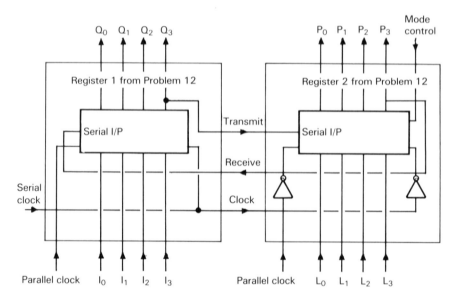

Satisfy yourself that you can transmit data in both directions. (See Chapters 10 and 12 for further details.)

(14) Verify the operation of the binary ripple counter shown in Figure 2.18.

CHAPTER 3

Peripherals

Chapter 1 introduced the concept of a computer being able to process data that has been presented to it in some way and of the computer presenting the results of its processing back to the outside world. The parts of the computer which are involved in the transfer of data to and from the outside world are known as peripheral devices and can be categorised as follows:

(1) *input:* devices used to transfer information into the computer.
(2) *output:* devices used to transfer information from the computer to the outside world.
(3) *input/output:* devices which can be used for both the input or the output of data.
(4) *television technology:* methods currently available of data transmission based on television.
(5) *specific transducers:* devices which will sense such things as pressure, temperature, etc., and pass information directly into the computer.

Within any one of these classes there may be devices of a similar type, some which may be used as peripheral devices to a small computer and some as peripheral devices to a much larger computer. The differences in the devices lie in their ruggedness, capacity, speed and cost. Clearly, devices intended to accompany a small portable computer will have to be smaller and lighter than similar devices which are permanently attached to a large static, general-purpose computer. In achieving the smaller size and lighter weight (and often lower cost), ruggedness, capacity and speed may have to be sacrificed.

3.1 Input peripherals

As indicated later in Chapters 5 and 6, data can be stored in character form in the main memory of a computer by using some appropriate numeric code. The purpose of an input peripheral is to transfer data from its real world representation into the internal character code of the computer. Because data in the real world exists in many different formats, several different input devices may be used under different circumstances.

3.1.1 Key to tape/disk

The data is keyed in at a keyboard but is stored initially in the electronic memory, thus allowing for easy correction. If the operator realises that a character has been miskeyed, the backspace is depressed, the correct character keyed in, and the memory's stored character is corrected. Once all the characters in the record (a record being a convenient collection of characters—see Chapter 4) are keyed in, the record can then be recorded on the magnetic tape or disk (see Chapter 4).

The main advantages are:

(1) increased productivity of punch/keyboard operators because of the ease of error correction;
(2) some automatic error checking can be built into the system;
(3) there is a ready visual check on the small TV screen (VDU);
(4) no expendable materials;
(5) the tape/disk thus produced provides a much faster read in to the computer system compared with punched cards or paper tape.

3.1.2 Point-of-sale (POS) systems

Advances in technology, in particular the microprocessor, have led to the development of point-of-sale devices, primarily for use in shops. The collection of data at the point of sale has been accepted for many years; Kimball tags, prepunched cards and by-product paper tape have been widely used in the retail trade. However, the introduction of micro-processors and low cost keyboard/display devices have led to a number of variations of this equipment, the most common being electronic cash registers and cash terminals.

Electronic cash registers

These are small computers with keyboard and simple display facilities to show price data. The cashier keys in an item identifier and price (although prices may be held in a memory). The cash register accumulates sales under a range of nominated codes for subsequent processing. Data may be collected on cassette tapes (see Chapter 4).

Cash terminals

These are usually connected to a small computer in the store. This central computer controls a network of terminals at pay-points, and has stock and price data usually stored on disks. The terminal is used to input details of each sale made. A common method of identifying items is by passing a magnetic/optical sensing wand over a tag on each item. Items are priced automatically and receipts printed on the terminal. Stock sales data is accumulated for later processing leading to automatic reordering.

3.1.3 Bar coding

Computer systems are becoming increasingly used by people never trained in the use of keyboards and used in places where keyboards were never designed to go. It is in these conditions where bar-code systems have their greatest potential. Bar-code technology is essentially a means of recording cheaply (on paper with ink) information for subsequent fast error-free entry to a computer. Virtually any application may use bar codes to advantage where the requirement is for fast recognition of a known item of data such as a product number, identity code, job number, parcel number or weight. (For an example of a bar code see the cover of this book.) These areas of application are fairly routine. Other more unusual applications handled using bar codes have been machine control, where bar codes replace keyboards in hazardous environments; questionnaire analysis, where pilot market research surveys had bar-coded answer boxes for direct entry of answers to the computer; and marathon race control, where every runner in the London Marathon is bar-coded to ensure fast check in and out of runners.

The essence of bar-code technology is simple in principle. A light is focused on and scanned across a pattern of black and white stripes of varying thicknesses. The stripes are arranged to encode data according to a symbology which is presented to a detector as a series of reflected light pulses of varying strength and duration. The signal conditioner timer and decoder in the reader compensates for varying speed and print density and checks the resulting data for accuracy before passing it on to the computer.

No special inks are required to print bar codes and many standard computer printers with graphics facilities may be used to produce machine readable data as part of normal printing routines on standard documents. Bar-code readers are becoming more and more sophisticated but generally rely on one of the following methods to achieve the desired scan across the code. The reader is moved across the code (as with most bar-code pens), or the code is moved past a fixed reader (typically used on conveyor belts where distance and code height are pre-determined), or the light spot is moved back and forth through an arc many times a second (the technique used by laser scanners). Hand-held pens are the most popular and they are the cheapest general-purpose device. They consist of a pen shaped barrel containing the electronics which feeds back to a base unit via a cable. The base unit may be anything from a full terminal with display to a simple transmit only device. Successful reads are signalled by a bleep whilst unsuccessful attempts get no response or a different bleep.

3.1.4 Optical character recognition (OCR)

Devices are available that, by a process of optically scanning documents, are able to recognise character shapes. They may be capable of reading whole pages (page reader) or merely one or two lines only. Generally, the characters to be read must be machine printed and of special character design or fount. In America, a character fount known as OCR 'A' has evolved while in Europe OCR 'B' has been developed. Figure 3.1 illustrates both these founts.

Below are some of the advantages and disadvantages of OCR.

Advantages

(1) Computers can produce pre-printed documents which can later be read.
(2) Data preparation errors are eliminated.
(3) Document is a visible record.
(4) Considerable range of document size is catered for.
(5) Can be on-line to the computer (but often data written to magnetic tape off-line for faster computer input).

Disadvantages

(1) Documents must be treated with care.
(2) Special measures are required to replace spoilt or lost documents.
(3) Equipment is very expensive.
(4) Print quality may be critical.

3.1.5 Magnetic ink character recognition (MICR)

In MICR specially designed characters are used which are printed in ink containing magnetic particles. The document is read by a document reader that recognises the particular character from the variation in magnetic flux which is induced by the shape of that particular character.

Banks are the main users of this system. By pre-printing the cheque serial number, the bank and branch sorting code numbers, and the

1234567890
ЈЧНIABCDEF
GHIJKLMNOP
QRSTUVWXYZ
⸗⸗ℿ⩢⟋⟨⟩⁒?&⹀

OCR 'A' fount

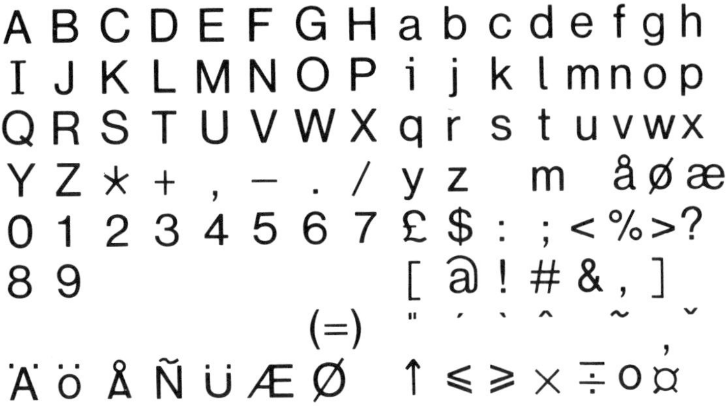

A B C D E F G H a b c d e f g h
I J K L M N O P i j k l m n o p
Q R S T U V W X q r s t u v w x
Y Z ✳ + , − . / y z   m   å ø æ
0 1 2 3 4 5 6 7 £ $: ; < % > ?
8 9   [ⓐ ! # & ,]
          (=)   " ´ ` ^   ~   �‚
Ä ö Å Ñ Ü Æ Ø   ↑ ≤ ≥ × ÷ o ¤

OCR 'B' fount

Figure 3.1

customer's account number in a single line along the bottom of cheques before issue, it is possible to sort the cheques, after they have been presented, by means of a MICR sorting machine. The amount of the cheque is encoded on the cheque in MICR fount by a keyboard machine called a magnetic ink encoder. The cheques are then read by the magnetic ink character reader which can verify the characters and then send the data directly to the computer or to magnetic tape or disk for later input to the computer.

Figure 3.2 illustrates the fount known as E13B that is common to the banking world in both America and the United Kingdom.

0 1 2 3 4 5 6 7 8 9 ⑈⑇⑆⑉

MICR E13B fount

Figure 3.2

Below are some of the advantages and disadvantages of MICR.

Advantages	*Disadvantages*
(1) Visual inspection possible with practice.	(1) One line of information per document only.
(2) Useful for document sorting.	(2) Cannot be produced by computer; printing requires special printing device.
(3) Forgery impeded.	(3) The quality of printing is important; the amount of ink in a character is critical.
	(4) Very limited character set in E13B.

3.2 Output peripherals

The purpose of an output peripheral is to transfer information from the internal character code stored inside the computer to an appropriate real world representation. This real world representation may be a printed page, a television tube, a diagram on paper, magnetic spots on plastic tape or even microfiche.

Society as a whole is very much geared to the use of the printed word and consequently the most common forms of output device are those which produce printed information on paper, commonly referred to as 'hard copy'. There are now a number of different types of printing device. Some printers operate like typewriters in that type strikes an inked ribbon which in turn strikes paper to transfer an image. These are known as *impact printers*. The advantage of impact printers is that multiple copies can usually be produced by using multipart paper interleaved with carbon, but their disadvantage is that they can be relatively noisy. Non-impact printers on the other hand are usually very quiet but it is not usually possible to produce multiple copies. Printers can also be classified according to the sequence in which printing takes place. Some devices, like a typewriter, print one character at a time working left to right across a page. These are known as *character printers* or *serial printers*. The other type print randomly along the print line, gradually building up the complete line. These are known as *line printers*.

3.2.1 Line printers

Some impact printer devices are based on the typewriter mechanism where the character strikes a ribbon which presses against the paper, so transferring the shape of the character to it. Other types use hammers behind the paper forcing it to press against the ribbon, which in turn presses against the type thus transferring the image.

Chain, train and belt printers use several complete sets of type which move horizontally past the print line, and are separated from the paper by an inked ribbon. In the case of the chain printer, the type characters literally form a chain, like the links of a bicycle chain. The train printer is very similar except that the type characters are not permanently joined together but can be individually attached to or removed from the train carrier, hence the character set can be varied very easily. The belt printer has a series of slim metal uprights that are secured to a horizontal rotating belt, the type character being on the top of the upright. Depending on the particular printing mechanism, chain, train and belt printers may be character printers or line printers.

The drum or barrel printer has complete character sets wrapped around the circumference of the barrel at every print position. If the printer is a 132-character width printer then there are 132 complete sets of type wrapped round the barrel. There are also 132 hammers, one for each print position, with the inked ribbon and print paper sandwiched between the hammers and the barrel. As the barrel revolves and brings a particular character in line with the paper in every print position, the hammer(s) corresponding to that position in which the character is required strikes the paper. Consequently in one revolution of the barrel, all the characters will have passed the paper, and the complete line will have been printed.

Table 3.1

	'Line' printers			'Character' printers		
	Speed	Character	Special paper	Speed	Character	Special paper
Chain/train/ belt	200– 2,000 LPM	Full	No	30– 400 CPS	Full	No
Barrel	125– 3,000 LPM	Full	No			
Dot matrix				30– 600 CPS	Dot	No
Daisy-wheel				30– 60 CPS	Full	No
Ink jet				100 CPS	Dot	No
Thermal				10– 30 CPS	Dot	Yes

Speeds for all these types of printers and other printing devices are shown in Table 3.1.

3.2.2 Dot matrix printer

The dot matrix printer prints a pattern of dots in the shape of a character. The position of these dots is formed, for example, by a matrix of seven vertical dot positions and five horizontal dot positions.

The print head contains seven wires that can strike an inked ribbon which is sandwiched between the print head and the paper. Each character is formed by the print head moving to each of the five horizontal dot positions and the appropriate wires striking the paper. Clearly because of the number of strikes per line required the speed is restricted.

3.2.3 Daisy-wheel printers

The print mechanism of the daisy-wheel printer consists of a flat disc with petal-like projections. At the end of each projection is an embossed character which on impact with the paper will transfer the image of the character.

The advantages of the daisy-wheel printer are that there are few moving parts, printing can be performed in either direction, paper can be fed up or down, it has a low noise level, the type fount is easily changed and the print quality is high.

3.2.4 Thermal printers

Thermal printers have print heads that convert electricity to heat. The image is created on special heat-sensitive paper by the heated wires in the print head, in a similar way to that of the dot matrix printer. There is no inked ribbon required since the images are created by heat.

These printers are generally used where the volume of output is small because the heat-sensitive paper is relatively expensive. Speed is low because the heated wires of the print head must cool before moving to the next position.

3.2.5 Ink jet printers

These printers employ a technique which consists of spraying a stream of electrically charged ink droplets on to ordinary paper to produce printed characters. Character formation is performed by electrostatic deflection plates that control the direction of the charged ink droplets in much the same manner as the electron beam movement is controlled within a television set. Although reasonably fast for serial printers, their disadvantage is that they are relatively expensive.

3.2.6 Drum and flatbed plotters

Plotters are devices that output line drawings on paper. They consist of a pen which is either touching the paper or may be lifted from it. It can be moved a short distance (e.g. 1 mm) either horizontally or vertically or, by moving both horizontally and vertically at the same time, generate a line at 45°.

A line, curved or straight, is represented as a series of very short incremental lines, each one at the angle which most closely approximates the desired line. Because of this principle, curved or straight lines can be produced, so that the plotter is able to produce bar charts, line graphs, engineering drawings, maps and many other two- or even three-dimensional illustrations, all fully annotated. The paper is usually plain although it could be pre-printed if necessary.

There are two types of plotter: the drum plotter and the flatbed plotter. On a drum plotter, in order to achieve the required movement of the pen relative to the paper, the pen moves across the paper left to right or right to left and the paper (one end of which is wrapped round a drum) rotates around the drum so that the paper and pen are moving relative to each other in an up and down direction.

On a flatbed plotter the paper is stationary and only the pen moves across and/or up and down the paper. The advantage of the flatbed plotter is that it can draw illustrations up to two metres square whereas the drum plotter is limited to drawings of only about one metre wide, although since the paper is on a continuous roll quite long drawings are possible.

3.2.7 Computer output microfilm (COM)

The adaptation of microfilm to the computer as an output medium was introduced a number of years ago and is still a valuable option in cases where large volumes of printed output have to be kept. Although microfilm media for data storage are available in several forms the most common is called *microfiche*. Microfiche is a small card of microfilm with many small images in a grid pattern. Usually the output from the computer is written first to magnetic tape; a special machine then reads the tape and transfers the data to microfiche. Subsequently microfiche can be inserted into a simple reader which enlarges the image and projects it on to a screen for the user to read. It can be duplicated, and multiple hard copies can be printed from it if required.

The following are some of the advantages and disadvantages of COM.

Advantages	Disadvantages
(1) Speed of output is ten to twenty times faster than high-speed line printers.	(1) Requires special viewing equipment.
(2) Very compact storage capability.	(2) If printed copy is required a special reader/printer is needed.
(3) Cost of developing microfilm is low compared to traditional paper costs.	
(4) Distribution costs are low.	

Because of the above disadvantages microfilm is generally economical only when a high volume of documents is regularly output or where large files of printed data must be retained.

3.3 Input/output devices

There are a number of peripheral devices which to the user are a combined input and output device. With these devices there is some means whereby the user can input data or commands to the computer, and there is also some means by which the computer can output information back to the user. These devices are particularly useful in situations which require a user to interact with the computer such as on a multiple terminal network system. It must be emphasised, however, that as far as the computer is concerned these are entirely separate devices. One is an input device, the other an output device. The fact that they may share the same cabinet is of no consequence to the computer. Two very common devices will be considered.

3.3.1 Visual display unit (VDU) and keyboard

The keyboard is essentially very similar to a typewriter keyboard except that depressing a key does not result in a character being punched, but in the character being transmitted directly to the computer. In most systems the character is also displayed on the VDU screen. Bearing in mind that the keyboard and display are two separate peripheral devices that share a common case, what actually happens is that when the computer receives the character from the input keyboard it sends this character back to the output display. This happens so quickly that the two operations appear simultaneous. This is known as *echoing*.

Visual display devices were developed as an alternative to printing devices for situations in which it is not essential to have a printed copy.

Their chief advantages are that they are virtually silent, and can, if desired, display information at far greater speeds than any printing device.

The visual display unit is essentially like a small television set. In a simple form they are inexpensive but more expensive ones may offer special features. These include colour, flashing characters, variable intensity, protected areas on the screen, and the ability to go back to a prior point to delete or correct characters. If the device has a built in memory (which it must have to allow the correction of characters) it will allow the user to 'roll back' or redisplay lines that have 'rolled off' the top of the screen.

3.3.2 Typewriter terminals

These are very similar in principle to the visual display unit except that the output side of the device is a hard copy printer rather than a display screen. On this printer, which uses a moving, rotating or pivoting print head, the print device moves serially across the print line, the print head striking an ink ribbon which is between the print head and the paper.

3.4 Television technology

There have been a number of developments in the transmission of data which employ a domestic television set as the peripheral device. Two of the main developments are known as *viewdata* and *teletext*.

The term viewdata was introduced to describe a new information service being developed by the British Post Office in the early 1970s. The information available through the service is stored on a computer system and is accessible to anyone who has a television and a telephone (and an adaptor). Since that time a number of other countries have either signed agreements with British Telecom or begun to design their own systems. Consequently the term viewdata has become a name for the type of service, British Telecom's System now being called *Prestel*.

Teletext is the general name given to such systems as those developed by the UK television companies. The BBC's version is known as *Ceefax* and ITV's version is known as *Oracle*. In a teletext system the data that can be transmitted to the user is also stored on a computer system. However, there is a very important difference between teletext and viewdata. In the case of viewdata the information is transmitted via the public telephone network whereas teletext information is transmitted with the television signals. One disadvantage of teletext is that to make the information available on demand, because it is transmitted with television signals, it must be transmitted continuously. Consequently the volume of data that is available is limited.

On the other hand, since viewdata is accessed by the public telephone network there is no theoretical restriction on the volume of information that can be accessed. There is of course a practical one, fixed by the size of the computer being used. More importantly, the user is allowed to enter data as well as use the data entry device to specify what information is required. When the system is fully developed, television sets will be available with adaptors and data entry devices already built into them rather than provided as extras for an ordinary television set. These new sets will be capable of receiving both viewdata and teletext transmission.

Similar systems are being developed by television and telecommunication companies throughout the world, and readers are encouraged to investigate the facilities available in their own countries.

It may seem that the television set is being used merely as a convenient visual display unit to receive information transmitted from a computer. In many cases it will be, and this will provide access to an enormous amount of information for the general public at their own convenience. However, one possible development is that of an 'intelligent' viewdata terminal. Such a device will be equipped with its own CPU and main memory, plus other peripherals such as a printer and perhaps floppy disk (see Chapter 4). This opens up the possibility of 'telesoftware'. With such a system, a program could be transmitted from the central computer system to the user's viewdata device and executed there. The advantage here is that the user does not have to pay for the connect time while the program is being executed but only during the transmission of the program into the viewdata terminal. This could be very useful in computer-aided learning (CAL) because students can learn at their own pace and at the same cost. It could also be used to give access to business programs, and so provide a cheap form of small business computer service. One of the obvious problems, however, is how to prevent people from extracting programs for their own use (a large part of the revenue for running viewdata is clearly from the connect time to it). When the system is fully available there will be a number of ways to overcome this.

3.5 Specific transducers

The advent of the microprocessor has highlighted the uses of computers for control of machine tools and other processes. This has entailed the development of devices which are able to measure some parameter of the product performance in a way which is readily converted to digital signals. A *transducer* is a device which is able to convert energy from one form to another. For example, a loudspeaker is a transducer which converts electronic signals to sound waves.

Most naturally occurring signals have an *analogue* nature, i.e. they vary continuously. In order that such signals can be processed by a computer, they have to be converted into a *digital* form. This conversion is carried out by sampling the input signal at regular intervals and passing a value corresponding to the sampled value to the computer. Such devices are called *analogue-to-digital converters* and will be a constituent part of any transducer sampling analogue signals. For example, a temperature sensor will require such a converter.

In the control of machine tools the digital output from the computer can be used directly to cause some on-off type action to be undertaken, e.g. the starting of a drill. The subsequent lowering and raising of the drill would also be controlled digitally by, for example, having switches which are activated by the lateral movement of the drill.

Other transducers include magnetic switches and light activated switches which can be interfaced directly with the circuitry of a computer. The advantages of such devices are their reliability and cost-effectiveness. The main problem with contact switches is that they can cause switch bounce which gives more than one response when there should only be one.

Robot arms used in many manufacturing systems are other examples of devices controlled by computer.

The output from a computer cannot be used to drive directly a machine tool and there usually has to be some form of interface circuitry to allow the tool to be activated.

3.6 Summary

This chapter has indicated the large range of peripheral devices that are available and their areas of application. It is important that in any situation careful consideration should be given to the most appropriate peripheral device to employ. Not only does it have an effect on the speed of the task being performed but it is often the basis by which 'users' judge the success or otherwise of a computer system, since it is their point of contact with the computer.

CHAPTER 4
File store

In Chapter 1 the file store of a computer was introduced as a means of holding information in bulk. The type of information held in a file store is either data or programs. This information is held there rather than in the main memory because the main memory is relatively small in comparison to the file store and would soon become full. Most of the information held in a file store is only required for a short period when compared to the life of a computer and it is therefore most cost-effective to keep the information in the file store. A file store also has the advantage of being a permanent storage medium so that when power is switched off the information is still retained. This is not the case with most memories where information is lost as soon as power is removed (see Chapter 6). A file store device can therefore be used as a storage medium upon which the permanent programs such as compilers and operating system used by the computer are stored. The file store can be considered to be the second level in a storage hierarchy with the main memory at the top level. Programs may only execute when the algorithm and the necessary data are in the main memory. The computer provides an efficient means of transferring information between file store and memory so that processing delays are reduced to a minimum.

The remainder of this chapter discusses how file stores can be organised and the types of devices which can be used to provide file store systems.

4.1 Files, records and items

The file store of a computer system is analogous to a filing system for storing paperwork in a filing cabinet. Consider, for example, the file held by a general practitioner; the file comprises all the patients' records, each record containing the notes pertaining to a particular patient. Each record is differentiated from the others by means of a unique identifier, usually the name and address of the patient. In the general practice environment there is only one such file, but in a hospital there will be many such files, each one associated with a different speciality within the hospital. Hence a hospital can be seen as a collection of files, a file being made up of similar records and the records each containing information about a patient.

The file store of a computer system is very similar in that it is split up into many named files each of which can be individually processed by just referring to the name given to the file. A file is a collection of similar records, that is within a file all records hold the same kind of information in the same structure. The structure of records can vary between files because different files hold different information to which different structures are appropriate. A record is constructed from data values from which information can be found for the user processing the file. Data has no intrinsic meaning; data only becomes information when it is surrounded by other symbols. The number '30' has no meaning because it has no context; it only becomes information when surrounded by '°C' for example. Within a record it is only necessary to store the data, because within the record it will be known that a particular data item is used to represent temperatures. The '°C' only needs to be added when the data is presented to the user who needs the information that the temperature was 30°C.

A paper file is usually organised into some order, known to the user of the file, so that a particular record in the file can be found quickly. For example, patients' records could be stored alphabetically by surname and forenames. The surname and forenames are data items within the record which are used to order the file and as such are called 'key' data items. The person's marital status would probably not be a key data item but would be stored in the record. In such a paper file the organisation of the file is usually held in the memory of the person using the file and the user also knows the most efficient way to access a piece of information in the file.

In a file store maintained by a computer system the files can be organised in many ways, of which three predominate. The choice of a particular organisation depends upon the use to which the file is going to be put. The organisations are known as sequential, indexed-sequential and random.

4.1.1 Sequential files

A sequential file is one in which the records are stored and maintained in a predefined order specified by the user. Within such a file there is no means of adding records into the middle of the file except by copying, into another file, the records of the file up to the position of the new record, adding the new record and then copying the remainder of the original file. A similar process is needed to delete a record from the file, except that the record to be deleted is not copied to the new version of the file. In order to be able to manipulate a particular record, the file is processed from the beginning until the desired record is found. There is no direct analogy between a paper file and a sequential file because human operators usually have some idea of the location of records, so that they do not always have to search the file from the beginning.

4.1.2 Indexed-sequential files

An indexed-sequential file is one which is maintained in the same order as a sequential file except that usually some space is left for the addition of records. This organisation is augmented by indexes which allow the search for a particular record to be started at some point within the file, thus reducing the time to search for a particular record in the file. An indexed-sequential file is split up into smaller sections, each of which is maintained in sequential order. An index maintains the range of records kept in each section. To access a record therefore involves searching the index to find in which section the record resides and then searching the indicated section for the desired record. In a large file a hierarchy of indexes may be maintained so as to reduce the search time through the indexes.

An indexed-sequential file can be processed in two ways; namely, sequentially or randomly. When it is processed sequentially, the index is ignored and processing commences with the first record in the file and proceeds in order to the last record. When the file is processed randomly the indexes are used to shorten the search time.

Such files are used a great deal because their usage reflects the requirements of everyday applications. For example, consider the current account system of a bank. When an account holder comes to the bank to withdraw some money an immediate response is expected from the teller and so the file is processed randomly. It is impossible to guarantee that processing for the file will be in account number order. However, when the file is being processed to generate a report of all overdrawn accounts this can be done sequentially.

4.1.3 Random files

A random file utilises the fact that every record location within the file has a unique address. This address is usually an integer ranging from 1 to the

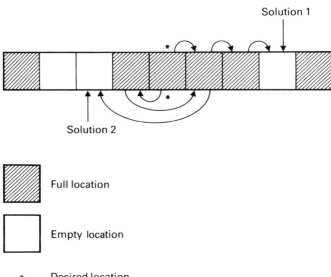

Full location

Empty location

* Desired location

Figure 4.1

number of records in the file. When a record is to be processed, the key value of the record is taken and processed by means of a *hashing algorithm*. The effect of the hashing algorithm is to map the range of key values on to the number of records which can be stored in the file.

The simplest mapping is 1:1 but this implies that there will be a location in the file for every key value. Normally this is not the case as most key fields contain some redundancy and therefore an n:1 mapping is employed. Redundancy within a key means that not all numerical combinations are used; for example, in a bank account number, part of it may represent the type of account. The net effect of such a mapping is that it is possible for the hashing algorithm to generate the same record address for records with different key values. Hence the algorithm has to be able to deal with this, a situation known as *synonyms*.

There are a number of ways of dealing with this. Two simple solutions are as follows. Either the record is placed in the next empty record location to be found as the file is read in order or, alternatively, the record is placed in the record location nearest to the desired location which is not occupied. The second solution involves accessing record locations to the left and right of the desired location whereas the first only requires access to records to the right. Figure 4.1 illustrates these alternatives.

4.1.4 Filing systems and privacy

A computer system is able to store and maintain many files for many different users and it is therefore vitally important that the different users are able to gain access only to those files to which they are entitled. Hence most computer systems use filing systems which enable users to maintain a record of the files which they own. In more flexible systems, users will be able to gain access to other users' files provided the owner of the file has granted the necessary access rights to the user wishing to gain access. Such systems usually involve the use of a password system.

When a file is created a user will have a set of access rights which he can associate with the file, and by allocating a password to a particular access right users who know the password will be able to gain that type of access to the file. Typically the access rights could be: private, read only, modify, execute only. If a file is given the access right *private* then only the owner of the file will be allowed access to the file. *Read only* implies that users who know the password will be able to access the file but only for reading. *Modify* implies that read and write access is allowed. *Execute only* means that the file contains a program which can only be executed by persons knowing the password. In a completely flexible system the owner of a file would be able to assign many different passwords to each of the access types in order to support the privacy requirements of complex filing systems.

4.2 Storage media

This section describes the techniques which can be used to implement the devices used to support file stores, and how the different file organisations can be implemented on the devices. The majority of these devices use some form of magnetic recording facility. In simple terms, a magnetic field can be applied to a magnetic material causing the material to store the corresponding field. Thus it is possible to store binary information by recording fields of different density or by storing fields of different orientation. Information can be read from such a magnetic material by passing the material in front of a detector which is able to detect the magnetic field.

The most common domestic use of magnetic storage techniques is in a tape recorder. The main difference between the domestic and computing environments is that a computer records information in binary form whereas a tape recorder records analogue information. The analogue information requires a range of magnetic densities large enough to discriminate between the musical or speech frequencies.

4.2.1 Tape storage

Historically tape storage was one of the first magnetic storage devices to be

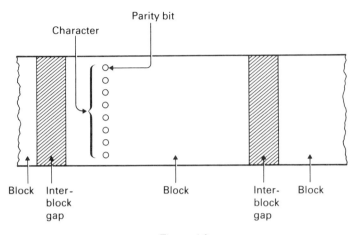

Figure 4.2

developed and it has been utilised by the computing industry in the following manner.

A character of information is stored as a bit pattern in parallel across the width of the tape (see Figure 4.2). The data is recorded together with a *parity bit*. A parity bit is a means of providing a check that the data has been stored correctly. If we consider an eight-bit character of which one is the parity bit then either odd or even parity can be used. In even parity systems the number of bits set to '1' in the character code is summed and if the number is even the parity bit remains at '0', otherwise it is set to '1'. Hence it is possible to detect when there is an error in a character, but it is not possible to correct errors. The correction of errors is dealt with in section 4.3

Data is recorded on magnetic tape at the rate of either 800, 1600 or 6250 bits per inch which, because a character is stored across the tape, is also the rate at which characters are stored. The tape passes through the drive mechanism at 75 inches per second giving a data transfer rate of 60 to 470 kb/s (kb means kilobytes or thousand bytes). A magnetic tape is usually no longer than 2400 feet and can be as short as 100 feet. The amount of data which can be stored on one magnetic tape is therefore very large, ranging up to 180 Mb (Mb = megabytes or million bytes). It is therefore impossible to transfer the whole tape into the memory of a computer at one time, so the tape is logically split up into blocks and the tape mechanism transfers one block at a time. The tape therefore has to stop after the transfer of each block and has to be able to get up to full speed before it encounters the next block. The part of the tape used for stopping and starting is called the inter-block gap and it contains no information. The inter-block gap is usually of the order of ½ to ¾ inch.

A block is used to store one or more records and the blocking factor of a particular file is the number of records stored per block. Some magnetic tape systems only have fixed length blocks, but the majority have variable length blocks because the user is best able to choose the size of the block commensurate with the application. There is a relatively simple trade-off: the larger the block the more data that can be stored on the tape because of the fewer inter-block gaps necessary, but the larger the block the more memory is required to store the block.

If more than one record is stored per block, a block only has to be transferred to memory when all the records in the memory buffer have been processed. The memory buffer is the place to which a block is transferred. Hence every read issued from a program may not cause a transfer from the tape because there may still be records to be read in the buffer. This aspect of memory buffer management is usually transparent to the user, and the current state of the buffer is maintained by that part of the operating system controlling the magnetic tape subsystem.

Magnetic tape is usually only used to store sequential files because there is no means of moving the tape forwards and backwards at a sufficient speed to be able to carry out the random processing required by the other file organisations.

Magnetic tape drives can take several forms. The most usual on mainframe computers is the reel-to-reel system using ½ inch wide tape. The tape is passed from one reel to another and when processing is complete the tape has to be rewound on to the original reel. Several mini- and microcomputers use a cassette mechanism which is very similar to an audio cassette and uses ¼ inch wide tape. These cassette mechanisms tend to be very much slower, as data is stored serially rather than in parallel but the tape and drives are very much cheaper.

There is also a cartridge system which employs ½ inch wide tape and uses the same technique as the reel to reel, except that the tape is totally enclosed in the cartridge. A mass storage device has been developed that accommodates many hundreds of such cartridges which can be automatically loaded into the drive mechanism. This device has a storage capacity measured in thousands of millions of bytes, but access to a particular byte is relatively rapid because the storage capacity is physically split up into the cartridges which can be loaded fairly quickly (10 to 15 seconds).

4.2.2 Disk storage

A disk storage system comprises two major parts, of which the first is a circular plate mounted on a central spindle. The plate is coated with a magnetic material, usually on both sides of the plate. The diameter of the plate can vary from 5 to 15 inches depending upon the disk system. Secondly there is a read/write head assembly which is able to move across the surface of the plate while the plate is made to rotate. In smaller disk

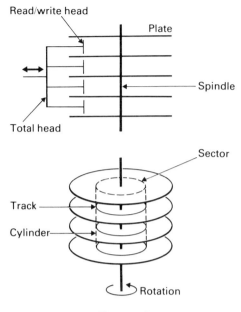

Figure 4.3

systems there will be one such complete assembly; however, in larger systems many plates will be stacked upon the same spindle, each surface having its associated read/write head assembly. The structure of a multiple plate disk is shown in Figure 4.3; in such a system all the read/write heads are attached to a common movement so that all heads are in the same position relative to the disk surface.

In order that the process of data transfer to and from the disk system can be understood it is first necessary to define some terms commonly associated with disk systems. A *track* is that part of the disk surface which can be read by one read/write head without moving the heads. On one surface the individual tracks make a series of concentric circles corresponding to the position of the head. The number of tracks per surface varies with systems but can be as few as 30 to as many as 400. In a multi-surface system a *cylinder* comprises all the tracks which can be read without moving the read/write heads. The system shown in Figure 4.3 has 8 tracks per cylinder. The quantity of data which is stored in a track is usually too large to be transferred in one read to the computer system's memory. A track is therefore subdivided into a number of *sectors*, a sector being the unit of data transfer between the disk and the memory. A sector may contain several, one or part of a record depending upon the application. The disk system has a means of determining the current position of the disk relative to the read/write heads so that it can process the correct sector. Between each sector there is an *inter-sector gap*, which contains addressing information and provides sufficient time for the disk electronics to switch between one track and another within the same cylinder. The inter-sector gap does not provide sufficient time for the head to be moved between one cylinder and another and also be able to read 'consecutive' sectors.

Every access to the disk could involve a head movement plus a time to wait for the appropriate sector to come under the read/write heads. There is usually a larger time penalty if many cylinders have to be traversed and it is therefore normal for files to be allocated to contiguous cylinders. To overcome some of the delays, disk systems are being constructed which have more than one read/write assembly so that it is then possible to read and write from each assembly at the same time.

In order that data can be accessed from the disk it is necessary for the software to provide the cylinder, track and sector values of the data to be processed. The disk system then moves the heads accordingly, and the data can subsequently be transferred. Most disk systems usually incorporate a 'retry' mechanism as a means of ensuring data accuracy. That is, when data is written to the disk it is immediately read back, after waiting one rotation, to ensure that the stored data is the same as that transmitted to the disk system. If it is not the same, several attempts are made to write the data on the disk. If none of these is successful, a disk error has occurred which will require maintenance to be carried out upon the system to ascertain the reason for the fault. Most systems do not employ a retry mechanism upon reading data because this process is not prone to errors.

Before a disk can be used, it has to be formatted; this usually means storing the cylinder, track and sector numbers in the inter-sector gap prior to each sector on the disk. This information is read at the same time as the following sector is processed, and thus provides an added check that the correct sector is being processed. That is, the sector address provided by the software matches that provided from the disk. If there was no match, it would usually imply that the disk hardware was not functioning correctly.

Disk systems take many forms which are commonly categorised as floppy, hard and fixed or exchangeable. Floppy and hard relate to the nature of the base material upon which the magnetic material is coated. If it is constructed from flexible plastic material the term *floppy* is used. If the material is rigid the term *hard* is used. Floppy systems tend to be much cheaper, not be so critical in their manufacturing tolerances but also have a much slower data transfer rate and smaller data capacity than hard disc systems. Floppy disks tend to predominate in microcomputer systems where the requirement for large fast disk storage is not necessary.

A *fixed* disk system is one in which it is not possible to remove the disk(s) from the drive mechanism. An *exchangeable* disk system is one in which the disk can be removed and replaced by a different disk. An exchangeable system allows for unlimited storage but only a part of the total can be accessed at any one time.

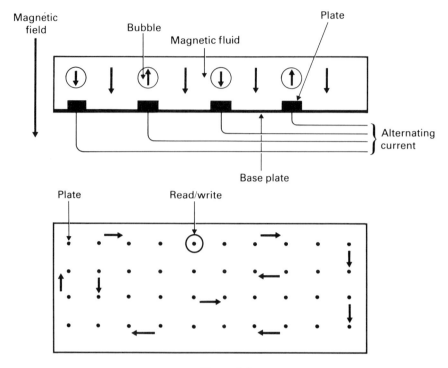

Figure 4.4

4.2.3 Bubble memories

A bubble memory is a magnetic device in which magnetic 'bubbles' can be manipulated in such a way as to store data. The device comprises magnetic fluid on a base plate upon which a pattern of electrical plates is arranged. An alternating current can be applied to each of the plates in turn so as to cause the movement of magnetic material from one plate to the next. The complete assembly is held in a magnetic field which ensures that the fluid particles are all aligned in the same direction. Within the assembly there is a means of causing a particle of the fluid to be magnetically reversed, thus forming a bubble of reverse magnetisation to the majority of the fluid. There is also a mechanism by which it is possible to detect the magnetisation of a particular bubble. The structure is shown in Figure 4.4.

The operation of a bubble memory is as follows. Data is written to the memory by sending it the bit pattern. Whenever there is a one bit the write assembly causes the current bubble to be inverted relative to the rest of the fluid. If there is a zero bit then the bubble has the same orientation as the rest of the fluid. The applied alternating current then causes the bubble to move to the next plate and so on until the whole of the data has been encoded. The choice of field and size of alternating current are critical so as

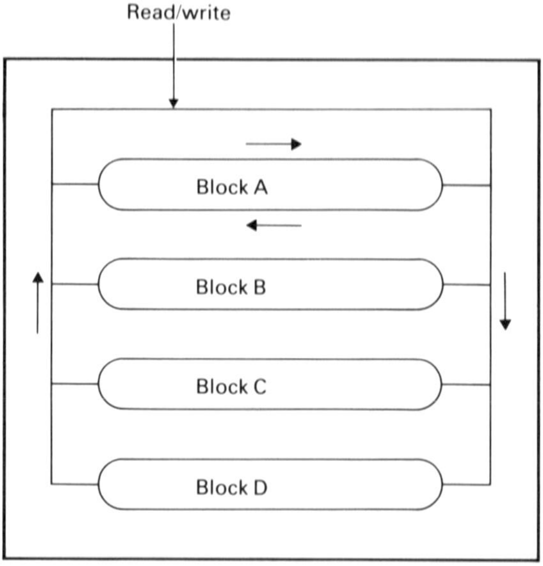

Figure 4.5

to ensure that the bubble does not change its state. Data is read by passing the stream of data bits past the read point. Hence the memory has to wait until the required data passes the read point. In larger memories data is organised into smaller blocks as shown in Figure 4.5. When data from a particular block is required it is shifted into the outer path and then back into the block.

Such devices, although cheap and small, are relatively slow, and tend to be used in applications where speed is not essential. Such an example is a portable terminal in which it is possible to store data, then connect the terminal to an acoustic coupler and thus to a computer. The stored data can then be transferred from the memory. Also, these devices are not volatile, which means that information is not lost when electrical power is removed, and so standard information can be maintained by the terminal at all times.

4.2.4 Charge coupled devices

A charge coupled device is very similar to a bubble memory except that electric charges are transferred rather than magnetic bubbles, and the whole device can be constructed by means of semiconductor techniques. The only further requirement is that because an electrical charge leaks away the electrical state of each charge has to be periodically renewed. The structure of a charge coupled device is shown in Figure 4.6.

Data is applied at the read/write point and a charge is either created or

Read/write

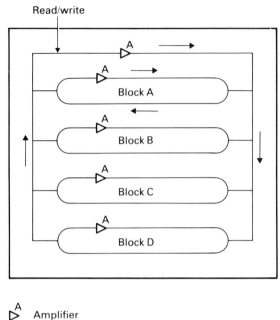

A
▷ Amplifier

Figure 4.6

not depending upon the state of the current bit. The charge is then made to move by applying an alternating current to plates within the semiconductor material in the same way as in the bubble memory. The data is then moved into one of the blocks in which it continually rotates through the amplifier thus ensuring that data is not lost. Data is read by passing charges from the appropriate block round the outer loop past the read point. The chief disadvantage of this memory is that it is volatile, i.e. when electrical power is removed data is lost.

Charge coupled memories are cheaper and faster than bubble memories and have a larger data capacity. In both cases, however, it is unlikely that they will be used as the main memory in a computer system due to the delay in accessing the data. However, they are quite likely to be used as a more reliable form of mass storage possibly replacing the disk and tape systems. The cost differential, however, is such that the replacement of disk systems is still a long time away.

4.2.5 Content addressable file store (CAFS)

Most data processing applications require records to be fetched from disk or tape storage and then processed to find out their current state; modifications are then made to only a few of the records, depending upon certain conditions, and the records are then written back. In such an application every record is read into main memory, interrogated and in a large number of cases immediately written back to the storage device. A content addressable file store is essentially a disk system to which has been added some processing capability. The system is designed so that only those records to be processed are transferred to the main memory; those requiring no attention are never transferred. In such a system holding many different types of data it is necessary for the programmer to be able to specify details about the records and the condition(s) under which records are to be passed to the main memory. Once the content addressable file store has been so 'programmed' it will access all the records in the file and select only those which satisfy the conditions. Programming such a system requires a mechanism that can identify the fields and sizes of a record together with field values of the records desired for processing. This type of device therefore reduces the amount of work which has to be undertaken by the central processing unit and allows the CPU to do other work, thus increasing the efficiency of the overall system.

4.3 Error checking

During the transfer of data from a disk or tape system to main memory data may become corrupted. It is therefore necessary to have some means of detecting errors which have occurred and possibly correcting them. These techniques can also be applied to the transmission of data in a communications link.

The first technique is to apply an augmented type of parity checking which thus ensures that the individual characters are correct. Other techniques generate a check-sum mechanism to a block of data and so provide a check on the whole data.

The simple parity system described earlier is only able to detect an error but not correct it, and it is possible for more than one error in a character to be missed. A simple expansion of the system is to have more parity bits which check only part of the character. Consider a four-bit code in which the bits are named a, b, c and d, and which has two parity bits P1 and P2. Parity P1 operates on bits a, b and c and parity bit P2 operates upon bits b, c and d. If P1 shows an error state then the error is known to be in bits a, b or c and similarly for parity bit P2 with b, c and d. If both parity bits are incorrect then it is known that bits b and c contain the error. By adding a third parity bit as follows it is possible to detect all errors and correct some of them:

P1   a   b   c
P2   b   c   d
P3   c   d   a

If P1 and P2 are in error, the implication is that bit b is in error and can therefore be corrected. In this example it can be seen that errors in bit c can be detected but not corrected.

Thus by adding more parity bits more checks can be undertaken, but as the number of parity bits increases the possibility of error in the parity bits themselves also increases. The advantage of these parity systems, however, is that when data correction can be undertaken it saves data transmission time because erroneous data does not need to be retransmitted.

The above system would, however, become extremely inefficient if in parallel transmission one of the transmission lines were to go down. Such errors are detected by the check-sum mechanism. A check-sum can be formed by adding together all the words to be transmitted, ignoring overflow. The resultant sum is called the check-sum. The check-sum is then transmitted after the data. On receipt of data the check-sum is recalculated and checked with the transmitted check-sum. If there is a discrepancy it is known that an error has occurred.

By combining these two techniques it is possible to detect errors at the character and the block level, and thereby provide a means of ensuring that stored data and transmitted data correspond.

4.4 Summary

This chapter has described methods by which bulk storage of data can be achieved. The organisation of the data so that it is held in a form useful to the programmer has also been considered in relation to the physical characteristics of the devices. Finally the concept of error checking has been introduced, and techniques have been briefly described that allow errors to be detected and in some cases corrected.

4.5 Problems

(1) Choose a suitable file organisation for the following applications and justify your answer. How would you organise the individual records of each file?
- current accounts for a bank
- hospital outpatients' clinic records
- an appointments system for a small firm
- a payroll system
- a students' record system
- a library's catalogues and indexes

(2) From current manufacturers' information find out the cost per byte of storage of the following storage media:
- hard disk
- floppy disk
- bubble memory
- charge coupled devices
- tape

From the same source of information find out:
(a) the dimensions of the storage media and associated hardware;
(b) the transfer rate;
(c) the delay between data being requested and the data becoming available for transfer;
(d) Total storage capacity.

NB: These figures will vary with manufacturer and type of media.

(3) A magnetic tape of total length 2400 feet has data recorded on it at 1600 bits/inch. It utilises an inter-block gap of ½ inch. A file is stored upon the tape which contains records of 400 characters.

What is the total capacity of the tape when the number of records per block is 1, 2, 3, 8, 10, or 16? How does this affect the size of memory buffer required?

Numbers and character codes

5.1 Number systems

Although in everyday life people generally use the decimal number system
for counting, it is more convenient to use the binary number system in a
computer, since, as explained in Chapter 2, electronic components are
usually in one of two states used to represent 0 and 1, the two digits used in
the binary number system.

The binary system can perhaps be best explained by considering first a
typical number in the decimal system. This system uses ten symbols 0 to 9.
The weighting of each digit is a power of ten determined by the position of
the digit within the number and consequently decimal numbers are said to
be to the base 10.

For example, the decimal number 4528.035 is made up as follows:

$$4 \times 10^3 + 5 \times 10^2 + 2 \times 10^1 + 8 \times 10^0 \cdot 0 \times 10^{-1} + 3 \times 10^{-2} + 5 \times 10^{-3}$$
$$\text{(1,000s)} \quad \text{(100s)} \quad \text{(10s)} \quad \text{(units)} \quad \text{(0.1s)} \quad \text{(0.01s)} \quad \text{(0.001s)}$$
$$\text{Decimal}$$
$$\text{point}$$

Remember that any number raised to the power of zero is 1. The binary
number system (base 2) uses two digits (binary digits or bits) 0 and 1 and a
number has the same structure as a decimal number except that the
weighting of each digit is a power of two. Thus $101101 =$

$$1 \times 2^5 + 0 \times 2^4 + 1 \times 2^3 + 1 \times 2^2 + 0 \times 2^1 + 1 \times 2^0$$

which is equivalent to 45 in the decimal system.

Other number bases encountered are octal (base 8) and hexadecimal (base 16). These are of importance because they can be used as a 'shorthand' for binary numbers. This is because three binary digits can be represented by the numbers 0 to 7, i.e. the octal range, while four binary digits can be represented by the numbers 0 to 15, i.e. the hexadecimal range (see Table 5.1 later).

The representation of a digit in the hexadecimal system creates a problem, since, if the normal decimal numerics were used, two characters would be needed to represent each of the values 10 to 15. This is overcome by using letters to extend the representation of numbers, i.e. A = 10, B = 11, . . . F = 15 (see Table 5.4 later in the chapter).

As an example of a number expressed in these different number bases, consider the decimal number 1984 represented in binary, octal and hexadecimal:

Binary:

$$
\begin{array}{cccccc}
1 & 1 & 1 & 1 & 1 & 0 \\
\end{array}
$$
$$(1 \times 2^{10} + 1 \times 2^9 + 1 \times 2^8 + 1 \times 2^7 + 1 \times 2^6 + 0 \times 2^5$$
$$
\begin{array}{ccccc}
0 & 0 & 0 & 0 & 0 \\
\end{array}
$$
$$+ 0 \times 2^4 + 0 \times 2^3 + 0 \times 2^2 + 0 \times 2^1 + 0 \times 2^0)$$

Octal:

$$
\begin{array}{cccc}
3 & 7 & 0 & 0 \\
\end{array}
$$
$$(3 \times 8^3 + 7 \times 8^2 + 0 \times 8^1 + 0 \times 8^0)$$

Hexadecimal:

$$
\begin{array}{ccc}
7 & C & 0 \\
\end{array}
$$
$$(7 \times 16^2 + 12 \times 16^1 + 0 \times 16^0)$$

Section 5.2 explains the process involved in converting from one number base to another.

The usefulness of octal or hexadecimal representation as a shorthand for binary numbers can be seen from the above example. The binary system results in numbers with a large number of digits. On paper this can be more conveniently expressed by the octal or hexadecimal systems which require fewer digits.

Note how that since some numbers could equally well be a number in decimal, binary, octal or hexadecimal, for example 101, it is usual to signify the base in which the number is represented by writing, for example, 101_2 for binary or 101_8 for octal.

5.2 Conversion between the number systems

Table 5.1 lists some examples that may be useful in converting numbers from one base to another.

Table 5.1

Decimal(n)	Binary	Octal	Hexadecimal	2^n
0	0	0	0	1
1	1	1	1	2
2	10	2	2	4
3	11	3	3	8
4	100	4	4	16
5	101	5	5	32
6	110	6	6	64
7	111	7	7	128
8	1000	10	8	256
9	1001	11	9	512
10	1010	12	A	1024
11	1011	13	B	2048
12	1100	14	C	4096
13	1101	15	D	8192
14	1110	16	E	16384
15	1111	17	F	32768

5.2.1 From binary to octal

Any octal digit can be represented by three binary digits. Consequently, to convert a binary number to octal, simply divide the binary number into groups of three binary digits, starting at the binary point (and working both ways if it is a fractional number), and represent each group by its equivalent octal digit.

Consider again the earlier example of the binary equivalent of 1984:

Binary:	11	111	000	000
Octal digits:	3	7	0	0

To convert from octal to binary is exactly the reverse procedure. Replace each octal digit by its 3-bit binary equivalent.

5.2.2 Between binary and hexadecimal

This is very similar to the octal conversions, except that each hexadecimal digit is represented by four binary digits. Consequently it is necessary to divide the binary number into groups of four digits and replace each of these by their equivalent hexadecimal value; the reverse procedure is used to convert from hexadecimal to binary.

Referring once more to our example of the binary equivalent of 1984 we have:

Binary:	111	1100	0000
Hexadecimal digits:	7	C	0

5.2.3 Between binary and decimal

To convert a number from decimal to binary, one of two methods can be used. One method is to consider the composition of a binary number as defined in section 5.1. The number to be converted must be decomposed into its various powers of 2 corresponding to bit positions.

For example, the decimal number 24.625 is made up of:

$$
\begin{aligned}
1 &\times 16 & (2^4) \\
1 &\times 8 & (2^3) \\
0 &\times 4 & (2^2) \\
0 &\times 2 & (2^1) \\
0 &\times 1 & (2^0) \\
1 &\times 0.5 & (2^{-1}) \\
0 &\times 0.25 & (2^{-2}) \\
1 &\times 0.125 & (2^{-3})
\end{aligned}
$$

Consequently the binary equivalent is 1 1 0 0 0 . 1 0 1.

An alternative method, which will only work for integer decimal numbers, is to divide the number by 2 repeatedly. The remainder at each stage (either a 0 or a 1) gives the next bit in the binary equivalent. As an example, consider the decimal number 207.

Quotient	Remainder	
207		
103	1	rightmost bit
51	1	
25	1	
12	1	
6	0	
3	0	
1	1	
0	1	leftmost bit

The resulting binary number is 11001111.

To convert binary to decimal sum up the powers of 2 that correspond to the 1 bits in the binary number. (As an example, refer to the conversion of a binary number in section 5.1.)

5.3 The representation of numeric information

5.3.1 Integer numbers

A decimal integer (whole number) can simply be converted to its equivalent binary value and stored in memory as the contents of, say, one word. However, if, as is usual, it is required to store negative numbers, some way has to be found of storing the sign. There are a number of ways, but two of the most common are *sign and magnitude* and *two's complement*.

Sign and magnitude

With sign and magnitude representation the most significant bit of the word is used to indicate the sign (0 represents positive and 1 represents negative). The remainder of the word holds the absolute magnitude of the number. For example, in a 16-bit word, the values $+11$ and -14 would be represented as

$$\text{Sign} \begin{cases} 0000000000001011 & +11 \\ 1000000000001110 & -14 \end{cases}$$

One of the disadvantages of such a representation is that there are two representations for zero: $+0$ and -0.

Two's complement

With this representation a positive number is stored with a sign bit (the most significant bit) of 0, the remainder of the word containing the binary value of the number.

A negative number, however, is stored as the two's complement of the binary pattern of the equivalent positive number. To obtain the two's complement of a binary number, replace all zeros by ones and all the ones by zeros (i.e. flip the bits) and add 1. For example consider the 8-bit representation of the number -4.

Take the two's complement of the following:

$$
\begin{array}{rl}
 & 00000100 \\
= & 11111011 \\
 & \underline{+1} \\
= & \underline{11111100}
\end{array}
$$

The most significant bit is still the sign bit, a 1 indicating a negative number.

There are two advantages of this representation. First, there is only one representation of 0 and this is $+0$. Secondly, in order to perform the computation of subtraction such as A − B, the two's complement of B is added to A. Thus the arithmetic unit of the CPU only needs to be able to complement (a simple bit flipping operation) and add. Consider as an example the calculation of 3 − 2:

= 00000011 − 00000010
= 00000011 + two's complement of 00000010
= 00000011 + 11111110
= 00000001 (the carry bit beyond the end of the word is discarded).

Clearly this is the value +1.

If the result of an operation involving two numbers exceeds the maximum number allowed, overflow has occurred. This can be detected by examining the carry bit (which is normally discarded) after an arithmetic operation has been performed.

As an example, consider the sum of two 4-bit unsigned numbers (which must be in the range 0 to 15):

$$1001 \quad (9 + 8 = 17)$$
$$+1000$$
$$\overline{10001}$$

Here, the result (17) is larger than can be contained in four bits and the carry bit (1 in this example) indicates that overflow has occurred. However, with signed numbers, setting the carry bit to 1 does not always indicate overflow because the carry notation can become confused with that used for negative numbers (two's complement). For example, if we use two's complement notation to represent a negative number, the calculation of −3 and −2 would result in a carry bit of 1, but the result could easily be stored in four bits, even with one bit indicating the sign.

When manipulating two numbers where negative numbers are stored in two's complement form, overflow has occurred if the two numbers being added have the same sign and the result has the opposite sign.

5.3.2 Floating point numbers

In mathematical notation, a representation of numbers known as floating point notation is commonly used, particularly to represent very large or very small numbers. For example, the mass of a hydrogen atom is 1.660×10^{-24} grams. Because the range of numbers that can be represented by integer notation is limited by the word length, floating point notation is convenient for representing non-integer numbers (often referred to as 'real' numbers) in a computer.

The following examples show the floating point representation of some 'real' numbers:

$$
\begin{aligned}
562.428 &= 0.562428 \times 10^3 \\
-62.018 &= -0.62018 \times 10^2 \\
0.000527 &= 0.527 \times 10^{-3} \\
110.11011 &= 0.11011011 \times 2^{-3} \\
0.00101101 &= 0.101101 \times 2^{-2}
\end{aligned}
$$

Such numbers can be represented as:

$$
\pm m \times r^e
$$

where m is known as the mantissa, r the radix, and e the exponent.

Within a computer, a binary floating point number can be represented by storing the values of m and e, the radix being assumed. Consider the following example:

$$
0.11011011 \times 2^3
$$

Only the values 11011011 and 3 need be stored, the others being assumed. In fact if the mantissa is adjusted so that the first digit to follow the assumed point is a 1, the number is said to be *normalised* and this 1 need not be stored. (Obviously the arithmetic and logic unit needs to be aware of it in order to perform the computations correctly.)

On the assumption that 32 bits are available (either a 32-bit word or two 16-bit words), a typical representation of a floating point number in a computer would be as follows:

Mantissa	Exponent
← 24 bits →	← 8 bits →

The mantissa can be stored in either sign and magnitude form or two's complement form, as in the case of integer numbers. In practice, since special hardware (or software) is necessary to perform computations on floating point numbers, there is no particular advantage in using the two's complement form, so the use of sign and magnitude is not uncommon.

With the exponent, however, a representation known as *excess* form is often used. For n bit numbers, the value is stored as the sum of itself and 2^{n-1}. For example, for $n = 8$ (the size of the exponent used in the earlier example) the system would be called excess 128 and the exponent would be stored as its true value plus 128. Since, for 8-bit exponents, the value of the exponent could lie between -128 and $+127$, storing it in excess 128 form means that the value lies between 0 and 255. The main advantage to be gained is that because the exponent usually only occupies part of a word its value will have to be extracted by using a suitable mask and logical AND instruction (see Chapter 7). If it were extracted and left in a word greater in size than 8 bits, the leading bits would be zero, and would have to be changed if the number had been negative in order to maintain the two's complement form of representation. With the excess form, no such change has to take place, the exponents always being positive. Consequently, processing of the number will be faster. When printing out a result, the binary floating point number will have to be converted to decimal, and it is an easy task at that stage to subtract 128 from the exponent.

The example discussed used 32 bits to store a floating point number. Although this is common, many machines provide facilities for defining 64-bit, 128-bit or even 60-bit and 120-bit floating point numbers. Increasing the number of binary digits available for storing the mantissa will clearly increase the accuracy to which a number can be stored. Increasing the number of binary digits available for storing the exponent will increase the range of numbers that can be stored.

5.4 Transmission codes

The transmission of data consists essentially of passing a stream of binary digits over a line connecting two devices. The information is transmitted as a sequence of characters, each character being in a particular code.

5.4.1 The Baudot code

A very common code is used in telegraphy and telex transmissions (the public system for sending telegrams and telex messages) is the *Baudot code* (see Figure 5.1). It is a 5-bit code and consequently it would appear that only 32 different characters can be represented. In order to get round this restriction there are two special characters called letter shift and figure shift which correspond to an upper and lower case form. After a letter shift character is received all the following characters are from the letter shift alphabet until a figure shift character is received, and vice versa. The main disadvantage with the Baudot code is that there is still a very limited character set and that there is an apparent lack of logic in the allocation of bit combinations to each character.

5.4.2 Binary coded decimal (BCD)

If the data to be transmitted consists of numbers only it may be convenient to transmit these in their binary form rather than convert to one of the

Table 5.2 The EBCDIC code

LSD \ MSD	0000	0001	0010	0011	0100	0101	0110	0111	1000	1001	1010	1011	1100	1101	1110	1111
0000	NULL				SP	&	−									0
0001							/		a	j			A	J		1
0010									b	k	s		B	K	S	2
0011									c	l	t		C	L	T	3
0100	PF	RES	BYP	PN					d	m	u		D	M	U	4
0101	HT	NL	LF	RS					e	n	v		E	N	V	5
0110	LC	BS	EOB	UC					f	o	w		F	O	W	6
0111	DEL	IL	PRE	EOT					g	p	x		G	P	X	7
1000									h	q	y		H	Q	Y	8
1001									i	r	z		I	R	Z	9
1010			SM		¢	!		:								
1011					.	$	,	#								
1100					<	*	%	@								
1101					(	)	_	'								
1110					+	;	>	=								
1111					|	¬	?	"								

Most significant digits (columns) / Least significant digits (rows)

PRE	Prefix
SM	Set mode
PN	Punch on
RS	Reader stop
UC	Upper case
EOT	End of transmission
SP	Space
NL	New line
BS	Backspace
IL	Idle
BYP	Bypass
LF	Line feed
EOB	End of block
NULL	Null/Idle
PF	Punch off
HT	Horizontal tab
LC	Lower case
DEL	Delete
RES	Restore

1	2	3	4	5	Lower case	Upper case
•	•				A	–
•			•	•	B	?
	•	•	•		C	:
•			•		D	who are you?
•					E	3
•		•	•		F	
	•		•	•	G	
		•		•	H	
	•	•			I	8
•	•		•		J	Bell
•	•	•	•		K	(
	•			•	L	)
		•	•	•	M	.
		•	•		N	,
			•	•	O	9
	•	•		•	P	0
•	•	•		•	Q	1
	•		•		R	4
•		•			S	!
				•	T	5
•	•	•			U	7
	•	•	•	•	V	=
•	•			•	W	2
•		•	•	•	X	/
•		•		•	Y	6
•				•	Z	+
					Blank	
•	•	•	•	•	Letters shift	↓
•	•		•	•	Figures shift	↑
		•			Space	
			•		Carriage return	<
	•				Line feed	≡

Figure 5.1

other more extensive codes. BCD is a system of coding in which each decimal digit is converted into its binary form and the whole number is then transmitted as a sequence of binary coded decimal digits. To represent any one of the decimal digits 0, 1, . . ., 9 requires four bits. For example, the decimal number 6 8 4 1 would be coded as:

$$0110 \quad 1000 \quad 0100 \quad 0001$$

5.4.3 The EBCDIC code

One of the major general codes in use is the EBCDIC Code. This stands for Extended Binary Decimal Interchange Code. Each character is represented by an 8-bit number and the complete code is given in Table 5.2. This code was initially developed by IBM for use on their range of computers but has since been used on a number of other computers.

5.4.4 The ASCII code

In an attempt to counter the threat of a proliferation of codes the American Standards Association (now known as the American National Standards Institute) defined a 7-bit code known as ASCII—the American Standard Code for Information Interchange (see Tables 5.3 and 5.4). This code has been widely accepted and is now in general use. It is often made into an 8-bit code by the addition of a parity bit. This involves the addition

Table 5.3 The ASCII code

		Most significant digits							
		000	001	010	011	100	101	110	111
	0000	NULL	DLE	SP	0	@	P		p
	0001	SOH	DC1	!	1	A	Q	a	q
	0010	STX	DC2	"	2	B	R	b	r
	0011	ETX	DC3	#	3	C	S	c	s
	0100	EOT	DC4	$	4	D	T	d	t
	0101	ENQ	NAK	%	5	E	U	e	u
	0110	ACK	SYNC	&	6	F	V	f	v
Least significant digits	0111	BELL	ETB	'	7	G	W	g	w
	1000	BKSP	S0	(	8	H	X	h	x
	1001	HT	S1	)	9	I	Y	i	y
	1010	LF	S2	*	:	J	Z	j	z
	1011	VT	ESC	+	;	K	[	k	{
	1100	FF	S4	,	<	L	\	l		
	1101	CR	S5	−	=	M	]	m	}
	1110	SO	S6	.	>	N	↑	n	~
	1111	SI	S7	/	?	O	←	o	DEL

NULL	Null/Idle	HT	Horizontal tab	NAK	Negative
SOH	Start of header	LF	Line feed		acknowlegement
STX	Start of text (message)	VT	Vertical tab	SYNC	Synchronous idle
ETX	End of message (text)	FF	Form feed	ETB	End of block
EOT	End of transmission	CR	Carriage return	S0-S7	Separator
ENQ	Enquire	SO	Shift out		information
ACK	Positive acknowledge	SI	Shift in	SP	Space
BELL	Audible signal	DLE	Data link escape	ESC	Escape
BKSP	Backspace	DC1-DC4	Device control	DEL	Delete/Idle

of the eighth bit such that the sum of binary 1s in any character is an odd number (odd parity) or an even number (even parity), both systems being in common use. This parity can be used as a crude check that the correct bits have been transmitted.

A number of characters in the ASCII code have special meanings. They are used as special control characters in connection with serial transmission of data from one machine to another (see section 13.5.1). The meanings of

Table 5.4 The ASCII code with hexadecimal bit pattern

Hex	ASCII	Hex	ASCII	Hex	ASCII
00	NULL	2B	+	56	V
01	SOH	2C	,	57	W
02	STX	2D	-	58	X
03	ETX	2E	.	59	Y
04	EOT	2F	/	5A	Z
05	ENQ	30	0	5B	[
06	ACK	31	1	5C	\
07	BELL	32	2	5D	]
08	BKSP	33	3	5E	↑
09	HT	34	4	5F	←
0A	LF	35	5	60	`
0B	VT	36	6	61	a
0C	FF	37	7	62	b
0D	CR	38	8	63	c
0E	SO	39	9	64	d
0F	SI	3A	:	65	e
10	DLE	3B	;	66	f
11	DC1	3C	<	67	g
12	DC2	3D	=	68	h
13	DC3	3E	>	69	i
14	DC4	3F	?	6A	j
15	NAK	40	@	6B	k
16	SYNC	41	A	6C	l
17	ETB	42	B	6D	m
18	S0	43	C	6E	n
19	S1	44	D	6F	o
1A	S2	45	E	70	p
1B	ESC	46	F	71	q
1C	S4	47	G	72	r
1D	S5	48	H	73	s
1E	S6	49	I	74	t
1F	S7	4A	J	75	u
20	SP	4B	K	76	v
21	!	4C	L	77	w
22	"	4D	M	78	x
23	#	4E	N	79	y
24	$	4F	O	7A	z
25	%	50	P	7B	{
26	&	51	Q	7C	|
27	'	52	R	7D	}
28	(	53	S	7E	~
29	)	54	T	7F	DEL
2A	*	55	U		

some of the control characters in Table 5.4 are as follows:

SOH (start of heading)	Used to indicate the start of control information at the beginning of a block of data.
STX (start of text)	Indicates the end of the heading and the beginning of a block of data.
EXT (end of text)	Used to indicate the end of a message text which started with an STX.
EOT (end of transmission)	Signifies the end of transmission.
ENQ (enquiry)	Used to request a response, such as the address or status of the receiver.
ACK (acknowledge)	Positive acknowledgement usually indicating a successful reception.
BEL (bell)	Character used to activate a visible, audible alarm at the receiving terminal device.
NAK (negative acknowledgement)	Indicates unsuccessful reception.
SYN (synchronous idle)	Used to identify a sequence of synchronising bits.
ETB (end of transmission block)	Used to indicate the end of a physical block of data where this may not coincide with the logical format of the data being transmitted.
CAN (cancel)	Used to signify that all preceding data in the block or message should be ignored.

5.5 Summary

Since the basic unit of information stored in a computer is an integer binary number, any other form of information has to be coded in some way. This chapter has explored how decimal numbers, both positive and negative, floating point numbers and character information may be coded. All of this information constitutes the data as described in section 1.2.2. Chapter 7 will describe how the computational operations (the algorithm) are coded in order to store these in memory.

5.6 Problems

(1) Convert the following decimal numbers to the equivalent binary numbers:

(a) 14	(e) 21	(i) 256
(b) 13	(f) 19	(j) 0.4375
(c) 15	(g) 63	(k) 512.5
(d) 6	(h) 103	(l) 131.5625

(2) Convert the following binary numbers to equivalent decimal numbers:

(a) 1101	(d) 1011	(g) 0.1011
(b) 1001	(e) 11011	(h) 111011.1011
(c) 10111	(f) 10101	(i) 11.01010111

(3) Perform the following additions and check by converting the binary numbers to decimal and adding:

(a) 1011.1 + 1011.11   (c) 0.1011 + 0.1101
(b) 100101 + 100101   (d) 1011.01 + 1001.11

(4) Perform the following subtractions in binary and check by converting the numbers to decimal and subtracting:

(a) 1111 − 1000 (c) 1011.1 − 111.1   (e) 111.11 − 111.1
(b) 1101 − 1011 (d) 1111.01 − 1011.1 (f) 1101.1 − 1110.01

(5) Convert the following hexadecimal numbers to decimal:

(a) B6C7   (b) 64AC   (c) A492   (d) D2763

(6) Convert the following octal numbers to decimal:

(a) 14	(c) 105	(e) 156
(b) 124	(d) 123	(f) 15.5

(7) Convert the following binary numbers to octal:

(a) 101101	(c) 10110111	(e) 011.1011011
(b) 101101110	(d) 110110.011	

(8) Convert the following octal numbers to binary:

(a) 56	(c) 231.2	(e) 454.45
(b) 43	(d) 231.4	(f) 32.234

(9) Convert the following decimal numbers to octal:

(a) 15	(c) 19	(e) 0.625
(b) 9	(d) 0.54	(f) 2.125

(10) Convert the following hexadecimal numbers to binary:

(a) CD   (b) 649   (c) A13   (d) AA   (e) ABCDE

(11) Convert the following binary numbers to hexadecimal:

(a) 10110111	(c) 1011111	(e) 101011.1011001
(b) 10011100	(d) 0.01111110	

(12) To convert a decimal integer X, whose value lies between 0 and 32767 into a 15-bit binary number, the following algorithm can be used:

(a) Is X ⩾ 16384? If so, set the most significant bit to 1 and subtract 16384 from X. Otherwise, set the most significant bit to zero and omit the subtraction step.

(b) Repeat step (a) using one half of the previous test constant to determine the next significant bit.

(c) Repeat until 15 bits have been obtained.

Write and test a program to implement the above algorithm.

(13) Find the two's complement of the following binary numbers:

00110101 and 01000000

(14) Add the binary number 01010000 to each of the two's complement numbers computed in Problem 13. Verify the results by converting all binary numbers to decimal and reworking the calculations in decimal.

(15) Perform the following subtractions using two's complement arithmetic:

(a) 00110110 − 00011101   (c) 01001001 − 01101000
(b) 00011111 − 11101010   (d) 00001110 − 00001111

(16) Consider the following addition problems for 3-bit binary numbers in two's complement. For each sum, determine whether overflow has occurred:

```
000   000   111   100   100
001   111   110   111   100

___   ___   ___   ___   ___

___   ___   ___   ___   ___
```

(17) (a) Describe one of the methods commonly used for representing signed integers in present-day digital computers. What are the maximum and minimum values which may be represented by your method?

(b) Express the contents of the 32-bit word containing hexadecimal 008150C1 as:
(i) four EBCDIC characters;
(ii) a fixed point integer decimal number.
How is a computer able to distinguish between the two?

(c) The following two integers have been printed in their binary coded decimal (BCD) representation. Convert them to a normalised floating point representation using six bits for the mantissa and five bits for the exponent.

Number 1: 000100011001
Number 2: 00100000

(18) Determine the accuracy and range of numbers stored in floating point format by using the representation described in section 5.3.2. What would be the effect on accuracy and range if the number of available bits were increased to 64 bits, the exponent remaining at 8 bits?

(19) (a) (i) Represent each of the decimal values 26, −37 and 19909 in their fixed point number format, assuming a word length of 16 bits.

  (ii) How would the words created in (i) above be interpreted as ASCII characters and EBCDIC characters?

 (b) What is meant by the term 'floating point number'? Explain how a floating point number may be represented by a fixed point mantissa and an exponent, indicating particularly the effect on range and accuracy of your representation.

(20) Decode the following text assuming that it is in:

 (a) ASCII;

 (b) EBCDIC code.

      11000011 11010110 11010100 11010111 11100100
      11100011 11000101 11011001 11100010 01101101
      11000111 11011001 11000101 11000001 11100011

CHAPTER 6

Memory

Chapter 1 introduced the concept of a memory that could retain information which could be used subsequently by the computer. This information
was identified as being of two types: first, sequences of instructions
corresponding to an algorithm, and secondly data upon which the algorithm was to operate.

In order that an algorithm can be processed it is necessary for both the
data and the instructions to be in the memory of the computer. In this
chapter we shall expand on this to show how different concepts in memory
design and technology can be used to generate different memory structures. Each of the basic structures will be associated with a particular
design criterion at which the computer architect has to aim. In particular,
the architect will choose a memory structure which satisfies the needs of a
particular environment in the most cost-effective way. The memory
technologies currently available follow the simple rule that the faster access
there is to the memory the more expensive the memory. Hence any
computer system will be constructed from a hierarchy of different memory
technologies reflecting the most cost-effective balance for a particular
computing environment.

6.1 The basic building blocks

Any memory is constructed from a collection of memory cells, each having
its own unique name, commonly called an address. It is normal for these

addresses to be assigned from the positive integers. Each of the memory cells contains a piece of data which is referred to as the contents of a memory location. Each memory cell or location usually holds one piece of data.

Figure 6.1 shows the normal structure of a unit of memory which is constructed from a number of cells. Each collection of memory cells has associated with it two registers in the CPU known as the memory address register (MAR) and the memory buffer register (MBR). Registers will be discussed in detail in section 6.2. A memory may be constructed from more than one such unit, in which case the MAR and MBR will be placed on a memory bus linking all the units together (see Chapters 8 and 10 for a description of the use of buses). The mode of operation of a memory unit is that the address of a particular cell to be processed is placed in the MAR.

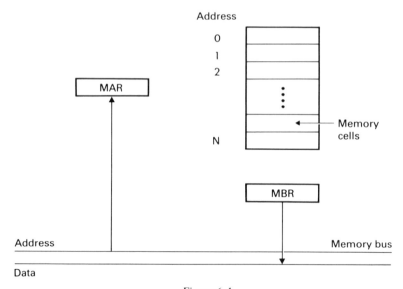

Figure 6.1

This address is decoded by some electronics (see decoders in Chapter 2) which then activate the correct memory cell in order that it may be processed. Because any of the cells can be processed at random, this type of memory is called random access memory (RAM). A memory cell can be processed in one of two ways. First, it can be read, that is the contents of the memory cell are placed in the MBR from where other parts of the CPU may process the data (see section 8.12). Secondly, the memory cell may be written into. This is carried out by a data value being placed in the MBR by some means external to the memory, and then copied into the addressed memory location. During a read the contents of a memory cell remain unaltered, i.e. the data is not destroyed. During a write the contents of a memory cell are replaced by the value in the MBR, and any data which may have been previously stored in the cell is thus destroyed. The memory cells themselves are therefore separated from the rest of the CPU by means of the two registers MAR and MBR. All communications between the CPU and memory is via these two registers.

The size of a memory cell varies from computer to computer. More precisely, if we interpret the contents of a memory cell as an integer, the modulus of the maximum value varies between memory units. If a computer system has more than one unit then, as a general rule, all the memory units will have the same cell size. The size of a memory cell is usually no smaller than eight binary digits (bits).

An 8-bit unit is commonly called a byte and has become the standard unit for storing a single character. A byte allows 256 different characters to be represented even though most character sets do not contain this number of characters. Obviously a computer would not be very useful if the modulus of the largest integer which could be represented was 255. Some memory units are not made up of bytes but of words. The word size, or word length, of a memory is usually a multiple of the 8-bit byte so that the word can efficiently store a number of characters. Hence more generally a memory cell can be referred to as a word of memory and the word can store one or more characters, it being the smallest piece of memory which can be uniquely addressed. An example of this is the HP21MX which has a word size of 16 bits, capable of storing two characters. The IBM 4300 and PDP-11 both have a word size of 8 bits but have another mechanism superimposed upon them. This mechanism uses different instructions to process different sized objects constructed from several bytes (see Chapter 7). The PDP-11 has instructions capable of processing two and four bytes, referred to as words and double-words. On the IBM 4300, bytes can be combined into two-, four- and eight-byte units. These are referred to as half-words, full-words and double-words respectively. However on both the IBM 4300 and PDP-11 the basic memory unit is the byte, even though other mechanisms are used to enable numbers of sufficiently large value to be manipulated. The Intel 8088 processor (used on the IBM PC) has a memory organised as bytes but these can be accessed in pairs as if they were 16-bit words.

It is in the decisions about word size and the way memory is to be manipulated by instructions that we can first see the role of the architect in memory design. If it is known that the machine is going to be designed for a data processing environment in which a lot of character information will be processed, the architect may opt for a byte-oriented memory. However, in numerical and process control environments it is more likely that a much larger word size will be used, e.g. 60 bits. The disadvantage of a large word size is that when storing characters space may be wasted or extra processing may be required. The disadvantage of byte- or character-oriented memories is that, in order to retrieve a number, several accesses to the memory will be required, unless there are some extra electronics associated with memory to allow sequences of bytes to be accessed. Obviously this extra facility increases the cost of the memory unit, and has to be considered when these decisions are taken.

6.2 Dedicated registers

Not all the memory in a computer will be accessed via the MBR and MAR. In order that the computer can function efficiently there may have to be registers which are special storage locations that are not part of main memory and consequently can be accessed without recourse to the MAR and MBR. Such registers are usually few, and have a fixed use within the overall structure and operation of the computer.

The use to which these registers is put is discussed more fully in section 8.1.1 and by implication in Chapter 7. During the processing of an instruction, data may have to be temporarily stored. For example, when adding two integers together the integers could be stored in two registers and the result in a third before it is transferred to some other location within the computer system. If these registers were in main memory, the above process would be impossible, because we can only access one location of memory at a time with the memory structure so far discussed. Perhaps more important is the fact that accessing a register is much quicker because no addressing mechanism is needed (see Chapter 7), the register being accessed directly as required by an instruction.

The registers which have been discussed so far are somewhat special in that, normally, the user of the computer is unaware of their existence. Further, these registers are designed to do a specific job and are not bound by the word size of the computer. There is no point in having an 8-bit register if a 2-bit one will do. There are within a computer many one-bit registers which are known as flags or flip-flops. These registers are able to store the state of some part of the CPU and can be tested by other parts of the CPU. Sometimes, for convenience, these one-bit flags may be collected together into a larger register such as a flag register.

It is also common for a computer to have one or more registers which are available for use by the user by means of his programs. Such registers, for example, can be used to hold intermediate data values when evaluating expressions. Hence the user's program will execute more quickly because these registers are directly accessible by a unique name inherent within the instruction. If there were no registers, all intermediate data values would have to be stored in the memory via the MBR and MAR, which is a very much slower process.

The role of the architect can be seen here again. By making a number of registers available to the user, the cost of the computer will be increased, but the ease and flexibility of use will be much greater than that of a computer which has fewer registers. The greater the set of instructions that are available to a computer, then probably the more internal registers will be used; the cost will rise but the computer will be more generally versatile.

6.3 Von Neumann memory organisation

John Von Neumann was one of the first people to put forward a mathematical theory that could be applied to the construction of a computer. A large part of this theory was concerned with the development of a memory which could be used to store the instructions and data of a program, the so-called stored program concept. Fundamental to this theory was the idea of a linear array of memory cells that could be used to store both the instructions of the algorithm and the data. This was a big step forward from early calculating machines in which the algorithm was remembered, or stored, by the operator. Unfortunately the theoretical design was somewhat deficient. Two important difficulties were that only one location of memory could be accessed at one time and there was no physical separation between instructions and data.

As has been seen in the case of the addition of two numbers, the computer needs access to two or three registers concurrently. Thus the restriction on access to the memory necessitated the use of registers which are probably not strictly necessary. Another effect of having an addressed linear array is that the address of every required memory location has to be known. It is easier to conceive of data records in which the remainder of the record can be processed when the value of part of the record is known. Finally, because there was no distinction between data and instructions, disastrous consequences could result from trying to obey or use data as instructions. Disasters should not occur when a program works correctly, but they may when programs are being tested. For example, a data value obeyed as an instruction may cause branching to an area of memory that is not supposed to be accessed by this program.

Up to the mid 1970s all commercially available computers had a memory structure similar to that propounded by Von Neumann. It is only since then that machines have become available which have attempted to remove the strait jacket imposed by the Von Neumann architecture. The remainder of this chapter discusses these techniques, many of which were developed before the mid 1970s but are only now being applied in situations unrelated to the Von Neumann architecture. The reason is that semiconductor technology has made it possible to mass produce the required memory structures. The final section of this chapter deals briefly with these technological developments.

6.4 Associative memories

An associative memory, or content addressable memory, is one which does not require the use of a MAR and MBR because data is accessed via the content of the registers used in the memory. Figure 6.2 shows the structure of a simple associative memory.

The associative and conventional fields comprise a memory location such that if the associative field is changed the conventional field has to be changed as well. These memory locations are filled with data. Subsequently a data value is placed in the interrogate register. This value is then compared in parallel with (that is, at the same time as) the contents of the associative field of all memory locations. If one of the associative fields

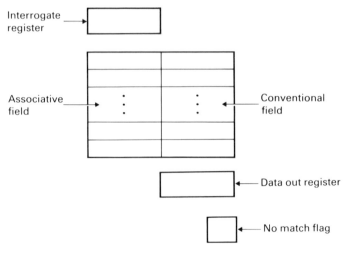

Interrogate register

Associative field

Conventional field

Data out register

No match flag

Figure 6.2

contains the same value as the interrogate register then the value in the corresponding conventional field is placed in the data out register for subsequent processing by the CPU. If none of the associative fields contains the required data value then a no-match condition is set in a flag associated with the associative memory. Thus this mechanism allows the processing of many memory locations in parallel based not on the address of the location but upon its content. Because processing is carried out in parallel, it is much quicker than using a linear array of addressable memory locations. In this form the associative memory is somewhat limited in that it cannot deal with multiple matches as it has only one data register. This deficiency could be overcome if there was a processor which was associated with each memory location in the associative process. Such systems are becoming more feasible with the development of cheap memories and processing units.

An associative memory using a single data out register was used in this form in the early 1960s in a computer called Atlas which used the memory to control an addressing mechanism called paging. Paging is described in section 6.8. Developments were undertaken to the simple system described here so that the facility could be made available to the user rather than remain an unavailable internal mechanism.

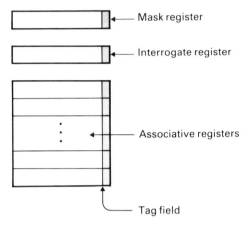

Figure 6.3

The structure of such a memory is shown in Figure 6.3. Its operation proceeds as follows. The associative registers are filled with data values and prior to a set of interrogations the associated tag fields, which are one bit long, are reset to 0. The interrogate register is filled with a data value such that the fields of the data correspond in position to the fields within the data stored in the associative registers, i.e. multi-field data can be processed. The mask register has bits set and cleared so that only those bits that are set in the mask will cause the corresponding bits to be compared in the subsequent associative processing. For example, if bits 8, 9 and 10 are set to 1 in the mask register the other bits being cleared to 0, then only bits 8, 9 and 10 in the associative registers will be compared with the interrogate register. This means that only selected fields within the data can be used. Those memory locations for which there is a match between the interrogate register and the associative registers will have their tag field set to 1. The interrogate and mask registers can now be changed and, by including the tag field, further passes through the associative memory can be undertaken which will produce logical combinations from the data values stored in the memory locations. When the desired sequence of interrogations has been undertaken all locations in the associative register which have a tag field of either 1 or 0, whichever is appropriate to the solution, can be processed. If only one processing unit is available, the data will have to be processed serially; otherwise it can be processed in parallel. Even if there is only one processing unit, there will be a speed advantage over a normal memory, because the processing unit has only to test the state of the one-bit tag field rather than the multi-field record. As an example of the sort of processing which can be undertaken by such a unit, consider the following. The data comprises three fields and it is desired to find those memory locations for which the following logical condition holds:

$$\text{not } ((\text{field}1 = 2 \text{ or field}2 = 3) \text{ and field}3 = 4).$$

Assuming the associative registers have been filled and the tag fields are reset to zero, and remembering that the tag field is set to one after an interrogation which finds a match in a particular location, the sequence of operations required would be:

- Set field1 of interrogate to 2
  Set mask so that field1 is considered, interrogate
  Set field2 of interrogate to 3
  Set mask so that field2 is considered, interrogate
  Set tag field of interrogate to 1
  Set tag field of mask to 1
  Set field3 of interrogate to 4
  Set mask so that field3 is considered, interrogate
  Process those records with tag field of zero.

A simple extension which can be added to the above scheme is to incorporate a mechanism which allows the relation to be varied from equality to include the usual arithmetic relational operators ($\leqslant \neq \geqslant$).

One of the major drawbacks of such associative memories is their limited size, in that the size of each associated register is fixed as is the number of associative registers in the memory. A simplification of the above mechanism is used in Prime 750 computers.

6.5 Cache memories

A cache memory introduces the concept of memory hierarchy. A hierarchical memory is one which is constructed from different types of memory. The type of memory is usually differentiated by the speed at which the memory is able to process data. Hence a three level memory could be constructed from high, medium and low speed memories, where the high speed memory would be a cache memory, the medium speed memory would be the main store and the low speed memory would be disks. The reasons for introducing memory hierarchies are many and will be discussed in more detail in section 6.8. The cache memory was introduced to solve a specific problem in computer architecture and was the first attempt at using memories of different speeds. The problem which had to be overcome was speeding up the execution of instructions. An analysis of programs revealed that the majority of programs used only a very few memory locations for the storage of variables (excluding arrays). Thus if these variables could be collected together in a special memory which was of higher speed the execution speed of the program could be increased. Such a memory is called a cache memory.

A cache memory holds the variables of the currently executing program. Obviously these variables have to be loaded from the main memory, where the instruction sequence is stored, before the program is executed. The size of the cache memory has to be chosen so that most programs will be able to fit their variables into the cache. The instruction set (see Chapter 7) will have to be augmented to take account of the situation where there is insufficient room in the cache. In this case, some of the variables will have to be held in main memory. A more sophisticated cache memory would have a facility for ensuring that the most frequently accessed variables would be held in the cache. This would be done by keeping a count of the number of accesses made to a particular variable. By sampling these counts at regular intervals the most frequently accessed variables can be moved to the cache. This technique is used on computers designed in the late 1970s onwards, such as the Harris S800, Prime 750, IBM 4341 and ICL 2900 computers.

Consider the operation of a cache memory. When a read request is received from the CPU for a word in main memory, the contents of a block of words are transferred to the cache memory, and the required word is then transferred to the CPU. When any other words in this block are referenced subsequently they are transferred straight from cache.

Correspondence between main memory blocks and cache blocks is by a *mapping function*. If the cache is full and a new word is required that is not in the cache, some block in the cache is replaced with the block from memory by a *replacement algorithm*.

Consider the access to words in memory:

(1) Access to a word in cache:
    Read— no difficulties.
    Write—either the cache and main memory are updated simultaneously or only the cache is updated but is flagged in some way so that when the block is eventually removed the main memory is updated at this point.
(2) Access to a word not in cache:
    Read— the appropriate block is brought into cache.
    Write—the word is written to directly in main memory.

To examine the possible mapping functions the following example will be used:

Main memory— 64K words addressable by a 16-bit address and split into 4K blocks of 16-bit words.

Cache memory—2K words split into blocks of 16-bit words (i.e. 128 blocks).

The simplest mapping function is the *direct mapping technique*. Here, block k of main memory maps on to block k modulo 128 of the cache memory (i.e. divide k by 128 and the remainder is the block number). Since more than one main memory block shares the same cache memory block position, contention may occur and is resolved simply by overwriting, even if the cache is not full.

A memory address is divided into three fields, a 5-bit tag field, a 7-bit block field and a 4-bit word field as in Figure 6.4. When a new block is

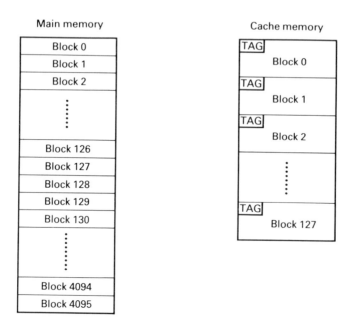

Interpretation of main memory address

Figure 6.4

brought into the cache memory the high order five bits are stored in the tag field of the cache block.

The following actions take place when the CPU generates a memory request:

(1) The 7-bit block address field is used to address the corresponding cache block.
(2) The tag fields are then compared.
(3) If they are the same, the required word is in that block and can be accessed by using the word bits of the address. If they are not the same, the word must be accessed from main memory.

A better mapping function is known as the *associative mapping technique*. In this case the layout of the cache memory is the same as above, except that the tag field is now twelve bits and a main memory address is interpreted as a 12-bit tag field and a 4-bit word field. A block from main memory is loaded into any of the block positions in cache (usually according to some replacement algorithm). When an address is received from the CPU the high order 12-bit tag field is *associatively* compared with all the cache tag fields to see if the required block is present (see section 6.4 for a discussion of associative stores). This technique is clearly more flexible in its use of the block positions in cache but is much more expensive because of the large associative compare.

The compromise solution often adopted is known as the *block set associative mapping technique*. In this technique, blocks are grouped into sets. Each block within a set has a tag field. A main memory address is interpreted as a tag field, a set field and a word field. The set field indicates which set the required block is in and the tag field is then associatively compared with the tag fields in that set. Figure 6.5 illustrates the situation when there are two blocks per set.

This technique eases the contention experienced in the direct mapping technique, since a block from main memory can reside in any block position in a particular set. The cost of the associative compare is lower than in the case of the associative mapping technique, since the associative compare is much smaller.

Notice that if the set size is reduced to one block per set it is equivalent to the direct mapping technique, and if the set size is increased to 128 blocks per set it is equivalent to the associative mapping technique.

With the block set associative mapping technique (or the associative mapping technique) there is a choice of where to place a block in the cache that is to be brought in from main memory. Clearly, if the appropriate set is not full (there are some block positions unused) the block can be placed in any of the empty block positions in that set. However, if the set is full, which is normally the case, there must be a replacement algorithm to decide which block to remove or overwrite. There are a number of possible

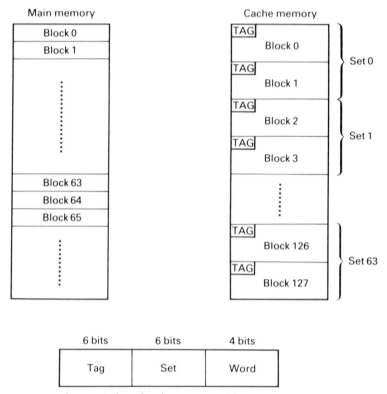

Figure 6.5

algorithms, but a fairly common one is known as the *least recently used* (LRU) algorithm. When using the LRU algorithm the assumption is that when it is necessary to replace a block the one that has gone the longest without being referenced is the right one to remove. As an example of how such an algorithm is used, suppose it is required to track the LRU block of a four block set (there is an alternative algorithm in Problem 14 at the end of this chapter). There is a 2-bit counter with each block in the set. Suppose a hit occurs (that is, a read for a block that is in the cache). The counter of the block referenced is set to 0, all the counters originally less than the referenced ones are incremented by 1 and the others are unchanged. If a miss occurs (a reference to a block not in cache) and the set is not full, the block is brought into the set, its counter is set to 0 and the other counters are incremented by 1. If a miss occurs and the set is full, the block with a counter of 3 is removed, the new block put in its place with a counter of 0, and the other block counters are incremented by 1. It is left as an exercise for the reader to verify that this works correctly.

6.6 Interleaved and segmented memories

6.6.1 Interleaved memories

An interleaved memory was first used on a CDC 6600 computer as a means
of speeding up access to the memory. In the mid 1960s memory access
speed was, and even now still is, a critical factor, which was slowing down
the overall execution speed of a computer. An interleaved memory is one
in which the memory is split up into banks, each with its own memory
address and buffer registers. Each bank is constructed from the same type
of memory. Thus it is possible to access as many words of memory as there
are banks in the interleaved memory.

Obviously such a system requires more complex control of the generation of addresses. When a piece of data is to be fetched from the memory
the address of the data item is generated within the CPU. In an interleaved
memory, part of the address is used to indicate which memory bank is to be
used. Before the address can be sent to the bank's MAR it must be
ascertained whether the bank is already busy. If the bank is not busy then
the address can be sent immediately to the bank. When the bank is busy

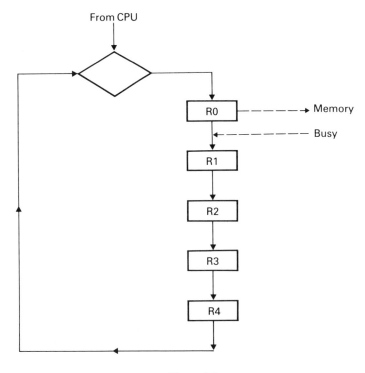

Figure 6.6

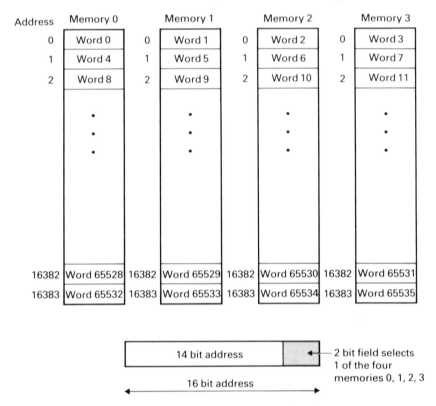

Address	Memory 0		Memory 1		Memory 2		Memory 3
0	Word 0	0	Word 1	0	Word 2	0	Word 3
1	Word 4	1	Word 5	1	Word 6	1	Word 7
2	Word 8	2	Word 9	2	Word 10	2	Word 11
⋮		⋮		⋮		⋮	
16382	Word 65528	16382	Word 65529	16382	Word 65530	16382	Word 65531
16383	Word 65532	16383	Word 65533	16383	Word 65534	16383	Word 65535

14 bit address

16 bit address

2 bit field selects 1 of the four memories 0, 1, 2, 3

Note that the MAR of each memory only needs to be 14 bits wide

Figure 6.7

the address cannot be sent and therefore it has to be retained within the memory control system. Obviously this could occur for more than one of the banks and the following solution can be adopted as shown in Figure 6.6. Registers R1 to R4 form a queue through which an address passes if it cannot be accepted by its memory bank. R0 is the register into which addresses are placed on entry to the mechanism. If the required bank is busy, a signal is returned to the control system, and the address passes into R1. If the required bank is free, the address passes to the appropriate memory bank. The priority mechanism ensures that if there is an address in R4 it is passed to R0 rather than allowing a new address into the mechanism from the CPU; in this way the address in R4 has another chance of being accepted. Obviously it is now necessary for the sequence in which operands are fetched from memory to be altered because a bank was busy and the bank for the next address in sequence was not. Hence addresses and operands from memory are given a tag which allows them to be processed in the correct order.

A program is a sequence of instructions, and therefore the best way of using an interleaved memory is to place the instructions in separate banks so that there is never any contention, except when data is being fetched. This can be achieved by making the bits of the address which indicate the bank the least significant part of the address, as illustrated in Figure 6.7.

Consider the example shown in Figure 6.7. Here, four memories, each of 2^{14} words are being used to implement an address space of 2^{16} words. The 16-bit machine-level address is divided into two parts. The rightmost two bits specify the memory to be used (0, 1, 2 or 3) and the other 14 bits specify a word within that memory.

The microprogram which examines the address prior to fetching a new word, examines the rightmost two bits to select the appropriate memory. It then transfers the other 14 bits of the address to the appropriate MAR and initiates a memory read.

While waiting for that read to complete, it could use one of the other memories to fetch another word. Note that in this example four consecutive items of information (instructions or data) are all located in different memories, so that up to four words (and possibly therefore four consecutive instructions) can be fetched in parallel. For an organisation having N memories, the term N-way interleaving is often used. To reduce further the contention for banks of memory it may be possible to store data in some of the banks and instructions in the remainder of the banks.

6.6.2 Segmented memories

A segmented memory is very similar to an interleaved memory except that it is not usual to distribute a sequence of instructions amongst several of the banks. Each of the banks of a segmented memory has its own memory address and buffer registers, and the CPU contains some control logic which ensures that some addresses are not sent to a segment until that segment is idle. This control logic is not as complex as that for an interleaved memory because each segment only holds information of a single type. It is usual to have data and instruction segments, and the data segments may be further subdivided by use. For example, the Zilog Z8000 processor chip includes a segmented memory in which segments are used for the operating system, programmer instructions, programmer data and a stack. The use of each segment is defined by the programmer. Because the segment has a singular use the contention problem is reduced, because the memory is alternately accessing an instruction segment and a data segment. (See Chapter 8 for further details of instruction processing.)

Another use to which a segmented memory can be put is that of *context switching*. In a computer system which is capable of supporting more than one user concurrently, it is necessary to switch from one user's program to another. In a simple linear memory this may mean that the memory holds each program in a different area of memory. If the memory is not sufficiently large, the programs may have to be swapped into memory from a file store. A more elegant and intrinsically safer solution is to put each program into a separate segment of memory. When it is the turn of a particular program to be allowed to process, all that is switched is the segment that is being addressed. Obviously there can only be as many concurrent users as there are memory segments. The system is much safer than a linear memory, because there is no way in which a program can overwrite part of another program. The two are in different segments of the memory and the segment information is appended to the address by the CPU and not by the user.

6.7 Tagged memories

This is a technique for labelling the contents of a memory location to indicate the type of data stored in the location. The label is called a *tag*. A tagged memory is a useful concept, because it can be used to ensure that data in the memory is protected from misuse.

The simplest type of tagged memory will differentiate between instructions and data and so ensure that instructions are not accessed as data and vice versa.This simple mechanism can be extended in many different ways. The type of data can be differentiated so that instructions designed to operate upon characters, fixed-point numbers and floating-point numbers only operate upon data of the required type. Some computers use variable length instructions, and a tagged memory can be used to indicate the length of an instruction. The Burroughs B5000 computers used a system similar to the technique described above.

6.8 Paged memories

One of the most important aspects of current memory technology (see 6.10) is that memory is becoming cheaper to produce in large quantities, but there is still a significant price differential between high speed and low speed memories.

Because of the price differential it became attractive to have memory hierarchies in which bulk storage was provided by large slow memories, while the data and instructions for the program being executed were moved to a high speed smaller memory.

A program is divided into fixed length pages. When the program is initiated, these pages may be on file store or in the bulk memory. At this stage, the first page will be copied into the fast memory and execution will begin. In due course, a reference will be made to a page which is not in fast memory. This page is fetched and placed in the high speed memory and execution will proceed. In due course, the high speed memory will become full, and a page will have to be removed to the bulk memory. Obviously such a mechanism has to be controlled by the CPU. Some of the properties of the control mechanism are as follows.

(1) The pages of a program in high speed memory do not have to be contiguous.

(2) A record of pages belonging to different programs must be maintained.

(3) A record of the most frequently accessed pages should be maintained.

(4) A record is kept of whether the page is of data or instructions.

(5) A record of where pages are stored in bulk memory must be maintained.

Property (1) is required so that pages do not have to be shuffled to maintain sequential order. They will probably not be required in sequential order in any case. Obviously addresses of memory locations within a program will relate to the start of the program and so there will have to be some means of translating a relative address into an address within the high speed memory. Relative addresses are normally stored as a page number and a word within a page. Hence all that is required is a mechanism which allows the CPU to find out where a particular page is stored in high speed memory and the word part of the relative address will give the offset from that location. The associative memory described in section 6.4 will carry out this function.

When a program terminates, some of its pages will remain in high speed memory and will only be removed when pages for the next program require space. Thus pages from more than one program may be in the memory at the same time, hence the necessity for property (2). This is further utilised when the following case is considered. A program is executing and then needs access to a page not in the high speed memory. Before the program can continue, this page has to be loaded into high speed memory. During this transfer time the CPU is idle, so another program can be given access to the CPU and allowed to execute. Thus within the same CPU it is possible to have more than one program in a state of execution but only one of the programs can actually be in the process of execution at any particular time.

Property (3) is required so that when a page has to be removed from the high speed memory because another page is needed, a page which has not been accessed for a long time can be chosen. This is also decided in conjunction with property (4). Pages which contain program instructions do not have to be written back to bulk memory because they will never be altered. However, pages which contain data will have to be written back, because data values may have changed. A variation of this technique is to keep a record of those pages which have been written to. The page most likely to be removed then is one which has not been accessed for a long time and which also has not been written to. The process which decides which page to remove is called the page turning algorithm. When a page is to be transferred from bulk memory to high speed memory and vice versa the location of the page in bulk memory has to be known, giving rise to the necessity for property (5).

The technique of paging has been described between two hierarchical memories but in fact it can be extended easily to a hierarchy of many memories. Further, paging gives rise to a concept known as *virtual memory*. The memory from which programs can be executed is necessarily much smaller than the bulk memory. It is possible in fact to construct programs which require far more space than is available to the high speed memory. The page mechanism ensures that only the pages currently required reside in high speed memory. We can consider the high speed memory to be the real (i.e. existing) memory in which the program can execute, and the program to exist in a virtual memory supported by bulk memory and file store. In fact some computers (ICL 2900) employ a technique where each program can have ¼ million pages each of ¼ K bytes. This gives a program space of 64 megabytes, which is far larger than the total memory space the computer can support; hence the term virtual. The virtual space that is available to a program can be used to ensure the modularity of the program, especially of instructions and data.

6.9 Read only memories

So far the memories which have been discussed are ones which can be written to and read from. There is, however, a different sort of memory called *read only memory* (ROM) which can only be read from. Read only memories can be used to store algorithms (i.e. the instructions of a program) when the memory is manufactured, and once tested these algorithms should not need changing. Obviously algorithms which are going to be changed are not stored in ROM as this would be a very inefficient way of using a ROM. In general once a ROM has been programmed it cannot be changed (see section 6.10). ROM is therefore used for special kinds of computers which carry out dedicated tasks.

In general-purpose computers, minis, mainframes and microcomputers ROM is often used to store part of the operating software of a computer system. When a computer is switched on there is nothing inside the RAM because such data is lost when the power is removed (see section 6.10). It is therefore necessary to have a program which can be loaded automatically and which will then load the necessary programs into the main memory. Such a loading program is called a 'bootstrap' loader. The algorithm stored in the ROM is obeyed and reads other programs from a peripheral device. In most cases the program read in is part of the operating system which then controls the subsequent operation of the computer system.

In dedicated computers all the algorithms will be stored in a ROM, because the contents of the ROM are not destroyed when the power is switched off. An example of this would be a point-of-sale terminal (see section 3.1.3). Such a terminal records the items being sold and the price payable, adds up the total and works out the change required for the cash tendered. Such a terminal can also be connected to a central computer which maintains stock control information. A dedicated computer will need some RAM, otherwise it could not store temporary data values, but there tends to be only a very little RAM in such a computer. This is in direct contrast to a general-purpose computer where the amount of ROM is very small and is used to hold the program which will initially load the computer with its operating system. With the introduction of cheap robust microprocessors there has been a trend to incorporate these devices in hostile environments where traditionally constructed computers could not be used, e.g. in machine tools or washing machines. Because these environments tend to be of a dedicated nature the use of ROM has increased significantly.

6.10 Memory technology

The technology of memory devices has progressed from magnetic techniques developed in the 1950s and 1960s to the semiconductor 'silicon chip' technology of the 1970s. This section will deal only with the semiconductor technology because no currently manufactured computers use magnetic techniques for main memory.

Early semiconductor memories could store only a few binary digits whereas modern memories can store hundreds of thousands. This increase in capacity has been achieved by improvement in the technology of semiconductor devices. The original semiconductor technology was capable of building one transistor on a ¼ inch square of silicon in 1960. By 1980 it became possible to build hundreds of thousands of transistors on the same piece of silicon. The original discrete semiconductor memories were static memories. That is once the memory had been written to, the information remained, provided that the power was not switched off. With the advent of integrated technology, dynamic memories were generated. A dynamic memory is one which has to be periodically refreshed because the electric charge used to store the data slowly leaks away. This is analogous to a bucket with a hole in it: it is possible to say when the bucket is full and also when it is empty, but there is an in-between stage where it is neither full nor empty. The refresh period ensures that all storage locations which should be full are filled up. The refresh mechanism takes place transparently and therefore the programmer is unaware that the process is taking place.

Read only memories are implemented in many different ways which give differing levels of flexibility. The simplest kind of ROM actually has the program built into it as the memory is manufactured. A more flexible approach is one which allows the ROM to be programmed by people other than the manufacturer. Such a programmable ROM (PROM) can be programmed by a special machine into which the desired program is previously read. Once the PROM has been programmed, it cannot be changed. A further level of sophistication is the erasable PROM (EPROM) which can be reprogrammed several times whilst retaining the read only characteristics of a ROM. Each type of ROM uses a type of semiconductor technology which allows the desired mode of operation. The PROM type uses the so called 'fusible link' which can be broken when a high enough current is passed through it. Initially, every bit is set to 1 and the programming requires that some of the links be changed to 0 by breaking the appropriate fusible link. An EPROM uses the same technique, except that the fusible link can be regenerated when the EPROM is exposed to ultraviolet light. The access time of a memory, whether RAM or ROM, is the amount of time it takes to process the memory in order to read some data from or write some data into it. With the technology available in the mid 1980s, the access time of memory varies from 30ns to 1000ns ($1ns = 10^{-9}s$). As usual, the faster the memory the more expensive it is. Thus 30ns memory is used for small high speed cache memories whereas 1000ns memory is used for bulk memory.

6.11 Summary

This chapter has described how memories can be constructed and how they have developed from the original linear string of locations developed by Von Neumann. Data is not normally just a linear string; it has other structures which have to be mapped onto a linear string. The development of large fast cheap memories has allowed designers to experiment with other memory strategies which try to overcome the restrictions of a linear string.

6.12 Problems

(1) Why would a computer be equipped with 262 144 words rather than 250 000 or 275 000 which are much easier to remember?

(2) Which of the following memories are possible? Which are reasonable? Explain.

	Bits in MAR	Cells in memory	Cell size in bits
(a)	10	1024	8
(b)	10	1024	12
(c)	9	1024	10
(d)	11	1024	10
(e)	10	10	1024
(f)	1024	10	10

(3) Describe two ways in which a computer memory could be organised so as to allow individual words to be read only, read/write, or execute only.

(4) Assuming an associative memory, as described in section 6.4 having mask and interrogate registers, show the sequence of operations needed to evaluate not ((field $1 \neq 2$ and not field $2 = 3$) or (field $3 = 1$)) and field $4 = 0$.

(5) Explain how the principle of an interleaved memory can be used to increase access speed to a memory if the data part of the memory bus is wider than each memory cell.

(6) Why is an hierarchy of memory types invaluable when designing a computer system?

(7) Investigate how modern computers utilise memory techniques in their design. How has this improved the performance of each system?

(8) Some implementations of paging do not use an associative memory, but instead maintain tables of the most recently used pages. These tables contain less entries than pages in real memory, the remainder being kept in main memory. Compare and contrast this with the technique described in section 6.8.

(9) In computers dedicated to a particular task the majority of memory is ROM. Why?

(10) By reading other publications find out how the cost, speed and size of memory has varied over the past seven years.

(11) A computer with a cache memory uses the direct mapping technique for cache organisation. The following are the pertinent parameters.

Main memory   64K words with a cycle time of 10 microsec
Cache memory   1K words with a cycle time of 1 microsec
Block size   128 words

Specify the number of bits in the tag, block and word fields in the interpretation of main memory addresses.

(12) A block set associative cache consists of a total of 64 blocks divided into 4-block sets. The main memory contains 4K blocks, each block consisting of 128 words.

(a) How many bits are there in the main memory address?

(b) How many bits are there in each of the tag, set and word fields?

(13) Suppose that the machine described in Problem 6.11 is used to run a program consisting of 2800 instructions each held in one word, which are all executed in simple sequence. Estimate the instruction fetch time for the whole program for both the machine with cache and the machine without cache. Explain the results.

(14) Consider the following LRU algorithm for a cache with B blocks. The cache hardware maintains a B × B matrix, with the rows and columns numbered 1 through B.

Whenever block N is referenced, row N is set to all 1s. After that step, column N is set to all 0s. At any point in time, the row with the lowest value (read as a binary number) is the least recently used row. Show that this algorithm works for a 4-block cache and the following sequence of block references:

$$1\ 2\ 3\ 4\ 4\ 4\ 2\ 3\ 1\ 3\ 4\ 2\ 1\ 3\ 4\ 4$$

(15) A program consists of two nested loops, a small inner loop and a much larger outer loop.

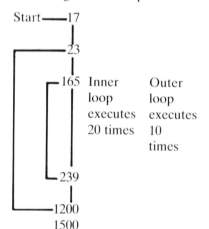

Start —— 17

23

165 Inner   Outer
    loop   loop
    executes executes
    20 times 10
             times

239

1200
1500

The numbers shown are the decimal addresses which indicate the start and end of both loops. All memory locations in sections 17–22, 23–164, 165–239, etc., contain instructions to be executed in straight line sequence.

The program is to be run on a computer that has a cache memory. The cache is organised in the direct mapping manner as follows:

Main memory   64K words with a cycle time of 10 microsec
Cache memory   1K words with a cycle time of 1 microsec
Block size   128 words

(a) Ignoring operand and result fetching and storing, compute the total amount of time needed for instruction fetching in the above program.

(b) Repeat the above calculation assuming no cache is available.

Machine codes and addressing techniques

Chapter 1 introduced the general concept that both program instructions and data are stored in the main memory. This chapter will consider the structure of instructions stored in a computer from the programmer's viewpoint.

Most instructions specify operations to be performed on data located either in the main memory or in general-purpose registers in the central processing unit (CPU). The reference to this data, whether it be numeric or character data, is said to be the operand of the instruction.

7.1 Instruction formats

Any program involves a number of functionally different steps. Obviously the machine instructions will reflect the different functions. The functions can be roughly classed as follows:

● Data transfers between the main memory and the CPU registers
● Arithmetic and logic operations on data
● Program sequencing and control
● Input/output (I/O) transfers

To examine possible formats for instructions, consider one of the fundamental instructions from the second of the above classes, an add instruction.

From the programmer's viewpoint, the simplest form of addition is C: =

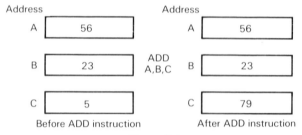

Figure 7.1

A+B where A, B and C are the names of variables. Assume the values of these three variables are stored in memory locations, their addresses being represented by the names A, B and C.

The above expression then has the following meaning. The contents of locations A and B are to be fetched into the CPU where they are added together using the arithmetic and logic unit (ALU). The resultant sum is then to be stored in location C.

If the whole of this expression is to be represented by one machine instruction, the machine instruction will need to contain three address fields (or three operands).

This 3-address instruction—which could be represented symbolically as 'ADD A, B, C'—would obviously require a large number of bits to accommodate three addresses. Figure 7.1 illustrates the contents of addresses A, B and C before and after the ADD operation.

An alternative is to use a 2-address instruction. Here there are only going to be two address fields or operands (and consequently the instruction will occupy fewer bits), but there needs to be an implicit assumption about where the result is to be stored. The result is stored back in one of the operands, thus destroying its original value.

The instruction 'ADD A, B' could add the contents of addresses A and B, storing the sum in address A. Figure 7.2 illustrates the contents of addresses A and B before and after this ADD operation.

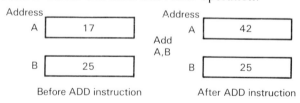

Figure 7.2

If it is important in a particular program to ensure that the sum is placed in C with the original values of A and B remaining unchanged then two instructions would have to be used, namely:

MOVE   C,B
ADD   C,A

This assumes that MOVE C,B performs the operation of copying the contents of address B to address C.

A further possibility is that of 1-address instructions. Here, since there is only one operand, not only is there an implicit assumption about where the result is going to be stored, but also about where one of the operands is stored. Usually a general-purpose CPU register, sometimes called an accumulator, is used.

The sequence of instructions:

$$\begin{array}{ll} \text{LOAD} & \text{A} \\ \text{ADD} & \text{B} \\ \text{STORE} & \text{C} \end{array}$$

could perform the operation C:= A+B. Here, the LOAD instruction copies the contents of address A into the accumulator, the ADD instruction adds the contents of address B into the accumulator and the STORE instruction copies the contents of the accumulator into address C.

Some computers have a number of general-purpose registers which can be used as an accumulator, and in this case a second operand signifies the register to be used. However, since the number of bits to signify the register to be used (say 3 or 4 since there are often no more than 8 or 16 of such registers) is considerably fewer than would be necessary to signify a second memory address, these types of instructions are sometimes called 1½ address instructions.

If a computer has a number of registers, there are usually some instructions to perform operations on data in registers only; that is, no reference is necessary to a main memory address. Since all operands are registers requiring only three or four bits each, these instructions obviously occupy only a small number of bits.

It is also possible to have instructions with no operands, and these are known as zero address instructions. Here the location of the operands is known implicitly. This will be discussed later in section 7.5.

7.2 Instruction sets

All the machine instructions that are provided by a given computer are termed its instruction set.

Within the instruction set instructions can usually be classified into one of three types:

(1) Memory reference instructions—these involve operations on data which is stored in memory.

(2) Non-memory reference instructions—these either require no data or operate on data stored within registers in the CPU.

(3) Input/output instructions (see Chapter 10).

7.2.1 Memory reference instructions

This class of instructions includes any instruction that references at least one location in memory, and consequently needs to hold the address of that location within the instruction.

It is not possible to give a definitive list of instructions that are available on any computer, since a computer manufacturer will design and provide a set of instructions that arise partly from other architectural considerations (for example, word size and available registers) and partly as a result of what he thinks is 'useful' in relation to the environment in which the computer is to be used. However, the following list is typical of memory reference instructions that may be found on a computer.

Load a register with the contents of a memory location.

Store the contents of a register into a memory location.

Add the contents of a memory location to those of a register.

Subtract the contents of a memory location from those of a register.

Compare the contents of a register with that of a memory location, skipping the next instruction if they are unequal.

Increment the content of a memory location and skip the next instruction if the result is zero.

Combine the contents of a memory location with those of a register by performing a logical operation on the corresponding bits (AND, OR, Exclusive OR).

Branch instructions—unconditional jump, conditional jumps and jumps to subroutines.

Shift instructions—a group of instructions which moves all the bits in a memory location either to the left or to the right with bits either being 'lost' off one end or coming back in at the other end of the memory location.

To examine the format of an instruction, consider a one-address computer which has two general-purpose registers (these could be called the A register and B register) and a memory word size of 16 bits. Typical instructions would be 'Load to A' (transfer the contents of a word in memory to the A register) or 'Add to A' (add the contents of a word in memory to the A register). The layout of such an instruction (e.g. a Hewlett-Packard 21MX computer) could be as shown in Figure 7.3.

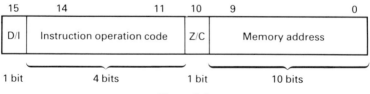

Figure 7.3

In a one-address machine the basic content of an instruction is the operation code which identifies that instruction and the address in memory of the word that contains the data being manipulated. As can be seen above, the operation code occupies four bits and the memory address ten bits. The purpose of bits 10 and 15 will become clear shortly.

If the address of the word in memory being referred to by this instruction can occupy a maximum of ten bits, the largest address that can be referred to would be $2^{10} - 1 = 1023$. Hence addresses can range between 0 and 1023, i.e. 1024 addresses.

Most computers, however, have memories much larger than this. If we allowed a computer to have a memory with a maximum size of, say, one million units of storage (words or bytes) then 20 bits would be needed for the address of a data item. This would make the instructions much larger and inevitably there would be a requirement for even larger memories.

To overcome this problem there is usually a limit to the number of words that can be directly addressed; that is, the instruction contains the absolute address of the data word in memory. To address other parts of the memory, other addressing techniques have to be used (see section 7.3).

7.2.2 Branching

Not all memory reference instructions are in fact manipulating data stored in memory addresses. There is a requirement for a class of instructions,

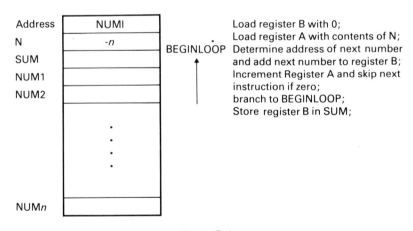

Figure 7.4

known as branch instructions, which refer to a memory address for the purpose of transferring control to this address.

The simplest form of branch instruction, an unconditional branch, can be represented symbolically as in the following code sequence.

BEGINLOOP Add (to a register) contents of X;
Branch to BEGINLOOP;

The branch instruction interrupts the normal sequence of instructions and causes control to return to the instruction at label BEGINLOOP. Obviously, this particular loop is an unending loop. Control is always going to return to BEGINLOOP. It is more usual for a branch instruction only to branch if some particular condition is satisfied; otherwise it allows the normal sequence to continue.

The following code illustrates this.

Load register A with value n;

BEGINLOOP ●
●
●
●
●
●

Decrement register A;
Branch>0 BEGINLOOP;

The DECREMENT instruction decrements the contents of register A, which has been set to an initial value of n, by 1 each time through the loop.

In the branch instruction, the condition under which branching occurs or not is usually related to the result of an arithmetic or logic operation. In the above example the condition is that the result of the most recent arithmetic operation is greater than 0. Since the DECREMENT instruction immediately precedes the branch, this means that a branch to BEGINLOOP will occur as long as the contents of register A remain greater than 0. After the loop has been executed n times, the register A will have been decremented to 0 and the branch will not occur.

Figure 7.4 illustrates a simple loop to add up a series of numbers stored in locations NUM1, NUM2, . . ., NUMn. This also illustrates an alternative way of controlling a loop. An 'increment and skip if zero' instruction increments a particular register by 1 and if the value then becomes equal to zero, control will skip around the next sequential instruction to the one after. Consequently, in the above example, while the A register contains a negative value, control will arrive at the branch instruction and then transfer back to BEGINLOOP. When the A register reaches the value zero, after n loops, control will skip around the branch instruction and continue with the store instruction.

7.2.3 Subroutines

A special form of branching or instruction sequencing is often necessary, when, for example, a particular task has to be performed a number of

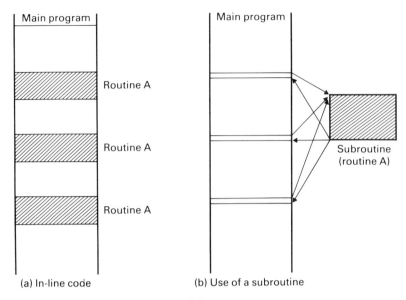

(a) In-line code   (b) Use of a subroutine

Figure 7.5

times on different data values. Instead of including the code each time it is required, it can be written as a subroutine and included only once as shown in Figure 7.5.

A special form of branch instruction is used to transfer control to the subroutine each time it is needed. At the completion of the subroutine, control must be transferred back to where it was 'called' from, so that processing can continue.

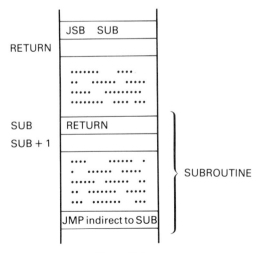

Figure 7.6

The need for a special form of branch instruction arises because it is necessary to save the address of the next instruction in the main program after the branch instruction, so that control can return to this point.

An example of such an instruction is a jump to subroutine instruction illustrated in Figure 7.6. Here, the jump to subroutine (JSB) instruction stores the address of the next instruction following it (RETURN) in the first word of the subroutine (SUB); it then commences execution of the instruction stored in the second word of the subroutine and continues the normal sequencing.

On completion of the subroutine, an indirect jump to SUB is required (see section 7.3.2 for an explanation of an indirect address) which will in this case then transfer control to RETURN.

7.2.4 Non-memory reference and input/output instructions

A non-memory reference instruction is one that does not need to contain an address of a memory location. Typical of such instructions are those that operate on data stored in registers. Because most computers have relatively few registers, it is only necessary to allocate three or four bits at the most to indicate the register being used; consequently these instructions are relatively short. The following is typical of such instructions.

(a) Register to register arithmetic and logical instructions such as ADD, SUBTRACT, MOVE, AND, OR, EXCLUSIVE OR. The logical instructions allow the programmer to isolate individual bits within a word. For example, an AND operation allows the modification of some bits such that certain of them remain as they are and others are set to zero. An OR operation allows the modification of some bits such that certain of them remain as they are and others are set to one, whereas the EXCLUSIVE OR operation selectively reverses the values of bits (see section 2.1).

(b) Shift instructions. This is usually a group of instructions which move all the bits in a register either to the left or to the right with bits either being 'lost' off the end or coming back in at the other end of the register.

As an example of the use of logical and shift instructions consider the following example. Suppose an 8-bit word W is composed of three fields, a two bit field IND, a four bit field X and a two bit field Y in that order. It is required to retrieve field X and put it in a register by itself.

The following instructions would achieve this, assuming that the MASK word contains the bit pattern: 00111100.

Load register R with the MASK;
AND register R with the word W leaving the result in R;
Shift right register R 2 places.

The contents of register R at the end of each of the above steps is

00111100
00field X00
0000field X

This particular example could also be achieved by just two shift instructions:

Shift left register R 2 places
Shift right register R 4 places

It is left to the reader to verify this.

7.3 Memory addressing

As was indicated in section 7.2.1 there is a need for more than one way of obtaining the address of a word in memory for an instruction, because of the length restrictions associated with the most obvious way of including an address in an instruction.

The effective address of an operand is the address that is used to access the memory, once all transformations and modifications have been carried out. We shall now consider some modification techniques.

7.3.1 Direct (absolute) address

The effective address of the location of the operand is given explicitly as part of the instruction. This usually places restrictions on the range of words that can be addressed in this way, depending on the number of bits allocated for the address within the instruction.

7.3.2 Indirect address

The effective address of the operand is stored in the main memory location whose address is in the instruction or in the register, if the operand of the instruction is a register rather than a memory address.

The purpose of bit 15 in the instruction layout defined in section 7.2.1 is to indicate whether the address field in the instruction is the absolute address of the operand or the address of a location in memory which contains the absolute address. It would be set to 0 if direct addressing was being used, and to 1 if indirect addressing was specified.

The advantage of indirect addressing in this context is that the memory location which contains the absolute address of the data can use all of its bits to indicate the address, whereas only the address field is available in the instruction, the other bits being used to define the operation code and other necessary information.

A more general advantage of indirect addressing is that it allows an instruction to refer repeatedly to a different item of data if the indirect address has been modified. For example, if each time round a loop the indirect address is incremented by 1 then the instruction using this address will be stepping through a table of data.

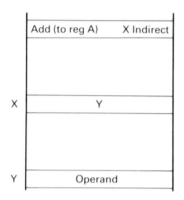

Figure 7.7

Figure 7.7 gives an example of indirect addressing. The execution of the ADD instruction starts by fetching the contents of location X from the main memory. The value, Y, is the absolute address of the operand and is then used to fetch the operand from the memory.

The following program repeats that given earlier (Figure 7.4 in section 7.2.2) for summing a series of values stored in consecutive locations but this time using indirect addressing. ADDR is a location containing initially the address of location NUM1; subsequently the contents of ADDR are incremented by 1 to step through the consecutive words containing the values to be added.

```
            Load register B with 0;
            Load register A with contents of N;
BEGINLOOP   Add to register B contents of ADDR (indirect);
            Increment ADDR;
            Increment register A and skip next instruction if zero;
            Branch to BEGINLOOP;
            Store register B in SUM;
```

7.3.3 Immediate address

The operand is given explicitly in the instruction rather than the address of where the operand is. This can be useful for dealing with data items that have fixed values but, again, the size of the constant is limited by the number of bits available for the operand.

7.3.4 Index addressing

The effective address of the operand is calculated by adding an additional value, the index value, to the address given in the instruction.

The index value is usually stored within a CPU register. On some computers this may be a dedicated register known as the *index register*. On other computers it may be any one of the general-purpose registers provided.

Figure 7.8 illustrates the use of the index register, assuming there is only one dedicated index register. The instruction operand refers to address S, but because indexing is specified the effective address is address S plus the contents of the index register. By varying the contents of the index register, the same instruction can be made to refer to a number of addresses. (This is a similar facility to that of subscripting within a high level programming language.)

The following program repeats the example taken from Figure 7.4 which sums the contents of a series of consecutive words, but this time using indexing:

```
                 Load register B with 0;
                 Load register A with contents of N;
                 Set X to zero;
BEGINLOOP   Add to register B NUM1 indexed by X;
                 Increment X;
                 Increment register A and skip next instruction if zero;
                 Branch to BEGINLOOP;
                 Store register B in SUM;
```

7.4 Addressing mechanisms

In addition to the addressing techniques that have just been described, many computer systems impose some fundamental addressing mechanisms on the programmer in order either to minimise the number of address bits required in an instruction or to allow programs to be relocated. Relocation is the ability to move a machine code program from one area of store to another without invalidating all the addresses.

We now examine some different mechanisms provided by computer manufacturers.

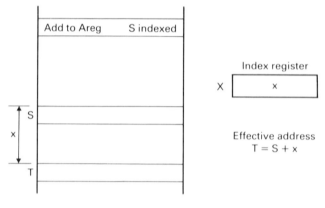

Figure 7.8

7.4.1 Base and current page addressing mechanism

The memory of a computer equipped with this type of mechanism is logically (not physically) divided into regions of a fixed length called pages. Take for example a 16-bit word machine with memory reference instructions of the form indicated in section 7.2.1. The memory could be divided logically into pages of 1024 words each. A page is defined as the largest block of memory that can be directly addressed by the memory address bits of a memory reference instruction. In this particular example the memory reference instructions have 10 bits to specify a memory address, thus the page size is 1024 locations.

Provision is made to address directly one of two pages: page zero (the base page) and the current page (the page in which the instruction itself is located). The memory reference instructions include a bit (bit 10) reserved to specify one or other of those two pages. To address locations in any other page, indirect addressing would have to be used.

The advantages of this mechanism are twofold. First the number of bits required for the address within an instruction is kept down to 10 bits plus one bit to indicate base or current page, and secondly, all direct addresses are actually relative either to absolute location zero, if on base page, or relative to the start of the page in which the instruction is located. Thus a program may be located or relocated on to any page of memory and the address fields are still valid.

7.4.2 Base addressing mechanism

On many computers, instead of storing any form of address within the instruction, all that is stored in the instruction itself is the number of a register, the actual address being stored in the register.

Table 7.1 Addressing modes

Bits in address field			Mode	Meaning
b5	b4	b3		
0	0	0	Register	A effective = Rn
				(i.e. operand = (Rn))
0	1	0	Autoincrement	A effective = (Rn)
				Increment Rn
1	0	0	Autodecrement	Decrement Rn
				A effective = (Rn)
1	1	0	Index	Fetch X
				A effective = X+ (Rn)
0	0	1	Register indirect	A effective = (Rn)
0	1	1	Autoincrement indirect	A effective = ((Rn))
				Increment Rn
1	0	1	Autodecrement indirect	Decrement Rn
				A effective = ((Rn))
1	1	1	Index indirect	Fetch X
				A effective = (X + (Rn))

Where () means 'the contents of'.

Consider for example the addressing mechanism on a PDP-11 computer. A 16-bit instruction is divided into two fields. The OP-code field is 10 bits long, leaving 6 bits for the address field:

Operation code field	Address field
10 bits	6 bits

15   6 5   0

The address field obviously cannot hold a useful actual address but is used to reference a register in various ways. The rightmost 3-bit field specifies one of eight registers R0 to R7. The other 3-bit field defines how the address in the specified register is to be treated. In addition to direct or indirect addressing this allows four basic addressing modes:

(1) *Register mode.* The operand is the contents of the register specified. In the indirect version, the specified register contains the effective address of the operand.
(2) *Autoincrement mode.* The effective address is in the specified register. After the operand has been fetched, the contents of the specified register is automatically incremented. In the indirect case, the effective address is contained in the memory location pointed at by the specified register.
(3) *Autodecrement mode.* The contents of the specified register are decremented and then used as the effective address, or as a pointer to the address in a memory location in the indirect case.

(4) *Index mode.* The effective address is generated by adding the contents of the specified register to the value X which is contained in the word immediately following the instruction. If indirection is specified, it is performed after indexing.

Table 7.1 summarises these addressing modes.

7.4.3 Base and displacement addressing mechanism

The two previous sections have given examples of addressing mechanisms used on computers of relatively small word length (16 bits). Many computer systems are designed with large memory space in mind and consequently have a large word length. A typical range for the word length in such a computer is from 32 to 64 bits. In this environment it is easier to store addresses within an instruction. However, having more bits available within an instruction may lead to the decision to have two address instructions rather than simply larger address fields. As an example of the addressing mechanism on a large computer system, consider the instruction formats used in the IBM 4300 series of computers.

This series resembles the PDP-11 minicomputer in that the base point for an address is the contents of some register. The IBM 4300 computers have sixteen 32-bit general-purpose registers that may be used for this function.

A program must arrange for one of these registers to contain the address of some convenient point in memory. An address within an instruction is then represented by two fields. A base field (4 bits long) defines the register which contains this 'base address' Rb. A displacement field D (12 bits long) contains a value representing the distance in bytes that the required operand is from this base address. The effective address of an operand then becomes:

$$A \text{ effective} = (Rb) + D$$

Although registers are 32 bits long, the effective address is computed by using only 24 bits but this permits accessing up to 2^{24} locations of approximately 16 million bytes of store.

The inclusion of the base register serves to assist relocatability of some programs. In some computers it is common to have several programs residing in the main memory at the same time. In this environment it is desirable that a program and its associated data can be moved into any available space in memory. In the case of the base and displacement addressing mechanism, a complete program can be located anywhere in the memory and executed correctly simply by loading an appropriate address value into the base register. Thus the value of the base register needs to be set only once at the start of each program.

Within the instruction set of the IBM 4300 series of computers some instructions also allow an index register to be specified. This is simply another of the 16 general-purpose registers Rx whose contents are also added to the address generated from the base register contents and the displacement. Thus the effective address of the operand then becomes:

$$A \text{ effective} = (Rb) + D + (Rx)$$

The IBM 4300 series of computers do not have indirect addressing facilities but this is not necessarily a drawback since indexed addressing can normally be substituted.

The fact that an address within an instruction is made up of a total of 16 bits on the IBM 4300, and that the word length is 32 bits, leads to an interesting point. A register-to-register instruction (non-memory reference) would only need 8 bits for the operation code (on the IBM 4300 computers all OP-codes are 8 bits) and 4 bits for each of the two register operands. Hence this class of instructions only requires half a word. Register/storage instructions, one operand being a register the other a store address, need at least 8+4+16 bits (i.e. 40 bits) and therefore will need one and a half words.

Not all the instructions, therefore, are of the same length and some require more than one word. This variable length instruction format is quite common, and found in a number of computers.

7.4.4 Memory segmenting

Another mechanism for allowing access to more words of memory without extending the address size is to use a memory segmentation process, as is implemented on the Intel 8088 (used in the IBM PC).

The 8088 microprocessor supports 1 M-bytes of external memory. The memory space is organised as bytes of data stored at consecutive addresses over the address range 00000 hex to FFFFF hex. Although the memory is organised as bytes, the 8088 can access any two consecutive bytes as a word.

Even though it has a 1 M-byte memory address space, not all of this memory can be active at one time. The memory is logically split into sixteen 64K byte *segments*. Only four of these segments can be active at a time. They are called the code segment, stack segment, data segment and extra segment. The location of these segments is identified by the value of the address held in the 8088's four internal segment registers: CS—code segment, SS—stack segment, DS—data segment and ES—extra segment. Each contains a 16-bit base address that points to the lowest addressed byte of the segment in memory. The code segment is used for the storage of program code (instructions), the data segment for data and the stack segment for a stack area (see section 7.5).

For a program to gain access to another part of memory, all that is necessary is for the contents of the appropriate segment register to be changed through software.

The logical addresses that occur in a program of the 8088 are always 16 bits long because all registers and memory locations are 16 bits long. However, the physical addresses used to access memory are 20 bits long in order to access the 1 M-byte of memory. The generation of the physical address involves combining a 16-bit offset value located in either an index register or pointer register, and a 16-bit base value located in one of the segment registers.

The following example illustrates how these are combined. The mechanism (which is done automatically by the hardware each time a memory access is initiated) is that the value in the segment register is shifted left by four bits with its least significant bits being filled with 0s. Then the offset value is added to the 16 LSBs of the shifted segment address. The result is the 20-bit physical address.

Suppose the segment address is 1234 hex and the offset address is 53 hex. Shifting the segment address left 4 bits and filling with 0s gives:

12340 hex.

The offset is 53 hex.

The sum is 12393 hex.

Thus the physical memory address is 12393 hex.

7.5 Stack computers

In the previous discussion on memory accessing it has been assumed that an instruction could access any location in memory merely by quoting its address. A stack (sometimes called a pushdown stack) is a list of data elements, usually either words or bytes, with the accessing restriction that items of data can only be added or removed at one end of the list. The term stack arises from the analogy with, say, a pile (or stack) of plates. New plates can only be added on to the top of the pile, and the only plate that can be removed is that on the top which was in fact the last to be added. This gives rise to another common term for a stack—LIFO, meaning 'last in first out'.

Stacks originated as a data structure which became widely used by systems programmers, especially when implementing compilers and interpreters. When a computer architecture is altered to accommodate a software device, it is a sign that the device has become generally accepted as an essential feature of a computer system.

While many computers still do not have an architecture that is built to accommodate stacks, new designs of conventional machines usually do include them. A system that makes use of a stack alongside a conventional set of registers could be called *stack assisted*. However, a system that uses a stack instead of the conventional set of registers is a *stack machine*.

7.5.1 The organisation of a stack

A stack can be organised as part of the memory with successive items in the stack occupying successive memory locations. Figure 7.9 shows how a stack could be organised in memory. SP, SL and SB are three registers containing addresses of memory locations as shown. The stack pointer (SP) is the address of the last data item to be entered into the stack. Since the stack is usually just a part of memory, it is important that no attempt is made to remove items from the stack when it is empty, or to add new items to the stack when it is full; otherwise memory locations will be accessed that are not part of the stack and will consequently be using invalid information. Hence, there are registers containing the address of the stack base (SB, the address of the first location of the stack) and the stack limit (SL, the address of the last location of the stack area).

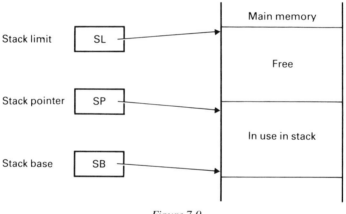

Figure 7.9

7.5.2 Stack instructions

The basic operations on a stack are those of putting a data item on to the stack (known as PUSH) or taking a data item off the stack (known as POP).

The machine instruction PUSH needs to carry out the following tasks:

● Increment the contents of the stack pointer register.
● Check that this value is not now beyond the limit of the stack area. This is a condition known as overflow and is generally an error.
● Insert the required data item on to the stack.

The machine instruction POP performs the following tasks:

● Checks that SP is not below base of stack. If it is, stack is empty and so a POP operation is not permitted; this condition is known as underflow and might be an error or a signal to terminate the process.
● Removes from the stack the data pointed to by the stack pointer.
● Decrements the stack pointer.

Some computers provide further instructions to perform arithmetic operations directly with the top two elements of the stack.

Consider the following instructions taken from the instruction set of the Hewlett-Packard HP3000 computer which provides extensive stack facilities.

LOAD   Performs a PUSH operation of a specified memory word on to the stack.
STOR   Performs a POP operation taking the top element off the stack and storing it in a specified memory location.
ADDM   Adds the contents of a specified memory location to the value at the top of the stack and replaces the top of the stack value with the resultant sum.
MPYM   Multiplies the contents of a specified memory location with the value at the top of the stack and replaces the value at the top of the stack with the least significant part of the product.

All of these instructions involve both the top of the stack and a location in memory. Because they contain a memory address they are one-address instructions. However, the instruction set also provides a number of zero address instructions, such as the following:

ADD   Add the contents of the top two words in the stack, delete these words from the stack and push the resultant sum on to the stack.
DEL   Delete the top word of the stack.

Because there is no address to be stored in the instruction, these instructions will merely consist of an operation code and can therefore be much shorter. The approach taken on the HP 3000 computer is to 'pack' two operations, where possible, into a word. Instructions normally occupy one word (16 bits): 4 bits for the OP-code leaving 12 bits for the other appropriate information.

The zero address stack instructions are identified by an OP-code of four zeros, the other 12 bits being split into two 6-bit fields each being a 'stack OP-code' specifying a stack instruction.

The second 6-bit field for specifying a second stack operation can only be used to advantage when two consecutive stack operations are specified. In other cases this part of the instruction remains unused.

In order to speed up the operation of such stack instructions, not all of the stack needs to be in main memory. Accessing of main memory locations is one of the most critical time constraints as far as the operation of the central processing unit is concerned. The time needed to fetch an item from main memory or to write an item to main memory tends to be very long compared with the time required for operations within the CPU, for example the transfer of data between registers. To hold all of the stack within registers would be expensive and would be an inflexible use of the registers. However, it is possible for the top few elements of the stack to be resident within registers, the remainder of the stack being stored in main memory. This certainly speeds up the operation on the top elements of the stack, and can be implemented so that the programmer need not be aware of the fact. On the HP 3000 computer there are four registers containing the top four elements of the stack. The remainder of the stack is stored in main memory, data being transferred into the fourth register as necessary.

7.5.3 Use of stacks

A stack is one of a number of data structures that are of interest in computing science and can be used in the solution of a number of problems. Two examples of the use of stacks are given here.

A stack can be used in connection with subroutine linkage. Section 7.2.3 explained the need for storing the address of the location following the instruction that branched to the subroutine in order to allow control to return to this address and processing to continue.

Since it is a reasonable and practical programming technique to allow one subroutine to call another, it is obviously important that each return address is stored separately so that addresses can be retrieved when necessary. The situation where one subroutine calls a second subroutine could obviously be extended to allow this second subroutine to call a third. This process is known as subroutine *nesting* and can be carried out to any depth. Eventually, of course, the last subroutine completes its processing and returns to the subroutine that called it. It is important here to note that the return address required will be the last one to be stored. That is, the return addresses are stored and recalled in a last-in-first-out order. This naturally suggests that these addresses could be PUSHed on to a stack and POPped off as required.

A stack facility is also useful for storing intermediate results when evaluating arithmetic expressions. Consider the following example. Assume that the values of the variables A, B, C, D, E are not stored in the stack initially but are stored in memory locations with addresses denoted by A, B, C, D, E.

$$X = (A + B)^* C + D^* E$$

The machine instructions necessary to perform the above computation (using the HP 3000 instruction set defined in section 7.5.2) are:

```
Step 1  LOAD   A
     2  ADDM   B
     3  MPYM   C
     4  LOAD   D
     5  MPYM   E
     6  ADD
     7  STOR   X
```

At the completion of Step 3 the top of the stack will contain the value of (A + B) *C. This will then be pushed down the stack as D is loaded on to the stack. At the completion of Step 5 the top of the stack contains the value of D*E. The operation of Step 6 adds the top two elements of the stack together, leaving the result at the top of the stack, which is then stored in location X in memory.

The stack then has provided a convenient facility for the temporary storage of intermediate results. Further, if the top elements of the stack are actually CPU registers (as described in section 7.5.2), the above arithmetic operations are taking place using registers, which will take significantly less time than the equivalent operations on memory locations.

7.6 Software

This chapter has been concerned with the machine instructions of the computer's native instruction set, which are stored in memory as a string of binary digits. However, as is clear from the earlier part of this chapter, coding and manipulating a string of binary digits is very difficult for humans and so programs have been represented here using a symbolic code. This technique of using a symbolic code rather than the fundamental binary string is in fact used in practice. However, there are degrees of symbolism and various aids are available for writing programs. These will now be briefly examined.

7.6.1 Machine code programming

Machine code is the native binary code used to represent the instruction set of the computer. This chapter has explained how the instruction set of the computer is defined by the designer of the computer system and constrained by the architecture chosen. Thus the exact details of instructions and addressing methods differ for different types of computer and as a result machine code programs cannot be transferred between one type of computer and another.

Since machine code programs are the actual binary code stored in the memory of the computer, a machine code program can be loaded into the computer's memory and executed directly. However, because writing programs in binary is very error prone and extremely tedious some simple aids are often available to ease these problems. The most basic of these is a facility to allow programs to be written using either hexadecimal or octal format notation. This simplifies conversion to binary while being much easier for the human programmer to deal with than a long string of binary digits. The facility is normally provided by a simple monitor (a very simplified operating system) which typically allows input from a set of hexadecimal keypads. The monitor is often stored in ROM so that it is permanently resident in memory.

However, although it is possible to write long and complex programs in machine code there do exist a number of serious problems which make it impractical. The most difficult tasks when writing in machine code are:

Working in binary (or hexadecimal/octal)
Using numeric OP-codes
Keeping track of all the addresses

Hence it is necessary to have available a more useable programming language which is much easier for the programmer to write in but easy to convert to machine code.

7.6.2 Assembly language programming

Assembly language is a symbolic language in which, for example, mnemonic codes are used to represent the OP-codes of the machine's instruction set. Thus there is a one-to-one correspondence between the assembly instruction and the actual machine instruction. An assembler is a program which converts assembly language statements (source code) into binary machine code (object code). It helps overcome the problems identified in section 7.6.1 as follows:

Data can be defined in decimal, binary, octal or hex, whichever is most convenient—the assembler performs the conversion to binary
OP-codes are replaced by mnemonics—they are easier to remember and read when debugging
Symbolic names are used for addresses—the assembler maintains a table of names and corresponding addresses

Most of the translation operations of an assembler are straightforward. For example, when translating OP-codes the assembler looks up the symbolic name used in the program in a table which contains all the mnemonics of the instruction set and their corresponding OP-codes.

However, the handling of addresses can present a problem. If a label is declared before it is referenced (that is, it will already have been allocated an address) then this presents no problem since its allocated address can immediately be inserted into the machine instruction (see the label BEGINLOOP in Figure 7.4 for example). If the reference to a label is to one which has not yet been assembled because it is further on in the program then it is not possible for the assembler to complete the machine instruction with this address because it does not know what the address is going to be. For this reason assemblers normally require two passes over a source program to generate the complete object code program. The first pass generates a symbol table containing all the label references in the program and their corresponding addresses, while the second pass is then able to generate the complete machine code program. The following outline algorithms for the two passes illustrate this.

Pass One
    procedure passone;
    begin
        repeat
            read a line of code;
            enter labels into symbol table;
        until opcode = 'END'
    end

Pass Two
    procedure passtwo;
    begin
        repeat
            read a line of code;
            look up mnemonic in table and output
                binary value;
            look up operand (data address) in symbol
                table and output binary value;
        until   opcode = 'END'
    end

Complete details of the syntax of a particular assembler and of all the debugging aids that are often available are beyond the scope of this book. As indicated in the preface, it is assumed that the reader is studying a particular assembly language in parallel with the computer architecture concepts being developed here, or already has knowledge of an assembler.

Though infinitely preferable to programming in machine code, assembly language programming even with good diagnostics and debugging software is still tedious and prone to errors. An assembly language program is still a 'low level' language firmly based on the particular architecture of a particular machine. Consequently when writing a program the programmer is often constrained by the available registers and other architectural considerations and less able to concentrate on the program algorithm. For this reason, a better solution to the task of programming is provided by the use of an appropriate 'high level' language, which allows the programmer the opportunity to exhibit good structure and readability in the program code.

However, there are occasions when the use of an assembly language is necessary, typically because it is necessary that the code executes in a given (short) time or the code has to be squeezed into a given amount of memory. Because of the close relationship between machine code and assembly language both of these features may be more achievable when writing at that low level.

Despite this low level, however, the techniques for program design or programming methodologies are *equally*, if not more, applicable when using assembly language, and the reader is urged to adhere to a proven, well structured methodology.

7.6.3 Relocation

Relocation means being able to move a machine code program about in memory, the addresses still being valid. More precisely it means being able to defer a decision on where in memory the program is to be loaded until loading time (that is, not at assembly or compilation time).

In order to achieve this, instead of addresses being absolute (that is, referring to a specific location in memory) they must be relative to something that will be adjusted at load time (when the program is loaded into memory just prior to execution).

How it is achieved depends on the mode of specification of main store addresses. There are three ways that are common:

● Direct addressing (many computers)
● Base addressing (DEC 10, Univac 1100, Honeywell 6000)
● Explicit base addressing (DEC 11, IBM 360/370/4300)

Direct addressing relocation

The assembler *tags* a relocatable address field to indicate that it has been assembled relative to zero and needs the actual start address adding on to it when it is loaded.

Consider the following example:

Reloc bits	Code		
0 1	12 17		12 57
0 1	13 05		13 45
0 0	03 18		03 18
As assembled			As loaded starting at address 40

Relocation bits:
    0 means not relocatable
    1 means add on start address

This obviously needs a loader routine to load the program into memory and perform the appropriate adjustments (see section 7.6.4).

Base addressing

All addresses in the program are relative to the start of the program. The loader places the actual load address into a special register called the BASE register at load time. At execution time all addresses are formed by the hardware adding the contents of this base register to the address given in the instruction.

Explicit base addressing

The best example of this is the base and displacement mechanism as used on IBM 360/370/4300 computers and described in section 7.4.3. This mechanism is inherently relocatable.

7.6.4 Loaders

A loader is a program to *load* any other program into main memory, usually from backing store. If the loading is always done to a fixed address point then the loader is very simple. If the code is relocatable then the loader needs to be told where to relocate the program to and has to incorporate an appropriate relocation mechanism (see section 7.6.3).

One of the major advantages of a relocating assembler is that with a very large program it can be split into a number of separate modules (maybe even written in different languages) and not all the modules need to be completely assembled every time some modifications are done to one particular routine or module. Hence we need to be able to bring together a number of program modules written and assembled or compiled separately. We now therefore need a *linking loader*.

There are two major features necessary in a linking loader:

(1) The ability to specify the base address of each object module so that each machine code module follows immediately the final address of the preceding module.

(2) A facility for resolving cross references between modules.

At assembly time the address of other modules are not known so any CALL to one cannot be completed; it can only be filled in at load time when the modules are 'linked' together. Thus the assembler needs some extra directives to define addresses which are outside or external to this routine. For example:

$$\text{XREF} \qquad \text{MOD9}$$

$$\cdot$$
$$\cdot$$
$$\cdot$$

$$\text{CALL} \qquad \text{MOD9}$$

As the linker gets each routine and loads it into memory it builds up a table of these external references. These can then all be resolved once the final memory addresses have been allocated to each machine code module.

7.7 Summary

The principal purpose of this chapter has been to introduce the representation of instructions at the machine code level as seen by the programmer and to discuss the problems of addressing memory locations.

A major point in the study of a particular computer is the method used for addressing memory locations. Inevitably the addressing scheme depends on the word length. Computers with a relatively short word length have to employ a more complex addressing mechanism and are, in general, less able to address a very large memory without resorting to multiple word instructions. The disadvantage of this is that it takes longer to process such instructions because they require multiple accesses to memory just to fetch the instruction. The instruction set is also dependent on word length, since the variety of instructions will depend on the utilisation of the bit space within each instruction. Instruction formats range from those with two operations within one word (some stack instructions) to those whose instructions require two or even three words each.

Examples of both instruction sets and addressing mechanisms have been drawn from a variety of machines and should, at least, indicate that there is no single approach to the problem but that each manufacturer decides individually what is felt to be appropriate both functionally and financially.

In order to understand thoroughly the main principles explained in this chapter it is necessary to write some simple programs in machine code or, perhaps, assembler code and examine the machine code version, for a particular computer. The differences between various computers can be readily understood once the common basic principles are grasped.

7.8 Problems

(1) (a) Explain what is meant by:
  (1) a zero address machine,
  (2) a one-address machine,
  (3) a two-address machine,
  (4) a three-address machine,
  indicating how the presence or absence of addresses is utilised and how the machine code reflects the machine structure.
  (b) What is an effective address? How is it achieved when addressing:
  (1) directly;
  (2) by indexing;
  (3) indirectly.
  Indicate further how indirect and indexed addressing can be combined.
(2) Explain what is meant by the following terms:
  (a) the effective address;
  (b) the addressing mode.
  Describe two simple addressing modes in common use. Specify their advantages and disadvantages and give a specific detailed example of each mode from a computer you are familiar with. Use diagrams where appropriate.
(3) (a) What factors have to be taken into account when the number of operands in an instruction is being specified and how does this affect the computer's architecture?
  (b) Describe four ways in which an effective address can be generated.
(4) (a) Explain the function of the base register in the addressing mechanism of the IBM 4300 machine instructions.
  (b) Explain how machine instructions refer to operands held in the main memory of an IBM 4300 computer. Include in your explanation the use of indexing.
  (c) Explain the term indexing in IBM 4300 assembler code.
(5) Show with examples how logical and shift operations can be used:
  (a) to replace part of a binary pattern by zeros leaving the rest unchanged;
  (b) to test for the occurrence of a 3-bit pattern in a particular part of a word or byte;
  (c) to pack a 5-bit pattern which is right justified in a register into bits 8 to 12 of the word labelled ODD.
(6) Discuss the relative merits of the addressing methods available in the PDP-11 and IBM 4300 computers. In particular, discuss how the

addressing method in each machine facilitates the following: relocatability, implementation of a stack, accessing an operand list.

(7) IBM 4300 computers do not have indirect addressing. Assuming that the address of an operand is stored in main memory, how would you access the operand?

(8) The following program written in IBM PC assembler language is not commented. Identify the segments of the program, deduce what the program is doing, and fully comment the program.

```
                NAME       EXAMPLE
    ;
    MY_STACK    SEGMENT    PARA 'STACK'
                DW         10 DUP(?)
    STK_TOP     LABEL      WORD
    MY_STACK    ENDS
    ;
    MY_DATA     SEGMENT    PARA 'DATA'
    SOURCE      DB         10,20,30,40
    DEST        DB         4 DUP(?)
    MY_DATA     ENDS
    ;
    MY_CODE     SEGMENT    PARA 'CODE'
    MY_PROG     PROC       FAR
                ASSUME     CS:MY_CODE, DS:MY_ DATA,
                ASSUME     SS:STACK
                MOV        AX,MY_DATA
                MOV        DS,AX
                MOV        AX,MY_STACK
                MOV        SS,AX
                MOV        SP,OFFSET STK_TOP
                MOV        DEST,0
                MOV        DEST+1,0
                MOV        DEST+2,0
                MOV        DEST+3,0
                MOV        AL,SOURCE
                MOV        DEST+3,AL
                MOV        AL,SOURCE+1
                MOV        DEST+2,AL
                MOV        AL,SOURCE+2
                MOV        DEST+1,AL
                MOV        AL,SOURCE+3
                MOV        DEST,AL
                RET
    MY_PROG     ENDP
    MY_CODE     ENDS
                END        MY_PROG
```

The central processing unit

The previous chapter has described the requirement for and the structure
of machine instructions. In order for the instructions to be obeyed there
must be a unit that will fetch each instruction in turn from memory,
examine it and arrange for the appropriate action to be taken. This is the
central processing unit (CPU).

The solution to any problem is defined by an algorithm. This algorithm is
then broken down further into a sequence of steps (that must be obeyed in
that particular sequence) known as the machine code instructions. The
CPU adopts the same approach. In order for it to fetch and execute a
particular instruction it must perform a sequence of more rudimentary
operations in a particular order. The operations and the means by which
they occur will be described in this chapter.

8.1 Component parts

The CPU can be thought of as being made up of a number of component
parts as illustrated in Figure 8.1. There are a number of special-purpose
registers (in addition to the general-purpose registers that are available to
the programmer), an arithmetic and logic unit (ALU) which can be
thought of as a 'black box' which performs actual computations, and a
control unit which is effectively the nerve centre of the machine, sending
control signals to all other units.

8.1.1 Internal registers

A program is made up of a series of instructions stored in the main memory of the computer. To execute this program, the CPU fetches the instructions one at a time and arranges for the appropriate actions to be performed. Instructions are fetched from consecutive locations unless a branch instruction of some form indicates that the next instruction to be executed is stored somewhere else.

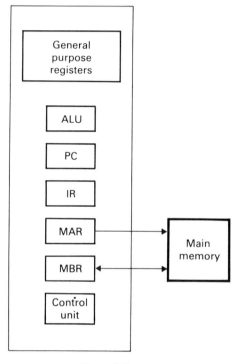

Figure 8.1

As we saw in Chapter 6, all communication with the memory is done via the two registers memory address register (MAR) and the memory buffer register (MBR). In order to fetch the next instruction, the CPU has to place its address in the MAR and issue a read memory command, as a result of which the instruction will be fetched and placed in the MBR. Having fetched it, the CPU may have to reference memory again to execute it if, for example, it is a memory reference instruction that requires data to be fetched from memory. To fetch the data the CPU will have to place the address of the data in the MAR and this will, of course, destroy the address of this current instruction which is stored in the MAR. The CPU would not know, therefore, the address of the next instruction.

Consequently, there is a need for a register to be dedicated to the task of keeping the address of the next instruction to be executed. This is known as the *program counter* (PC). The PC register is initially loaded with the address in memory of the location of the first instruction of the program, and then, after each instruction has been fetched, it is incremented to point to the next location, unless the instruction is a branch instruction.

When an instruction has been fetched from memory, it will be left in the MBR. However, since the control structure of the CPU will need to have access to the instruction during execution, and the MBR may be needed for data during execution, in a memory reference instruction, for example, it is also necessary to have a register dedicated to holding the current instruction being executed. This register is known as the *instruction register* (IR).

A program, then, is obeyed by the CPU carrying out the following sequence of events:

(1) Copy PC contents into the MAR and initiate memory read
(2) Increment the PC
(3) Copy the instruction now in the MBR into the IR
(4) Decode the IR (i.e. examine the instruction to determine what instruction it is)
(5) Execute the instruction
(6) Repeat from step (1)

This can be represented by a symbolic notation as follows, where [x] means 'contents of x', and M represents a main memory location:

[PC]   → MAR
[M]   → MBR
[PC] + 1   → PC
[MBR]   → IR
Decode IR
Execute the instruction

The 'Decode IR' step is achieved by the means of a decoder. This is essentially circuitry which examines the operation code field of the instruction in the IR and outputs a signal that indicates which particular instruction is being requested (see section 2.2.4).

Obviously, step (5) above also consists of a number of steps, depending on the instruction, and this will be examined in section 8.2.

8.1.2 The arithmetic and logic unit

The arithmetic and logic unit (ALU) is that part of the CPU where all the arithmetical and logical operations are performed. Constructed from high speed electronic components, it is a sophisticated piece of circuitry which will perform some specified operation on the data presented to its inputs. Typical of the operations that an ALU is able to perform are:

● Arithmetic operations such as ADD and COMPLEMENT
● Logical operations such as AND, OR, Exclusive OR
● Manipulation operations such as SHIFT, TEST

Note that specific details of number systems, sign conventions and their manipulation are given in Chapter 5.

The arithmetic operations to be found in the ALU are basically those of add and one's complement. Subtraction is usually performed by taking two's complement of the number to be subtracted (one's complement plus one) and adding it to the other value. Multiply and divide operations are much more complex than either addition or subtraction. On some machines these operations are provided at the machine instruction level and on other machines both multiply and divide are provided as software routines. These routines basically implement multiplication as a sequence of adds and shifts, and division as a sequence of subtracts and shifts.

Logical operations provided are usually those of AND, OR, Exclusive OR (see sections 2.1 and 7.2.4).

The type of shift instructions provided are also discussed in section 7.2.1 and are essentially of two kinds, arithmetic or shift and rotate. The rotate instructions are shift instructions where the bits that disappear off one end of the word come back in at the other end of the word. An arithmetic shift is one which preserves the sign bit. The test operations provide the facility for testing the relative size of values, although the operations themselves are usually simple arithmetic ones. There are often a number of single bit registers (flip-flops) associated with the ALU which can be set as a result of an arithmetic operation. Examples of these are the N bit, Z bit and O bit, set to binary 1 if the result of an arithmetic operation is negative, zero, or results in overflow respectively. The registers can then be tested by instructions to determine conditional jumps in the program sequence. For example, to determine the relative sizes A and B, the operation $A - B$ is performed. Instead of the normal value of $A - B$ being output to the ALU, it will merely set the values of the N bit and the Z bit to the appropriate values. If $A > B$ then $N = 0$ and $Z = 0$. If $A = B$ then $N = 0$ and $Z = 1$. If $A < B$ then $N = 1$ and $Z = 0$.

8.1.3 Floating point unit

The provision of floating point arithmetic in a computer is of great convenience to a lot of users. Apart from having an extended range of values available, the fact that the programmer does not have to worry about scale factors and aligning binary points is an important aspect.

However, the implementation of a floating point unit can be expensive.

One way to reduce the cost is to provide the facilities by software routines, but these routines may require hundreds of main memory locations to store instructions and data tables.

In machines where the use of floating point arithmetic is to play a significant part, it is usually provided by an additional hardware feature, the *floating point unit* (FPU). Although the FPU is expensive, it can reduce execution times significantly when compared with software implementations.

8.2 Execution of a complete instruction

As we saw in section 8.1.1, a program stored in the main memory of a computer is obeyed by the CPU carrying out the following sequence of events, described with the symbolic notation introduced earlier:

(1) [PC] $\rightarrow$ MAR
(2) [M] $\rightarrow$ MBR
(3) [PC] + 1 $\rightarrow$ PC
(4) [MBR] $\rightarrow$ IR
(5) Decode   IR
(6) Execute this instruction
(7) Repeat from step (1)

By examining this sequence it can be seen that steps (1) to (5) are concerned with FETCHing the instruction from the main memory, and that step (6) is concerned with EXECUTing this instruction. Each of these steps is called a micro-instruction.

These two stages are known as the fetch phase and the execute phase, or alternatively the fetch/execute cycle. Obviously, the fetch phase is the same regardless of what instruction is being fetched, although if an instruction occupies more than one main memory location, the fetch phase will have to be repeated as many times as necessary to fetch the complete instruction. The execute phase, however, is dependent on the particular instruction. To examine the sort of sequence necessary in the execute phase, consider the following instruction types.

8.2.1 Execution of a non-memory reference instruction

The execution phase of a non-memory reference instruction is straightforward in that it does not require any information to be fetched from main memory. We noted in section 7.2.4 that these are often instructions which manipulate data stored in a CPU register. In this case, all that is required is to present to the ALU the bits in the particular register defined and the signal from the decoder which indicates what particular action is required.

When the ALU has completed its task, the resulting bit pattern will be left in the appropriate register.

8.2.2 Execution of a memory reference instruction

In this case the execution phase is a little more involved, because a memory read is required to fetch the appropriate data from memory before the required actions can be carried out. The execute phase for an instruction which fetches some data from memory and performs some arithmetic on it can be represented symbolically as follows:

$[IR]_{address\ field} \rightarrow MAR$
$[M] \qquad \rightarrow MBR$
Perform appropriate action using ALU and MBR

If the instruction is one which writes to memory, e.g. 'store contents of register A in addressed memory location', the sequence would be:

$[IR]_{address\ field} \rightarrow MAR$
$[A] \rightarrow \qquad MBR$
$[MBR] \rightarrow \quad M$

In all the examples in this chapter it is assumed that the action described symbolically as:

$[IR]_{address\ field} \rightarrow MAR$

involves taking account of the basic addressing mechanism in use on a particular computer, such as base and displacement addressing, or base and current page addressing, as described in section 7.4.

Some instructions both read from and write to memory during their execution. Consider, for example, the 'increment and skip if zero' instruction. The effect of this instruction is to take the contents of some memory location, increment its value by 1 and if its value is now zero skip the next instruction in sequence; otherwise execute the next instruction in sequence. Symbolically this is:

(1) $[IR]_{address\ field} \rightarrow \quad MAR$
(2) $[M] \qquad \rightarrow \quad MBR$
(3) $[MBR] + 1 \quad \rightarrow MBR$
(4) $[MBR] \qquad \rightarrow \quad M$
(5) If $[MBR] = 0$ then $[PC] + 1 \rightarrow PC$

Having read the value of the data from memory in step (2), step (3) increments this value, and at step (4) it is written back to memory at the same address, since the contents of the MAR have not been altered. The skip if zero part of the instruction is carried out in part (5). It must be remembered that the PC has already been incremented during the fetch phase to point to the next instruction in sequence, so the only modification necessary is to increment it by a further one if the incremented value which is still stored in the MBR is now equal to zero.

8.2.3 Branching instructions

Branch instructions are a particular subset of memory reference instructions that reference memory for the purpose of transferring control rather than doing some arithmetic or logic.

Consider an unconditional branch instruction. The required effect is to transfer control to the address defined in the branch instruction. The instruction which will be executed after the current one is pointed to by the contents of the PC register. This is incremented by 1 during the fetch phase of every instruction on the assumption that the next instruction to be executed is going to be the next one in sequence. In the case of a branch instruction, however, the address of the next instruction to be executed is contained in the branch instruction, and so all that is necessary is for this address to be transferred to the PC. Consequently, the execute phase for an unconditional branch instruction can be represented symbolically as:

$$[IR]_{address\ field} \rightarrow PC$$

If the branch is a conditional branch, all that is necessary is for the condition to be examined to decide whether to transfer the address field of the IR to the PC or not, as illustrated by the 'increment and skip if zero' instruction considered in section 8.2.2.

8.2.4 Indirect and indexed addressing

If indirect addressing is specified for an instruction, this will introduce an additional memory read into the sequence of actions.

For example, consider again an instruction to fetch some data from memory and perform some arithmetic or logic function on this data, where the address is defined as being indirect. The sequence would be:

$$[IR]_{address\ field} \rightarrow MAR$$

$[M] \quad \rightarrow MBR$
$[MBR] \quad \rightarrow MAR$
$[M] \quad \rightarrow MBR$
Perform appropriate action using ALU

So far as the CPU is concerned, the main effect of indirect addressing is to slow down the execution of an instruction by requiring an additional memory read cycle.

If indirect addressing is specified, there is the additional step of adding the contents of the index register to the address defined in the instruction before the memory access can be made. For the same instruction as just described, but using indexing rather than indirect addressing, the sequence would be·

$$[IR]_{\text{address field}} \qquad \rightarrow MAR$$

$$[MAR] + \begin{bmatrix} \text{index} \\ \text{register} \end{bmatrix} \rightarrow MAR$$

$$[M] \qquad\qquad \rightarrow MBR$$

Perform appropriate action using ALU

For both indirect and indexed addressing there is also the additional requirement of identifying whether these addressing techniques are being used or whether direct addressing is specified. Consequently, the sequence of actions described above may well require a series of steps which entail testing whether one of the above addressing techniques is specified or not, and conditionally branching to the appropriate sequence of steps.

8.3 Architectural considerations

This chapter has so far discussed features of a CPU that are normally found on most computers. From the user's point of view what makes computer systems differ from each other is essentially the instruction set provided. From a performance point of view, in addition to the facilities provided by the instruction set, it is important to look at how the basic components are structured and interconnected. These are the factors that will determine how a computer will perform. It is in this area that the term 'architecture' can be sensibly applied. The word is directly analogous to the more familiar meaning of architecture applied to buildings. All buildings are constructed from the same basic components: bricks, cement, glass, door frames, etc. What makes buildings quite different from each other both visually and functionally is the way in which these components are put together, and the overall design is the work of an architect. All computers can be said to be constructed from the same basic components (memory, registers, ALU, etc.), but they are functionally different because of the way in which they have been structured and interconnected by the computer architect.

In this section we will consider ways of arranging for the basic components of the CPU to be controlled and connected.

8.3.1 Synchronous and asynchronous processors

Section 8.2 examined the sequence of steps that the CPU must perform in order to fetch and execute an instruction. Certain of these steps must wait until the previous step is complete before commencing. For example, during the fetch phase the instruction cannot be moved from the MBR to the IR until a previous step ([M] → MBR) has completed, which is dependent on the time for completion of a memory read. This is not necessarily true for all steps, however. The PC, for example, can be incremented at any stage during the fetch/execute cycle after its value has been transferred to the MAR. Since incrementing it is an operation purely internal to the CPU and involves the PC and perhaps the ALU, it takes less time to complete than a memory transfer operation. Since nothing else can proceed until the memory transfer, transferring the instruction from memory to the MBR, is complete, the incrementing of the PC can be done concurrently with this memory transfer. This is the reason why the PC is incremented for all instructions even though for some, such as a branch instruction, it is not really necessary because they are going to alter the value of the PC during execution.

The total time required to execute an instruction depends on the instruction itself. The fetch phase is the same for all instructions, but the execute cycle may require either one or a number of steps. Also the time for each step in the fetch/execute cycle is not necessarily the same. As has just been indicated, the time for a memory transfer will be relatively large compared to the time for an operation on an internal register. Also, operations involving simple register transfers, such as those which would occur in executing a branch instruction, will take less time than those operations on registers requiring arithmetic or logic to be performed. The timing for each of these steps can be done in one of two ways.

A *synchronous processor* has an internal processor clock. This is an electronic circuit which generates electronic pulses at regular and accurate intervals of time, and is usually based on a crystal controlled oscillator for accuracy and stability. Each step must commence operation on a clock pulse and although each transfer step always requires the same amount of time each time it is performed, some steps may require more than one clock period (the time between consecutive pulses) to complete whereas other steps will require less than one clock period to complete.

This leads to a relatively simple processor construction, but has the disadvantage that since not all steps need the same amount of time, some operations cannot commence until the next clock pulse, even though the preceding step is complete.

An *asynchronous processor* is one where initiation of the next step takes place immediately the previous step is completed. This will remove any idling of the processor as it waits for the next clock pulse and consequently

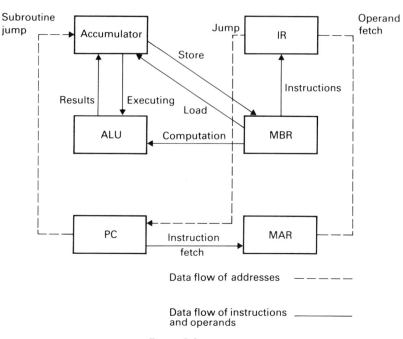

Figure 8.2

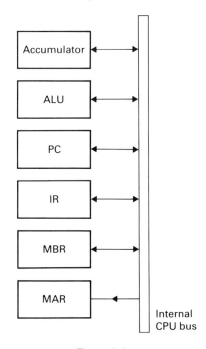

Figure 8.3

should result in an increase in speed of the processor. However, this is tempered by the fact that extra logic circuitry is required to detect the end of each event. Not only does this extra logic make an asynchronous processor more expensive (the cost of the logic circuits to detect the end of a step will usually be greater than that of a simple clock), but the fact that the end of an event has to be detected will take some time, and reduce the time saved over a synchronous processor.

Asynchronous operation of the CPU is, however, generally faster but more complex and costly than synchronous operation because more hardware is required.

8.3.2 Interconnection methods

The central processing unit is made up of a number of component parts described in section 8.1. These component parts can be interconnected in several ways and the way the components are connected can have a significant effect on the machine instructions that can be provided and on the speed of operation of the CPU. Consequently it is one of the architectural features that can distinguish one machine from another.

If you examine the individual information transfer steps that make up machine instructions as described in section 8.2, then for a simple CPU, with just one register known as the accumulator, some of the transfer paths are shown in Figure 8.2.

In this example, there is a requirement for four address transfer paths and six instruction and operand transfer paths, a total of ten paths. Obviously, the more registers there are available and the more machine instructions that are to be provided, the more information transfer paths will be required.

These transfer paths can be implemented in one of three ways, either using a point-to-point connection, a common bus, or a multiple bus system.

If a computer is to achieve a reasonable speed of operation it must be organised in a parallel fashion. This means that in order for a component to handle a full word of data at a time, the data transfer between components must be done in parallel (all the bits of a word are transferred simultaneously) which implies that a considerable number of wires (lines) are needed for the necessary connection. Such a collection of wires which have a common identity is called a *bus*.

In the case of a point-to-point bus system, every information transfer path required is provided by a dedicated bus. In the simple example shown in Figure 8.2, each data flow path would be implemented as an individual bus. The advantage of such a system is that many transfers could be taking place simultaneously, thereby tending to lead to a fast CPU. The disadvantage is that it would be very expensive to provide all the buses. On studying the transfers that are necessary for the operation of a machine instruction,

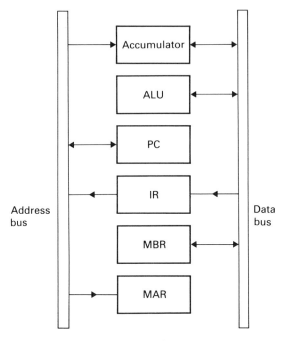

Figure 8.4

it can be seen that a lot of the transfers cannot logically take place simultaneously, even though it is physically possible. Consequently a full point-to-point bus system for internal CPU organisation is almost never used.

At the other extreme there could be a common bus system. Implemented with a common bus system, the simple CPU whose data flow paths are shown in Figure 8.2 would be as shown in Figure 8.3. All data transfers take place along this common bus. To enable information to be

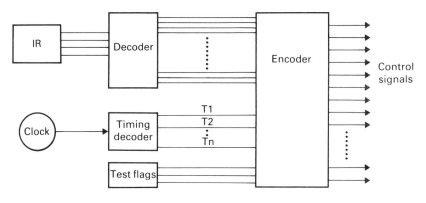

Figure 8.5

transferred from one register to another, there need to be some logic gates (on/off switches) which enable only the required registers to be actively connected to the bus at the appropriate time. The advantage of the bus system is that it is very inexpensive, but the disadvantage is that only one transfer can take place at once. There is therefore no possibility of concurrent operations and consequently this type of computer can be slow.

The most common form of internal CPU bus found on many machines is the multiple bus system, which is a compromise between the two extremes just described. Here there is more than one bus to which a number of components are attached, sometimes with some registers connected by a point-to-point bus if necessary. Often the data flow requirements are implemented with two buses, an address bus and a data bus. For the machine described in Figure 8.2 implemented as a multiple bus machine the structure might be as in Figure 8.4. This system would allow more than one transfer simultaneously, although allowing only one transfer on each bus at any time.

8.4 Control unit

To execute instructions the CPU must have some means of generating the appropriate control signal to initiate the next step in the correct sequence as discussed in section 8.2. The various ways that have been developed fall into one of two categories:

● Hardwired control
● Microprogrammed control

8.4.1 Hardwired control

Consider the sequence of steps in the fetch/execute cycle as defined in section 8.2. Each step will require a time period, defined by the clock if the processor is a synchronous one. The particular action at each step is defined by the state of

(1) the output of the decoder—this defines the machine instruction to be executed;
(2) the clock, relative to the time period at the start of this machine instruction;
(3) any test flags set in the ALU (see section 8.1.2).

The particular operation carried out by the CPU is controlled by a complex logic circuit known as an *encoder*. This, as illustrated in Figure 8.5, has as input a series of lines from the decoder, the clock and the ALU test flags. Only one line from the decoder will have a signal on it indicating which particular instruction is to be executed, and only one line from the clock will have a signal on it indicating which step period is the current one (the signal reverting back to line T1 at the end of execution of this instruction). Only the lines from the test flag set will have signals on them. Each output line corresponds to a particular control signal, a combination of which will result in one of the transfer steps that the CPU is capable of performing. As was indicated in section 8.3.2, all registers are connected to a bus system to allow information to pass between appropriate registers. Connections to the bus system are through gates which are normally inhibited (this means that there is no connection to the bus), but can be enabled by the application of a control signal. Thus to transfer information from one register to another, the output gate of one register and the input gate of the other register would need to be enabled, requiring two control signals. According to the combination of input lines to the encoder with signals on them, only the appropriate output lines will generate control signals which cause that particular step to be performed.

8.4.2 Microprogrammed control

An alternative way of generating the appropriate control signal at the appropriate time is by a software technique known as microprogrammed control.

Consider a control word whose individual bits represent the various control signals in Figure 8.5. Within the control word a one bit would indicate the presence of a control signal, a zero the absence of that control signal, there being as many bits as control signals. This is, in fact, a simplification of a realistic system, but it is useful for illustrating the concept. A particular combination of 1s and 0s in a control word would define a particular transfer step. The control signals and transfer operations that the machine is capable of are, of course, fixed at the design stage. A sequence of control words would correspond to a machine instruction, typical sequences being described in section 8.2. The individual control words are known as micro-instructions and the sequence of micro-instructions as the microprogram for that machine instruction. The microprograms corresponding to the instruction set are held in a special memory called the microprogram memory. The control unit generates the control signals for any machine instruction by sequentially reading the control words of the corresponding microprogram from micromemory. To read the control words sequentially, and at the correct time, a micropro-gram counter (μPC) and a clock is required. In order to take account of the condition of any status flags that exist (see section 8.1.2) there is a need for conditional branching in the microprogram.

Not all microprogrammed computers allow the user to write his own microprograms. Sometimes the microprograms, which are supplied by the manufacturer, are stored in ROM and cannot be altered. On other computers, for example, the Hewlett-Packard HP21MX, the microprogram memory can be altered, and consequently users can define their own microprograms for machine instructions. These machines are said to be microprogrammable.

The following points are important.

(1) Microprograms define the instruction set of the computer. If the microprogram memory can be written to, then the instruction set is not irrevocably fixed but can be changed by altering or adding microprograms. This can offer flexibility to the designer and user of the computer.

(2) Hardwired control units are inevitably faster than microprogrammed ones because there is dedicated circuitry for the control functions.

(3) Since execution of the machine instruction involves a number of fetches from the microprogram memory, the speed of this memory determines the overall speed of the computer. Consequently the microprogram memory is usually implemented in a small, very fast dedicated memory rather than the main memory.

8.5 Enhanced processors

Improved technology has led to a dramatic increase in the speed of processing over the years, but the question still remains, given a particular technology, how can the speed of the processor be increased? This section looks at some enhancements to the processor design which will help to increase the apparent processor speed.

8.5.1 Lookahead processors

It can be seen from the earlier part of this chapter that the process of fetching and executing machine instructions consists of a sequence of micro-instructions. During the time of a memory access, the processor is idle (unless there are other tasks for it to do, such as incrementing the program counter). Conversely, during periods when the processor is busy, particularly when computation is proceeding in the arithmetic and logic unit, the memory access mechanism is idle. During these periods the processor could be 'looking ahead' and fetching (and perhaps decoding) the next instruction(s) so that they are already available on completion of execution of the current instruction. Clearly the number of instructions that can be *prefetched* depends on the time available, and this in turn depends on the type of instruction being processed, but between three and twelve instructions is quite common.

Effectively the time for execution of one instruction and the time for fetching the next instruction are overlapped and so there must be an increase in the speed at which a program is processed. The disadvantage of this approach is that it assumes the next instruction required for processing is the next one in sequence in the memory. For an unconditional branch instruction this is not true and for a conditional branch this may not be true. In both these cases the processor may be prefetching the wrong instruction. When this is discovered, during the execute phase of the branch instruction, the processor must 'throw away' the instructions that have been prefetched and continue with the correct ones. A typical example of a prefetch machine is the Prime 750. Here, the instruction prefetch unit prefetches and decodes up to four instructions from cache memory, in parallel with the processor's execution unit.

8.5.2 Pipeline processors

With a pipelined processor, the idea of overlapping the fetch and execute phases is extended so that each of the following phases has its own processor:

● instruction fetch
● instruction decode
● address calculation
● data fetch
● instruction execution

This is illustrated in Figure 8.6.

When the machine starts, the first instruction is fetched by the instruction fetch unit. After that, the instruction decoder will decode this first instruction while the instruction fetch unit is fetching the second instruction. The next step will be to make the address calculation for the first instruction, decode the second instruction and fetch the third instruction, all in parallel. Clearly the potential throughput of such a pipelined machine must be greater than that of a sequential machine because of all the concurrent operations. However, it requires much more complex hardware to ensure the correct timing of all the operations on the pipeline. There is also the same problem of branch instructions as on a lookahead machine (in fact, a lookahead machine is a very simple pipelined machine). If a control transfer occurs as a result of either an unconditional branch instruction, or a conditional branch instruction for which the condition is met, then all the prefetched instructions must be abandoned. Thus a large gap appears in the instruction stream. The net effect of this on the performance of the processor depends on the frequency with which branch instructions occur, and a number of studies of the performance of

CPU

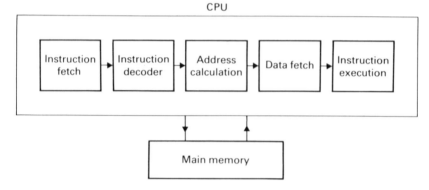

Figure 8.6

computer systems indicate that this may be as high as 20 per cent of all instructions obeyed.

A possible modification of the pipeline to ease this problem is to have a number of special buffer registers which contain the first few instructions at the destination or 'branched-to' addresses of recently obeyed control transfers. Access to these registers is via an associative search on the addresses of the instructions they contain. The pipeline mechanism proceeds normally until a branch occurs and the destination address is then presented to the associative store. If a match is found, the appropriate instructions are extracted and discharged into the pipeline. If no match is found, there is a hold up while instructions are fetched from memory, and the buffer registers are updated with these instructions also.

An example of a machine with a pipeline facility is the Harris 800. This computer has two separate processors, the instruction processor and the execution processor. The instruction processor maintains the instruction and operand stream to the execution processor and transfers the results to main memory. The execution processor simultaneously performs instruction decode, initialisation and execution. The two processors allow up to seven instructions to be in the pipeline of prefetch, decode, initialisation and execution.

The IBM 360/195, CDC Star, Cray-1, and the MU5 use sophisticated forms of pipelining.

8.6 Parallel machines

It can be seen from the previous sections that the way to increase the speed of a computer over and above that which results from improved technology is to introduce parallelism into its operation.

A useful classification of parallel computer systems, known as the Flynn classification, makes use of the ideas of parallelism in the instruction stream and parallelism in the data stream. The instruction stream is the sequence of instructions that are executed in a processing unit. The data stream is the sequence of operands being manipulated. There are four classes of parallel computer systems, illustrated in Figure 8.7.

SISD is a single instruction, single data stream machine. At any given time during the execution of a program, there is at most one instruction being executed, and that instruction affects at most one piece of data. This

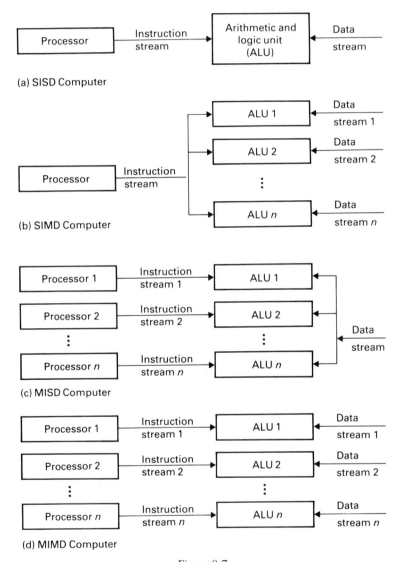

Figure 8.7

is the type of computer described in this book.

SIMD is a single instruction, multiple data stream machine. At any given time during the execution of a program, there is at most one instruction being executed, but it affects an array of data (a data vector) rather than a single operand. For example, a weather prediction program might read hourly temperature measurements taken from five hundred weather stations and then compute the daily average at each station by performing exactly the same computation on each set of twenty-four hourly readings. For each station it would load the first value into a register then add the second value and the third and so on, finally dividing the sum by twenty-four. Since the same program is used on each data set, a processor with one PC and one instruction decoder but N arithmetic units and N register sets could carry out computations on N data sets simultaneously. This type of processor is also sometimes known as an *array* processor. A common example of a SIMD system is the associative store described in Chapter 6. The same task (in this case a comparison) is performed on every word in the store in parallel.

MISD is a multiple instruction, single data stream computer. Each operand is operated on by several instructions simultaneously. This does not seem to be a useful concept.

MIMD is a multiple instruction, multiple data stream computer. There are N instruction streams and N data streams, one data stream per instruction stream. Because there are N processors, there needs to be some form of communication between them, so that they can co-operate within the required processing. The MIMD organisation can be implemented so that all the data share the same primary memory (a multiprocessor organisation), or each processor has its own primary memory (a multi-computer organisation).

Even a simple computer with a DMA or channel processor (see Chapter 10) is a MIMD system. The main CPU and the DMA processor are processing in parallel, each with their own data stream.

A typical MIMD system that is now very common is that of a distributed system or network. Here, there are a number of processors each processing their own data stream and communicating with each other over the network communication system (see Chapter 11).

A special case of this distributed function organisation is the pipeline described in section 8.5.2. Suppose we have a process P made up of two subprocesses P1 and P2. If both are executed on a single processor, the time the processor is occupied is t1 + t2 units. With a pipeline machine the processor is free to start a new task every max(t1,t2) time units. Thus the throughput is increased, although the complete problem still takes t1 + t2 time units to complete.

Pipelining does not provide more throughput than an equivalent parallel organisation. If two MIMD processors each execute P1 and P2, then a new problem can be executed every $(t1 + t2)/2$ time units on average. The pipeline can do no better than this because:

$$\max(t1,t2) \geqslant (t1 + t2)/2$$

However, in a pipeline machine the processors are dedicated to a particular task and so may be less expensive to produce.

8.7 Summary

The architecture of a CPU is decided by:

● the control functions that it is capable of initiating and consequently the instruction set that can be provided;
● the method of interconnection of component parts; and
● the availability of a hardware floating point unit.

Inevitably the design of a particular CPU is a compromise between cost and speed. The faster components and transfer methods tend to be more expensive, and so the designer has to have a clear idea of the requirements for the machine in order to make it process information quickly at a reasonable cost. However, the speed of hardware continues to increase and its cost decrease, and consequently the difference in speed between hardwired control units and microprogrammed control units is becoming less significant. Consequently the flexibility provided by microprogrammed control is becoming more significant.

8.8 Problems

(1) Explain and comment upon the effect of each of the micro-instructions given below. What is their total effect and what can you deduce about the memory of the computer? You can assume that the computer is a two-address asynchronous computer with the following registers which are referred to by the mnemonics given.

Register	Mnemonic
Memory buffer register	MBR
Memory address register	MAR
Program counter	PC
Instruction register	IR
Accumulator	ACC
First operand address	OP1
Second operand address	OP2

OP1 and OP2 within instruction register

Micro-instruction sequence:

Pulse	Micro-instruction
1	Read memory
2	PC=PC+1
3	Transfer MBR to IR
4	Transfer OP1 to MAR
5	Read memory
6	–
7	Transfer MBR to ACC
8	If ACC=0 transfer OP2 to PC
9	Transfer PC to MAR
10	End

(2) (a) What is a micro-instruction?

(b) How does the implementation of micro-instructions allow a manu-facturer to build a range of computers each with the same set of machine instructions but with different processor speeds?

(c) A two-address computer contains the following registers:

A	an accumulator
IR	the instruction register containing the fields:
	f the function code
	i the index bit
	OP1 the first operand address
	OP2 the second operand address
MAR	the memory address register
MBR	the memory buffer register
PC	the program counter
I	an index register

Describe, with reasons, the effects of each of the following micro-instructions and the effect of the sequence as a whole.

Transfer PC to MAR
Read memory
Increment PC by 1
Transfer MBR to IR
Decode for f
Transfer OP1 to MAR
Read memory
Add I to MBR giving A
If A=0 then PC=OP2
    else decrement I by 1

How could the complete machine instruction be used and what other machine instruction, if any, would be required to make this instruction function in the way you have described?

(3) The CPU of a two-address byte computer contains the registers defined in Problem 1 and 16 general-purpose registers R0, . . . ,R15. Define the sequence of micro-instructions needed to implement the fetch and execute phase of each of the following two instructions:

BALR R1,R15   (PC+2 to R1, branch to address in R15)

and

A R1,THREE   (add contents of location THREE to R1)

(4) Write the sequence of micro-instructions required to implement each of the following three instructions:

(a) Add the number N to register A.
(b) Add the contents of memory location N to register A.
(c) Add the contents of memory location whose address is in memory location N to register A.

Assume that each instruction consists of two words. The first word specifies the operation and the addressing mode, and the second word contains the number N.

(5) Consider the store instruction described in section 8.2.2, 'store contents of register A in addressed memory location'. Assume the CPU is driven by a continuously running clock such that each transfer step is 200 ns in duration. How long will the CPU have to wait in each of the two memory access steps assuming that a read or write operation takes 0.9 microsecs to complete? Also estimate the average percentage of time that the CPU is idle.

(6) Discuss and give examples of the Flynn classification scheme for the parallel computer systems SISD, SIMD, MISD and MIMD. Explain how a pipeline machine fits into such a classification.

Interrupts

During the execution of a program by a computer, many situations can arise which require prompt attention, either to utilise the whole computer system efficiently or to prevent a serious mishap occurring. In order to ensure that such situations are dealt with as quickly as necessary, the execution of the current program is interrupted. The computer is then able to execute a program which determines the cause of the interrupt and deals with it accordingly. After this interruption has been dealt with, the original program can be resumed at the point of interruption, unless a computer error or programming error caused the interrupt.

This chapter will describe the interrupt system and how it operates. Not only will it describe ways of handling a single interrupt but it will also describe techniques for dealing with the situations of either multiple interrupts occurring simultaneously or interrupts occurring before a previous interrupt has been fully dealt with.

9.1 Causes of interrupts

This section examines several situations which could require the processor to be interrupted. They are not in any order of priority, since the priorities are not the same for every computer system. The question of priorities is dealt with in section 9.4.

9.1.1 Hardware fault

The hardware circuitry carries out various checks for its own malfunction. Two examples are power failure and memory parity.

The electricity needed to operate a computer is usually supplied by the national or local power company via its existing power distribution system. In the event of a mains power failure, processing must be suspended. It is desirable that when supplies are resumed, processing can continue from where it was suspended. Because of the volatile nature of registers and of some main memory systems (see Chapter 6) an orderly shutdown procedure is required; otherwise data can be lost, erroneous information can be written into the memory and other malfunctions can occur during the fraction of a second that power is being lost. To guard against such an occurrence, the voltage supplied to the computer is monitored continuously. If it drops to, say, 85 per cent of its nominal value, the assumption is that a power failure is occurring and an interrupt request is generated. If this power fail interrupt is serviced immediately (it will have to be assigned the highest priority as described in section 9.4) there will be sufficient time for the computer to save the contents of all its registers and shut itself down. When power is restored the contents of the registers can be reloaded (either by the operator or sometimes automatically) and operation resumes from where it was interrupted. If the main memory is non-volatile, the registers can be stored in special memory locations reserved for this. In the case of a volatile main memory, the situation is more difficult. Back-up battery supplies are often used, switched on by the power fail detector. This will stop corruption of the data for hours, particularly as, with processing halted, it is not being accessed.

For detecting memory errors a parity bit is provided for every word in the memory. If on a memory access, either a read or write, one of the bits of a stored word is written into or read from incorrectly then the word transferred will not have the correct parity. In this case, an interrupt is generated.

The action on receipt of this interrupt could be to try the memory transfer again a number of times. If this is successful, processing can continue from where it was interrupted. Alternatively, if it is not successful the original program cannot be continued because either incorrect data would be used in a calculation, or an instruction which differs from that intended by the programmer would be executed.

9.1.2 Program errors

There are a number of errors that can be committed by a program as a result of an error situation introduced by the programmer.

Errors which occur while using the arithmetic and logic unit often generate an interrupt. An overflow error is one such condition. Usually an overflow occurs because the programmer did not anticipate that a computed result would exceed the range of the machine. On receipt of this interrupt the action would be either to terminate execution of the program or to transfer control to a user-supplied subroutine which might allow processing to continue despite the overflow condition.

Another condition is that of memory protection violation. It is possible for a program to generate an address which is outside the range of that program. Some areas of memory should be protected, such as the operating system routines used by many programs. Obviously a program must be prevented from overwriting such an area of memory. A memory block is protected by the supervisory programs executing a special PROTECT MEMORY instruction and can be unprotected by execution of an UNPROTECT MEMORY instruction. These instructions are privileged instructions which mean that only the supervisory programs can execute them. If a user program tries to write to an address which is in a protected part of main memory, an interrupt will be generated. On receipt of this interrupt the action is usually to terminate execution of the program and generate an appropriate error message.

Attempts can be made by a program to perform operations on data that is not compatible with the way data is stored. An example would be to interpret the contents of a word as a series of characters when in fact the bit pattern within the word does not correspond to characters in the character code being used. It is also possible to branch to a word, to continue execution from that point on, when the word branched to does not contain a valid instruction operation code. All of these are examples of conditions which could generate an interrupt to indicate that something is wrong.

9.1.3 Real time conditions

Computers are often used for the monitoring and control of real time processes. These are processes in which the computer is expected to respond to some situation in a realistic time scale (often very quickly).

In medicine for example, a computer may be used to monitor a patient's heart beat. If there is a significant reduction in the frequency or power of the heart beat an interrupt can be generated which enables the computer to take immediate action such as the triggering of alarm bells.

A potentially costly real time situation can occur during the control of a machine tool by computer. If an expensive part is being machined and the cutter breaks, both the part and the machine may be damaged. By detecting that tool breakage has occurred immediately and putting the equipment onto standby, consequent damage to the part and the machine can be prevented.

9.1.4 Input/output

Even though most peripheral devices seem to the user to operate at very high speed they actually operate very slowly compared with the rate at which the CPU operates (see Chapter 10). The slower peripheral devices such as printers and typewriter terminals transfer characters one at a time. In order to be able to make use of the CPU during the time the peripheral is transferring the character it is necessary that the peripheral device is able to interrupt the CPU on completion of the transfer. The CPU can then initiate the transfer of the next character. In the case of faster peripheral devices, such as magnetic disk, a block of characters can be transferred, and an interrupt only takes place on completion of the block transfer (see Chapter 10).

Consequently the interrupt facility is very important as an aid to maximising the use of the CPU during input/output.

9.2 Interrupt handling

Suppose the CPU is running a program when it receives a request from, say, a peripheral to interrupt its processing and deal with the peripheral. This will involve transferring control to a second program which will deal with the peripheral. This second program is often called an interrupt service routine. On completion of the interrupt service routine, control will have to transfer back to the original program at the point at which it was interrupted in order for it to continue. There must, therefore, be a mechanism to allow for error-free şwitching between the program that is being executed when an interrupt occurs, and another program to deal with the interrupt and back again.

Since the main purpose of an interrupt system is to utilise the CPU to the full, it is obviously important that the response to an interrupt be very quick. Since it is totally unreasonable to expect every user program to include an instruction to test the state of some interrupt flag after every instruction in case something requires attention, it follows that the interrupt mechanism must be automatic and provided by the CPU. However, as we shall see, there may be a case for using software to assist the hardware in the provision of the interrupt mechanism.

The problem of transferring control from a program to an interrupt service routine, while remembering the position in the interrupted program so that a return can be made, is essentially the same problem as that faced when writing a subroutine (see section 7.2.3). However, as we have just seen, the transfer of control from the interrupted program to the interrupt service routine must be performed by the hardware automatically on receipt of an interrupt and not as a result of the CPU executing an instruction. On completion of the interrupt routine, control has to be given back to the interrupted program, and this can be done by software in just the same way as with a subroutine.

In addition to the requirement that the response must be quick, it is also important that it is error free so that the program is not corrupted. The condition of the CPU must be exactly the same on return from the interrupt service routine as it was before the interrupt occurred.

9.2.1 The state of the CPU

In order for the CPU to be in the same state after an interrupt has been serviced as it was before, it is necessary to be able to preserve the state of all the components of the CPU when the interrupt occurs. The CPU consists essentially of a series of registers and lines containing control signals (see Chapter 8). To preserve the registers will require the execution of some instructions to store the contents of the registers in some area of main memory. However, since the actions required to preserve the control signals would destroy them, the signals cannot be preserved. The solution lies in the fact that in the brief instant between completing the execute phase of one instruction and the fetch phase of another instruction, the CPU control signals are always in the same state, regardless of which instructions have been executed. Consequently, when an interrupt occurs the CPU finishes executing the current instruction before it accepts the interrupt. It is then merely necessary for the interrupt service routine to store the appropriate registers immediately it is given control and to reset the registers back to these values immediately before giving control back to the original program.

9.2.2 A simple interrupt system

In order to see what is required of the hardware when an interrupt occurs, consider in more detail the situation of the CPU executing a program, the only other program involved being the interrupt service routine. We will also assume that there can only be one reason for the interrupt, and that a further interrupt cannot occur while this one is being dealt with. Although this is a false situation, it enables a clear picture to be seen of the actions to be taken on receipt of an interrupt. The other complications are dealt with later. Figure 9.1 shows the program in memory at the point where an interrupt occurs.

Assume that an interrupt occurs while the CPU is executing the instruction stored at the memory location with address n. The PC register will, of course, contain the address of the next instruction to be executed, namely $n+1$. In order for control to be given to the interrupt service routine, the address of that routine must be transferred into the PC so that

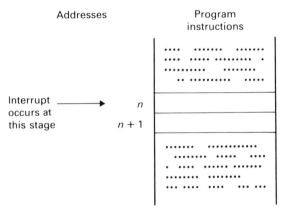

Figure 9.1

the next instruction fetched is the first one of the interrupt service routine. This unfortunately would destroy the address $n+1$ already in there, and so the contents of the PC will have to be preserved (by the hardware) in a particular memory location. Also, it is possible that we may wish to hold the interrupt service routine in any part of memory that is convenient and so the address of the start of it must also be stored in a special memory location. These two memory locations are often at 'one end' of memory, say at locations 0 and 1. This results in the situation where the hardware always uses fixed addresses, but the service routine can be placed anywhere in main memory. To recap—when an interrupt occurs, the following events will take place:

(1) The CPU will complete execution of the current instruction.
(2) The hardware will:
    (a) transfer the contents of the PC register to memory location 0;
    (b) transfer the contents of memory location 1 to the PC.
(3) The CPU will continue by fetching the instruction whose address is in the PC, i.e. the first instruction of the interrupt service routine.

The first instructions in the interrupt service routine will be to store all the general registers in some memory locations. In fact, it is only necessary for it to store away those registers that it is making use of during its processing.

Just before the interrupt service routine is finished, the last instructions will be to restore the general registers from the memory locations used for their preservation. Finally, control can be transferred back to the original program by executing a branch instruction which will branch indirect through memory location 0. This will cause the contents of location $0(n+1)$ to be put into the PC register, and processing will continue from where it was interrupted.

9.3 Identification of interrupt source

To explain the fundamental ideas of dealing with an interrupt, the previous section was restricted to situations where there was only one reason for the interrupt. The mechanism for handling interrupts must now be extended to deal with a number of interrupt causes. Section 9.1 described some of the possible causes of interrupts, and since it is reasonable to assume that the action required on receipt of an interrupt will be dependent on the cause of that interrupt, it follows that there need to be a number of interrupt service routines, one for each cause of an interrupt. Consequently it is necessary to identify the precise cause of the interrupt.

One way this can be done is to have multiple interrupt lines. Each type of interrupt will generate an interrupt signal on its appropriate interrupt line. Each line has its own pair of main memory locations, one of which contains the address of the service routine as described in section 9.2.2. However, there are some circumstances which require more than one type of interrupt on one line. If an interrupt from a particular peripheral device, for example, is considered to be a unique interrupt source then it could have its own interrupt line. But this would mean that the design of the CPU hardware fixes precisely the peripheral devices that can be attached to it. Obviously this reduces the ease with which different peripheral devices can be attached to the same CPU. Consequently, particularly in respect of input-output, it is usual to have a number of devices (interrupt sources) all attached to the same interrupt line. When an interrupt signal occurs on such an interrupt line, the particular device requesting the interrupt has to be identified. This can be achieved either by a software technique or implemented as a hardware function. Because of the potential delay in responding to an interrupt (either because the interrupt is not responded to until completion of execution of the current instruction or because it has to wait its turn as described in section 9.4), an interrupt line actually consists of two lines. One is the interrupt request line, this being the line which will transmit the interrupt request signal to the CPU. The other line is an interrupt acknowledge line. When the CPU is ready to accept it will send an interrupt acknowledge signal so that the interrupt request signal can be turned off by the source of the interrupt.

9.3.1 Identification by software

When a device signals an interrupt request, the hardware causes control to transfer to a service routine as described in section 9.2.2. In that section it was assumed that this would be the device service routine. If, however, there can be a number of devices attached to this line, the routine will be an interrupt service routine whose task is to identify the device requesting the interrupt and then to transfer control to that particular device's service routine. In order to determine which device is requesting the interrupt, the routine will examine all the devices on that line, one at a time. This is known as *software polling*. A common technique is to make use of a special skip instruction which allows examination of a particular peripheral device interface (see Chapter 8). On a peripheral device interface there is often a flag bit which is set to one when an interrupt request is generated and back to zero when the interrupt has been dealt with. One of the set of input/output instructions examines this flag and skips the next instruction when it is set to 0. An example of a software polling interrupt service routine is shown below. It assumes that four devices are attached to the same interrupt request line, that memory location 0 is used to store the PC and that the address of the interrupt routine is stored in location 1.

Address	Contents	Comment
0		Location for saving PC.
1	500	Start address of interrupt routine.
2	1575	Start address of service routine for device 1.
3	1625	Start address of service routine for device 2.
4	1650	Start address of service routine for device 3.
.		
.		
.		
500	SKDEV1	Skip next instruction if device 1 is not requesting interrupt.
501	BR 2 (indirect)	Indirect jump to location 1575 (device 1 requesting interrupt).
502	SKDEV2	
503	BR 3 (indirect)	
.		
.		
.		
506	SKDEV 4	
507	BR 5 (indirect)	
.		
.		
.		
1575		Start of service routine for device 1.
.		
.		
.		
1624	BR 0 (indirect)	Return to original program being executed before interrupt occurred.
1625		Start of service routine for device 2.
		Etc.

9.3.2 Identification by hardware

The above solution to the problem of identifying the source of the interrupt is relatively cheap to implement but slow in operation because of the time taken to execute the instructions, particularly in the case of the device that is polled last. However, in the days when the hardware was expensive, this was an acceptable solution. Since hardware costs are now relatively low, many interrupt systems use a hardware identification system.

This hardware system is called *vectored interrupts*. In general, this name refers to all interrupt handling techniques that allow the interrupting device to identify itself to the CPU by supplying a special code or address to the CPU.

When the CPU is ready to accept an interrupt, it sends an interrupt acknowledge signal. Of the devices attached to that interrupt line, only the device requesting the interrupt will respond. It does so by sending to the CPU an address. This address could be the start address of the service routine for that particular device. However, this would impose the restriction that the interrupt service routine for a given device always starts at the same location. An improvement would be for the address that is sent to the CPU by the device to be that of a word in memory in which the PC can be saved, the following word containing the start address of the service routine. Each device would have associated with it a unique pair of main memory locations.

The following, then, is the sequence of events:

(1) A device generates an interrupt request signal.
(2) The CPU completes execution of the current instruction and then sends an interrupt acknowledge signal.
(3) The device requesting the interrupt will send to the CPU (usually via the I/O data bus as described in Chapter 8) an address of a location in memory, and then turn off the interrupt request signal.
(4) The CPU hardware stores the current value of the PC in this memory address and loads the contents of the next word in store into the PC and commences processing again. The instruction now being executed is the first instruction of the device service routine.

The name 'vectored interrupts' stems from the idea that the specification to the CPU of a unique memory location for that device causes a specific directed change in processing sequence.

In contrast to the software polling method, the process is very quick, requiring not much longer than the two memory cycles required for the main memory access. Also the time taken to enter a particular device service routine is independent of the number of devices attached to that interrupt line. The disadvantage is that it requires more specialised hardware, in particular in the peripheral interface.

9.4   Priority systems

Section 9.3 extended the mechanism for handling interrupts to allow for a number of interrupt sources by looking at methods for identifying the source of the interrupt. This section will extend the mechanism even further by examining the situation in which an interrupt occurs before the previous one has been fully serviced, or when multiple interrupts occur simultaneously. Although the chance of more than one interrupt occurring at precisely the same instant is not very high, it must be remembered that an interrupt is not accepted until the machine instruction being executed when the interrupt occurs is complete. During this brief delay there may have been a number of interrupts generated, all of which require servicing simultaneously. Consequently the often used term of interrupts 'occurring' simultaneously in fact refers to interrupts requiring 'servicing' simultaneously. In this latter case the interrupt handling system is faced with the decision of which interrupt to service first. In the other case, that of interrupts occurring before a previous one has been fully serviced, the mechanism must decide whether to finish the servicing of the interrupt it has already started, or whether to leave off and accept and service the new interrupt request. Obviously there needs to be some system of priorities in order to resolve these questions.

9.4.1   Nested interrupts

There are many occasions when an interrupt occurs while a previous one is being serviced. If, as discussed later, it is necessary to process this second interrupt immediately, the processing of the first interrupt will have to be suspended. We have already seen (section 9.2.2) that when an interrupt is accepted the address of the instruction that would have been executed next is stored away so that control can be transferred back to it after the interrupt has been serviced. If a second interrupt occurs that must be dealt with immediately, it is important that the address that is now stored away (the address of the next instruction in the first interrupt service routine) is not stored at the same location as the first address that has been stored away (the address of the next instruction in the original program), otherwise control would not be able to return to the original program. Therefore these addresses must be stored in separate locations. This ability to allow interrupts to interrupt previous interrupt service routines safely is called *nested interrupts*. This is why, in the vectored interrupt system described in section 9.3.2, each device has associated with it a unique pair of main memory locations.

   If the computer has a stack facility (see section 7.5), the return address can simply be PUSHed on to the stack. This is discussed more fully in section 9.5. Each time an interrupt is accepted the PC will be pushed on to the stack. They will of course, be POPped off the stack in the reverse order, this being the order in which the interrupt servicing will now be completed. So long as the stack is sufficiently large, interrupt routines can be nested to any depth.

9.4.2 Enabling and disabling interrupts

There are a number of occasions when it is necessary temporarily to prevent an interrupt occurring. Consequently there needs to be provision for disabling the interrupt mechanism and also, therefore, provision for enabling interrupts so that they may continue to occur.

There are essentially three levels of interrupt disable:

(1) *Disabling of interrupts from a particular peripheral device.* Usually this can be achieved by the inclusion of an interrupt inhibit bit on the device interface.

(2) *Disabling of interrupts from sources of lower or equal priority.* When there is a system of priorities given to the various interrupt sources, it must be possible to delay an interrupt that comes from a source of equal or lower priority than that currently being serviced. In some computers, this selective inhibiting of interrupts can be achieved by setting the appropriate bits in an interrupt mask register (see section 9.4.5).

(3) *Disabling of all interrupts from any source.* This can be achieved in two ways. The first is a temporary inhibit imposed by the hardware, so that after acknowledging an interrupt the CPU will execute at least one instruction before allowing further interrupts. This ensures that the first instruction in the interrupt service routine is executed. If there is a need for more instructions in the service routine to be executed without interruption, the first instruction must be an interrupt disable instruction. This is, in fact, another way of disabling interrupts. An interrupt disable instruction is usually provided, which, when ex-ecuted, causes the CPU to ignore all interrupts. An example of the use of this can be seen by considering again the software polling system explained in section 9.3.1. The device requesting the interrupt is not acknowledged until it is addressed by the CPU. Since a device requesting an interrupt is not always on top of the polling list, a number of instructions in the interrupt service routine need to be executed before this device is addressed. Unless interrupts are disabled during this period, the device will continue to interrupt the CPU, causing the system to repeatedly re-enter the interrupt service routine.

9.4.3 Software allocation of priorities

If the recognition of the interrupt source is achieved by a software polling routine (see section 9.3.1), the priority is inherent in the order in which devices are examined or polled. If two devices interrupt simultaneously, the first one that is examined is the one accepted first. Even for interrupts that do not occur simultaneously it is interesting to note that the one that interrupts first may not be accepted first. If, after having switched to the interrupt service routine because of a device interrupt, an interrupt from another device occurs, and the second device is polled before the original one, then the second interrupt is accepted first.

Because the priority system is determined by the polling order, the priorities can be easily changed by rewriting the interrupt service routine to poll in a different order. Also it is possible for a device with a very high priority to be polled more often than other devices.

9.4.4 Hardware allocation of priorities

There are two basic methods of allocating priority by hardware. The first method is concerned with the priority amongst devices attached to the same interrupt request line. Instead of the interrupt acknowledge line being a common line to which all devices are attached in parallel, the interrupt acknowledge line passes from one device to the next in turn. A signal from the CPU on the interrupt acknowledge line will only be passed to the next device if the current device is not requesting an interrupt as in Figure 9.2.

This technique, known as *daisy chaining*, has its priority system built into the order in which the devices are attached to the interrupt acknowledge line, those closest to the CPU having the highest priority.

The second method of providing a priority system by hardware lies in the ability to have multiple interrupt lines. Each interrupt source is allocated to one particular interrupt line (there could be a number of interrupt sources attached to the same line). Priority between lines can be achieved simply by a priority arbitration circuit to which all lines are attached. If simultaneous interrupt request signals occur this circuit will send the acknowledge signal to the line with the highest priority. The allocation of priority

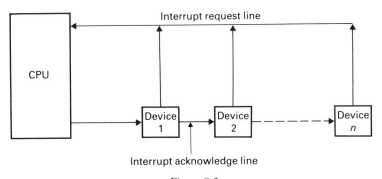

Figure 9.2

is sometimes fixed and sometimes programmable. If there is only one interrupt source to each interrupt line, total priority between sources is achieved. In practice, it is usual to have a number of interrupt sources (for example, peripheral devices) attached to each line. Priority between lines can be achieved by the arbitration circuit just described, and priority between devices on each line can be achieved by daisy chaining the interrupt acknowledge line between the devices. In this multi-level inter-rupt system, device recognition is usually achieved by vectoring.

9.4.5 Interrupt masking

The advantage of a software priority system is that it can be modified at any time merely by polling in a different order. In contrast, however, the faster hardware system is fixed by the wiring of the circuits. In order to combine flexibility with speed, a combined software/hardware system has been developed called *interrupt masking*. Here, all interrupt lines attached to the CPU are associated with a bit position in an interrupt register. If an interrupt on a line is generated, it will only be recognised by the CPU if the corresponding bit in the interrupt register is a 1. In order to allow the pattern of bits in the interrupt register to be changed there is an associated register, the interrupt mask register, which is program addressable. This register is permanently ANDed with the interrupt register so that only if there is a 1 bit in the mask register can an interrupt on that line be recognised. If a particular interrupt service routine wishes to inhibit interrupts of a lower priority, then at the beginning of the service routine it must load the interrupt mask register with an appropriate pattern of bits. Only those bit positions corresponding to interrupts that are to be allowed are set to 1, all other bits set to 0.

9.5 Other interrupt facilities

We have seen how it is necessary for the contents of the PC and any general-purpose registers being used to be saved at the commencement of dealing with an interrupt in order to allow control to return to the interrupted program. Stacks can be used for this purpose just as they can in subroutine handling (see section 7.5.3). The CPU can PUSH the PC on to the stack and the service routine can PUSH all the general registers on to the stack at the start of the service routine. On completion of the service routine, these values can be POPped off the stack. If interrupts are nested, the stack mechanism will ensure that the values are retrieved from the stack in the correct order (see section 9.4.1). However, there is still the requirement for a dedicated memory location to keep the address of the interrupt service routine.

We have seen the need to keep the address of the interrupt service routine in a dedicated memory location so that on acceptance of an interrupt the CPU can load this address into the PC and then recommence execution by fetching what will be the first instruction of the service routine (9.2.2). An alternative to this is to place an instruction in the dedicated memory location. The CPU then merely needs to transfer the contents of this location to the IR and then to continue. This instruction would usually be a branch instruction which would cause control to transfer to the first instruction of the interrupt service routine.

9.6 Examples of real interrupt systems

Having gradually developed the requirements for an interrupt system and seen various alternative ways of implementing such a system, it will be interesting to look briefly at the interrupt handling mechanisms actually used on some existing computers. The examples chosen are from a large mainframe computer, a minicomputer and a microprocessor, although it is important to note that these examples are not necessarily typical of each class of computer. It is left as an exercise for the reader to investigate the interrupt handling mechanism of the computer to which access is available.

9.6.1 The interrupt mechanism of the IBM 4300 series of machines

On an IBM 4300 computer the program that is currently being executed (regardless of whether it is a user program or a supervisor program) is described by a double word data item that is a register in the CPU called the *program status word* (PSW). Amongst many other things (the length of the PSW is 64 bits) the PSW holds the address of the next instruction to be executed; in other words it incorporates the PC.

There are six interrupt lines, each line having associated with it a pair of storage locations, one being a place to store the *current* PSW, the other containing a *new* PSW, the PC field of which contains the address of the interrupt service routine.

When an interrupt occurs, the CPU performs the following actions:

(1) The current PSW is stored in the appropriate store location, called the old PSW.
(2) The current PSW is replaced by a new PSW which is held at another store location.
(3) The CPU continues processing according to the new current PSW.

Clearly the new PSW should be set up to describe a program that will deal with the interrupt, that is the interrupt service routine. After this routine has serviced the interrupt, it replaces the current PSW by the old PSW and the interrupted program is resumed.

Each interrupt line is associated with an interrupt type. The six types are:

Restart   An interrupt caused by depression of the restart key on the operator's console.
External   Caused by a signal from outside, such as an external clock or timer, or a line attached to another computer.
Supervisor   Caused by an execution of an SVC instruction. This
call   allows a user's program to enter the operating system.
Program   A user's program error (section 9.1.2).
Machine check   Detection of machine malfunction (section 9.1.1).
Input/output   An input or output interrupt. Note that I/O is primarily performed by a channel (see Chapter 10). The CPU is only interrupted on completion of transfer. Since there is only one I/O line the interrupt service must first determine which I/O device is interrupting by examining information stored in memory by the channel. Then it can call the appropriate device service routine.

In the case of interrupted interrupts, suppose an interrupt of the same type has occurred. In order to prevent the old PSW being replaced by the current PSW (thereby ensuring that control could not revert to the original interrupted routine) the interrupt of the same type is masked out by a field in the PSW which indicates whether or not an interrupt of a certain type can occur or not. (If interrupts are inhibited they are queued until they can be accepted.)

Priority is assigned by the hardware to the processing of the interrupt lines in the following order:

High priority: 1. Machine check
               2. I/O
               3. External
               4. Program
               5. SVC
Low priority: 6. Restart

9.6.2 The interrupt mechanism of the Hewlett Packard HP21MX

The vectored priority interrupt system has up to sixty distinct interrupt levels, each of which has a unique priority assignment. Each interrupt level is associated with a numerically corresponding interrupt location in memory. Of the sixty interrupt levels, the two highest priority levels are reserved for hardware faults (power fail and parity error), the next two are reserved for block data transfer channels and the remaining levels are available for I/O device channels.

As an example, an interrupt request from I/O channel 12 will cause an interrupt to memory location 12. This request for service will be granted on a priority basis higher than afforded to channel 13 but lower than that afforded to channel 11. Thus a transfer in progress via channel 13 would be suspended to allow channel 12 to proceed. On the other hand, a transfer in progress via channel 11 cannot be interrupted by channel 12.

Any device can be selectively enabled or disabled under program control, thus switching the device into or out of the interrupt structure. In addition, the entire interrupt system, except power fail or parity error interrupts, can be enabled or disabled under program control using a single instruction.

It is assumed that when control is transferred to the corresponding memory location on receipt of an interrupt, this location contains a branch to subroutine instruction which will transfer control to the service routine. The hardware will also store the return address (the contents of the PC) in the first word of the service routine. The storage of all registers is the responsibility of the service routine.

9.6.3 The interrupt mechanism of the Intel 8086/8088 and the IBM PC

With the Intel 8086/8088 CPU chip there is only one interrupt line. If an interrupt flag is clear (IF=0) then it will ignore any incoming signals. Only when the interrupt flag is set (IF=1) will it respond to interrupt requests (there is a special non-maskable interrupt that is recognised regardless of the state of IF).

When an interrupt occurs the processor will save the current status of the machine by pushing relevant information onto the stack (the flag register, code segment register, the offset address of the next instruction to have been executed) and then clear the interrupt flag, so preventing another interrupt occurring.

It also expects to be provided with a one byte TYPE code, specifying one of 256 interrupt sources. This type code is used to vector into a table of interrupt service routine addresses which is stored in the bottom 1K bytes of memory.

The first five table entries (type codes 0–4) are reserved for specific conditions such as divide by zero, overflow, non-maskable interrupt and single step facility interrupt.

Because the processor has only one input line on which to receive an interrupt signal, the IBM PC provides a support chip, known as an 8259 interrupt controller chip. This support chip can accept up to eight independent interrupt signals numbered 0 to 7. The chip will accord priorities to these inputs and present a single interrupt to the CPU along with the unique interrupt type code associated with that interrupt source. Interrupt source 0 has the highest priority and 7 the lowest. After the processor has dealt with one of the interrupts any others that have occurred will be presented immediately, again in the order of priorities accorded.

On the IBM PC this support chip is mounted on the system board and provides this interrupt prioritisation mechanism for the following eight interrupt sources:

Timer
Keyboard
Colour graphics interface
Secondary serial interface
Serial (RS-232) interface
Fixed disc
Floppy disc
Printer

This chip also incorporates an interrupt mask register so that interrupt sources can be selectively masked out by writing an appropriate bit pattern into the mask register prior to enabling interrupts.

9.7 Summary

This chapter has presented the need for and means of achieving an interrupt system. In many computer applications it is necessary to be able to interrupt the normal execution of programs in order to service higher priority requests that need urgent attention. Most computers, large and small, have a mechanism for dealing with such situations, although the complexity and sophistication of interrupt handling schemes vary from computer to computer.

However, as the cost of hardware continues to decrease there is a move to hardware implementations rather than slower software facilities.

9.8 Problems

(1) Investigate the interrupt handling mechanism of a computer to which you have access.
(2) (a) Explain what you understand by:
      (i) an interrupt, suggesting reasons for the cause of an interrupt;
      (ii) interrupt vector and interrupt service routine.

(b) Explain the sequence of events when the following interrupts occur, assuming:
   (i) the second and third interrupts occur before the servicing time of the first interrupt has elapsed;
   (ii) an interrupt with priority 1 has the lowest priority.

The sequence of interrupts is:

Interrupt number	Time of occurrence	Priority
1	t1	1
2	t2	2
3	t3	3

(3) An interrupt handling routine usually masks out interrupts of the type that it is handling. If, however, an interrupt of type A occurs, followed by type B, followed by another interrupt of type A, it is necessary to ensure that this second type A interrupt does not wipe out information on the first type A interrupt. Using the priority structure given in section 9.6.1 determine which interrupt handling routines should allow which other interrupts. What special provisions would you make for machine-check interrupts?

(4) On a machine using base registers, it is necessary for the interrupt handling routine to save one base register for use by the interrupt routine itself. However, the instruction to store a base register itself requires the use of a base register to address the word where the base register is to be stored. Because an interrupt can occur at any time, the value of all the base registers are unknown at the start of the interrupt handling routine, and this means it has no base register available to use for the store base register instruction. Devise a solution to the problem, and if you are using a base register computer, check to see the manufacturers' solution.

(5) Explain why the nesting of interrupts is desirable and what the necessary requirements are of a system which allows nesting. Explain two ways of achieving these requirements.

(6) A 16-bit minicomputer has a multi-level interrupt system with twenty levels. Describe how the interrupt priorities of peripheral devices can be resolved by hardware to give each device a unique priority. If the system is vectored, explain how control can be passed to the interrupt service routine of the highest priority interrupt.

(7) Assuming a machine with a vectored interrupt system and a stack on which CPU registers can be stored, describe the sequence of events from the time a device requests an interrupt until execution of the

interrupt service routine is started. If machine instructions require one to four memory cycles to execute, estimate the maximum number of memory cycles that may occur before the execution of the interrupt service routine is started.

CHAPTER 10

Data transfers

The architecture of a computer will now be discussed in relation to the
ways in which it communicates with the outside world. One of the basic
features of a computer is its ability to send and receive data to and from
other devices. These range from slow peripheral devices which transfer one
character at a time, for example a teletype device, to very fast devices
which require a whole block of data to be transferred, such as a magnetic
disk device or even another computer if the machines are part of a
distributed network. Also, the devices may be very close to the computer,
in which case connection can be by a simple cable (multi-conductor cable if
information is transferred in parallel), or they may be some considerable
distance away, in which case the provision of multi-conductor cables
becomes too expensive.

This chapter will look at the above features as they relate to software,
e.g. input/output as it affects the programmer, and to some of the
hardware aspects of peripheral and 'line' transfers. The software aspects of
input/output are introduced initially in our discussion of the simpler
methods which apply directly to many micro- and minicomputers (sections
10.1 to 10.3) through to the more sophisticated techniques used on larger
mainframe computers (section 10.4). On the hardware side, transferring
data over lines is important not only in dealing with input/output along an
I/O bus or channel, but also in connection with the distribution of
processing and data over a network, as we shall see in Chapter 11.

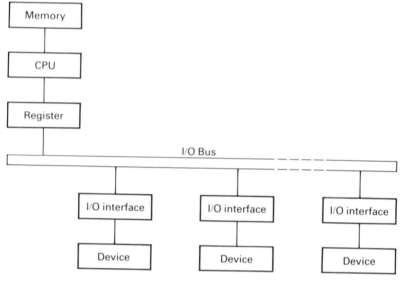

Figure 10.1

10.1 Input/output bus and the input/output interface

Since a number of peripheral devices are usually connected to a computer, there has to be some means by which only one of these devices can be selected to perform some input or output task. This can be achieved through the use of an input/output bus—the I/O bus. In some respects, the I/O bus is similar to the internal CPU bus system described in Chapter 8. Connected to the wires which form the bus are registers in the peripheral device interface. However, unlike registers in the CPU which are completely under the control of the CPU, those in the peripheral device act in an autonomous way. The CPU initiates their actions, but does not subsequently have any control over their operation.

A bus to which I/O devices are connected consists of three sets of lines used for the transmission of address, data and control signals. When the CPU wishes to send data to a particular I/O device it places a unique identity code, or address, onto the address line. Only the device that recognises that code will respond to the command that is placed on the control line. Figure 10.1 shows a typical structure of a computer system with a single I/O bus. In many so called 'single bus systems', the I/O interface can be identified uniquely by allocating it a specific memory address, and transfers of information to or from a register on an interface can be achieved by any of the appropriate instructions in the instruction set, rather than by a limited number of specific I/O instructions.

In a system such as that illustrated in Figure 10.1, reading data from a peripheral device and storing it in memory is a three stage process (output being the reverse):

(1) Device → I/O interface
(2) I/O interface → register
(3) Register → memory

A device is attached, by cable, to an I/O interface. The interface is plugged into one of a number of I/O slots, each of which is assigned a fixed address. The interface is the communication link. It includes three basic elements:

(1) *A control bit*—this is a one-bit register (flip-flop) which when turned on generates a start command to the device to start its I/O.
(2) *A flag bit*—this is set on by the device when transmission between the device and its interface is complete. It can be tested or cleared under program control.
(3) *A buffer register*—this is the register in which the data that has been read, or which is to be written, is stored.

When a start command is generated, one character is transferred between the interface buffer register and the device or vice versa.

10.2 Connecting lines

10.2.1 Parallel transmission

In parallel transmission, each bit position of a word or character code is associated with its own transmission line. Consequently all the bits of one word or one character are transmitted simultaneously. Obviously a large number of separate lines are required, and so, although it is a very fast way of transmitting data, its use is usually limited to very short-distance connections. For transmission over long distances, the cost of providing these multiple lines is usually prohibitive. Another problem which limits the distance is that of *skew*. The propagation delay is not identical for each line (bit), and so the greater the distance the greater the difference in time of arrival of the different bits.

Computer systems sometimes use parallel interfaces for connecting to their peripheral devices. This interface is often provided in the form of an LSI chip, which provides the facilities to control and transfer data between these devices and the processor, e.g. the Motorola peripheral interface adaptor (PIA). There are also some standard interface specifications, such as the IEEE-488, which are also available as LSI chips.

10.2.2 Serial transmission—asynchronous

If parallel transmission is too costly in terms of the number of lines required, the alternative is to use only one line and to send the bits that make up a character or a word one bit at a time. This is known as serial transmission.

In order that the receiving device can decode a character properly, it must know when to look for a signal and which bit is the first bit of a character. This problem is called synchronisation and there are two techniques used to deal with it. The first technique, asynchronous transmission, is suitable for low speed communications where keyboards or serial printers are directly connected to the line.

Each character transmitted is preceded by a 'start' bit and followed by at least one stop bit (hence it is sometimes called start-stop transmission). Some devices (particularly electromechanical equipment) will require two stop bits in order to give them time to resynchronise, whereas others require only one stop bit. The start and stop bits are always of opposite value. The stop bit is the same state as the line idle state, so that synchronisation can be achieved by the receiver detecting the transition from the stop or idle state to start.

The start bit 'wakes up' the receiver so that the receiver is aware that some data bits are following that it needs to record. The stop bits allow both the transmitting and receiving devices to get ready for the next character.

The transmission of data from a register in bit serial form down a line, or the receipt of serial bits and the assembling of these into a register, is usually performed by an LSI chip known as a UART (universal asynchronous receiver/transmitter). As an example of the operation of such a device consider the asynchronous receive process as illustrated in Figure 10.2.

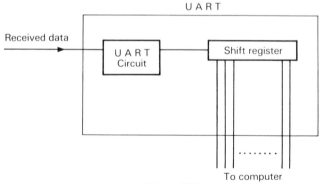

Figure 10.2

The circuit contains a 16× clock which samples the incoming line at 16× the anticipated bit rate. It detects the transition from idle to active soon after it occurs. This enables another circuit which counts eight ticks of the 16× clock and checks to see if the line is still active. If so a valid start bit has arrived, but if not the initial transition was probably due to line noise.

When a valid start signal is detected, a counter is enabled which divides the 16× clock rate by 16 to produce a sampling clock rate, ticking once every bit at approximately the centre of the bit. As bits are received they are clocked into a shift register. When eight bits have been received they are transferred to the processor in parallel. If in fact characters are sent continuously there is only the stop bit(s)' time to move the bits out of the register before the next character starts to arrive. Consequently this register is often double buffered.

10.2.3 Serial transmission—synchronous

The main drawback of asynchronous transmission is that a large proportion (about 30 per cent) of the transmitted bits are not data bits but synchronising bits. For faster devices sending blocks of data rather than individual characters, an improved transmission technique is synchronous transmission. In this case the devices are synchronised by the transmitting of a stream of synchronising bits at periodic intervals. In between will be blocks of data.

In order for the synchronising bits to be distinguished from the data bits, they must be sent in a predetermined order, and usually there will be a number of such timing characters (synchronising bits) so that one of them cannot be generated as a result of random noise on the line.

The various characters that are used for synchronisation and message control are described in section 5.4.4. There is a definite sequence in which the synchronising characters and message control characters must be transmitted, and this sequence is known as 'hand-shaking' or protocol. It is described in Chapter 13.

As with asynchronous transmission, the mechanism for synchronous transmission and receipt is often provided in the form of an LSI chip. Frequently this is provided as a system capable of operating in either synchronous or asynchronous format and known as a USART (universal synchronous/asynchronous receiver/transmitter).

10.2.4 Serial interface standard RS232-C

Because the connection of devices (printers, plotters, modems, etc.) to a computer is such a fundamental requirement, yet if each manufacturer of such equipment defined their own interface, the industry would be in chaos. Hence there are some generally accepted standard interfaces, one of which is known as RS232-C. Essentially it is the interface between data terminal equipment (a computer or a terminal) and data communication

equipment (a modem), employing serial binary data interchange.
The complete standard defines:

● Electrical signal characteristics
● Interface mechanical characteristics
● Functional description of interchange circuits

More details of the use of this in communications is given in 13.2.2.
However, the interface can be used for very simple connections between a
device and a computer by using only three of the connecting pins—signal
ground, received serial data and transmitted serial data. Thus it has
become commonly used to interface devices not connected through a
modem.

10.3 Programmed input/output

Programmed input/output is achieved entirely by the execution of input
and output instructions in the user's program. The execution of an input
instruction causes data (one character) to be transferred in from an input
device to a processor register, whereas execution of an output instruction
will cause a character to be transferred from a processor register to a
peripheral device. The transfer of a group of characters can be achieved in
one of two main ways.

10.3.1 Wait for flag programmed input/output

The simplest I/O system is one in which the processor commands the
device to operate and then waits for the completion response. Completion
of transfer is indicated when the flag bit on the interface referred to in
section 10.1 is set. Thus the 'waiting' for a response is in fact a repetitive
test of the state of this flag bit by the CPU.

The following two examples illustrate the sort of code necessary to
transfer a single character. They use instructions which refer to the
interface at a particular address.

INPUT

```
      wait  IN    20      ; read in the status register
                            (which includes flag bit)
            ANI   01      ; test to see if bit 0 is set
                            indicating interface buffer is full
            JZ    wait
            IN    21      ; read in character from interface buffer
```

OUTPUT

```
wait   IN    20        ; read in status register
                         (which includes flag bit)
       ANI   01        ; test to see if bit 0 is zero
                         indicating buffer is empty
       JNZ   wait
       MOV   A,B
       OUT   21        ; output character from register A
```

The test and loop instructions cause the processor to test repeatedly the state of the flag bit until it is set to 1, indicating that the transfer is complete. To transfer a group of characters would require a further loop around the above code, since the examples given only transfer one character.

Although this method of achieving input/output is very simple to program, the disadvantage of it is one of slowness. It might not be obvious at first why it is necessary to test repeatedly the flag bit to see if the character has been transferred. Obviously it is important to ensure that one character has been transferred before attempting to transfer the next, but why does the program have to loop, apparently 'waiting' for this to occur? To answer this, consider the following example of the timing of the character transfer process. Suppose the computer is reading data over a low speed line from a terminal at 1000 characters per second. Further, assume a memory cycle time of one microsecond and that consequently the following input code takes, say, 10 microseconds from the time a character is available (i.e., the IN 21 instruction is executed) until the next character needs to be transferred (i.e. the next time it arrives at the IN 20 instruction):

```
Loop      IN    20
          ANI   01
          JZ    Loop
          IN    21
          STA   Memory    (Store the contents of the accumulator
                address   in the addressed memory location.)
          JMP   Loop      (This would actually have to be a
                          conditional branch, depending on
                          whether the end of the data had
                          been reached or not.)
```

The terminal device transferring data at a speed of 1000 characters per second will transfer one character in 1000 microseconds. Consequently, after every 1000 microseconds, the CPU is to take 10 microseconds to deal with the character obtained and then wait another 1000 microseconds for the next character to arrive.

Not only does this explain why an idle loop is necessary (because the peripheral device is so very slow compared to the speed of the processor) but it also illustrates the disadvantage of this method of input/output. In the above example, the CPU is only usefully active for 10 microseconds in every 1000. That is, it is only being used for about 1 per cent of the time and 99 per cent of the time it is idling, waiting for the character to be transferred.

10.3.2 Interrupt programmed input/ouput

This method makes use of an interrupt facility (see Chapter 9). It removes the time spent testing the status of the flag bit of the interface by allowing the input/output transfer of data to be initiated by program instruction and allowing the hardware to cause an interrupt when the transfer is complete. In this case, the interrupt service routine would perform the task of transferring the character between the interface buffer register and the processor register (an accumulator, for example) and would then initiate the transfer of the next character. While the character is being transferred the processor is free to be used for other tasks, with the provision that it will be interrupted when the next character has been transferred.

The following example shows an interrupt routine for reading fifty characters from an input peripheral device. The mainline program has to set up the address of the interrupt service routine, initialise a count of the number of characters to be transferred and initiate the transfer of the first character. While the character is being transferred the processor can continue with another task. On the completion of each character transfer, the interrupt service routine is entered which initiates the transfer of the next character. The program runs as follows:

MAIN PROGRAM
Set up address of interrupt service routine

	IN	21	Set control bit to start the transfer of the 1st character.
	—		
	—		
	—		
	—		
	—		
Charcount	DEC	—50	The number of characters to be transferred.

INTERRUPT SERVICE ROUTINE

	IN	21	Transfer character from interface buffer to A register.
	STA	Memory location	Store this character in memory.
	INC	Charcount	Increment the character count.
	JZ	END	All characters are transferred if charcount = 0.
	IN	21	Initiate transfer of next charac-
	JMP	RETURN	ter.
			Return to interrupted program.
END	CALL	SUB	Branch to subroutine to process.
RETURN	JMP	0 (indirect)	Return to interrupted program.

On completion of the transfer of all fifty characters it is assumed that some processing of the characters is necessary and so control is transferred to a subroutine, SUB, to do the required processing.

10.4 Autonomous input/output—DMA

Programmed input/output (particularly interrupt driven) is suitable for transferring relatively few characters to or from slow peripheral devices. If, however, there are a large number of characters to be transferred, the CPU will be spending a large portion of its time just dealing with the individual characters, since each character still passes through the CPU and its MAR and MBR on its way to the memory. Also, some of the faster peripherals, such as magnetic tapes or disks, may be able to transfer characters at such a rate that there would not be time to process the interrupt service routine for one character before the next character had arrived. Consequently there is a need for some sort of system for allowing a peripheral device to transfer characters directly to memory, without going 'through' the CPU. Such a facility is known as *direct memory access* (DMA). This is achieved by incorporating many of the functions which are performed by software in a programmed I/O method into a hardwired controller. This controller will need:

(1) a register for generating the memory address;
(2) a register for keeping track of the word count;
(3) a register to store the command received from the CPU specifying the function to be performed;
(4) a register to be used as a data buffer between the peripheral device and the main memory.

Since DMA is used for connecting high speed devices it must be

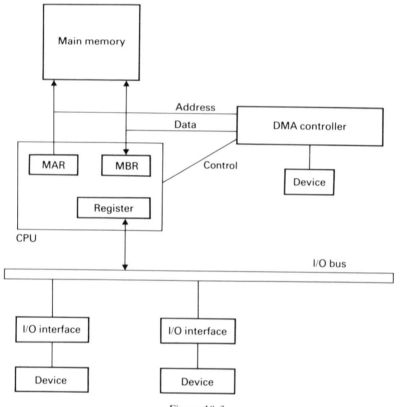

Figure 10.3

remembered that with devices such as magnetic tapes and disks there is no need to convert information to and from character format. Consequently the usual unit of transference is a word.

On a single bus computer the memory bus and I/O bus are in fact the same, and a peripheral device is connected to the bus by the DMA controller rather than by an interface.

On a computer with a separate I/O bus, however, the DMA controller will need to be connected directly to the memory, bypassing the CPU. Figure 10.3 illustrates such a connection. It is still necessary for the CPU to be connected to the DMA in order for control signals to be sent to the DMA controller to initiate the data transfers.

To start an I/O operation using the DMA it is necessary for the program to do the following:

(1) load the initial memory address;
(2) load the count of the number of words to be transferred;
(3) load a control word defining input or output;
(4) execute a START command.

On receiving the START command the DMA will proceed with the data transfer independently of the CPU, so enabling the CPU to continue processing another part of the same program or another program altogether. There is, however, the possibility of a conflict when both the CPU and the DMA controller wish to access memory at precisely the same time. Because the transfer of data from very fast peripheral devices attached to the DMA cannot be held up, priority is usually given to the DMA in preference to the CPU. In most cases the CPU will originate the majority of memory access cycles, and hence in the case of contention the DMA can be thought of as 'stealing' a cycle from the CPU, an event indeed often known as *cycle stealing*. It must be remembered, however, that in any program not all the instructions are memory reference instructions, and so, although all instructions involve a memory access to fetch them, only a proportion will access memory during execution. Consequently cycle stealing will only take place occasionally, although it is not possible to predict the effect of the DMA facility on the execution time of an instruction and it therefore follows that the execution time of a program will be unpredictable.

10.5 Input/output channels

The two methods of input/output described, programmed I/O and DMA, are adequate for the requirements of most micro- and minicomputers. DMA is usually associated with high speed peripheral devices, whereas programmed I/O is used with low speed devices. With large mainframe computers, however, the size of the system and the cost of the CPU make it desirable to get the maximum use out of the CPU. Consequently it seems reasonable that all input/output operations should be provided through a DMA facility rather than have the slow CPU consuming programmed I/O. Since it would be uneconomic for each peripheral device to have its own DMA controller, particularly when not all peripherals will be involved in data transfers simultaneously, it seems reasonable that the DMA facility should be shared between a number of peripheral devices. The concept of a small processor acting as a shared DMA facility to a number of peripheral devices is known as a *channel*. Strictly speaking, the term channel was introduced by IBM on their 360/370 range of computers and has since come into common use, although in fact not all computer manufacturers use the term 'channel' to describe their equipment of a similar type. On most large mainframe computer systems, all communication with external devices is through one or more channels, there being three basic types of channel:

(1) Selector channel

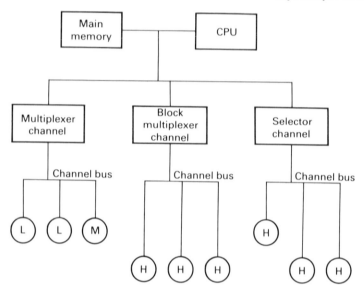

L = low speed device

M = medium speed device

H = high speed device

Figure 10.4

(2) Multiplexer channel
(3) Block multiplexer channel

An example of a system configuration is shown in Figure 10.4.

10.5.1 Selector channels

The selector channel provides an exclusive input/output path for a single high speed peripheral device. There may be a number of devices attached to the selector channel but at any time it is totally dedicated to the selected device and, until released, cannot be used for another input/output function. It is used to transfer a block of words to or from memory and provides the necessary synchronisation between the speed of transfer of words from the device and the speed of transfer of words to or from main memory. Additionally it performs parity checking or parity insertion. It generates a 'transfer complete' interrupt on completion of the block transfer, or an error interrupt on detection of bad parity or on receipt of an error signal from the device.

10.5.2 Multiplexer channel

A multiplexer channel is used for connecting a number of slow and medium speed devices. Since the rate of transfer of data over the channel to the memory is very much greater than the rate at which a device can supply data to the channel, a multiplexer channel is able to operate with a number of peripheral devices simultaneously. It is, in fact, able to operate in either one of two modes. The channel can be totally dedicated to one medium speed device for a burst transfer, in which case it acts like a medium speed selector channel. In the multiplex mode the channel will poll around the devices connected to it and transfer the next character or word from each device in turn that is ready for a transfer. Parameters relating to the operation of each of these devices, such as character count and memory data address, are usually kept in fixed locations in the main memory. When the channel is attached to a specific device, it fetches the appropriate parameters from memory and on disconnection the updated values are placed at the same location.

10.5.3 Block multiplexer channel

The block multiplexer channel combines the best features of both the selector and multiplexer channels. It operates in a very similar way to that of a high speed multiplexer channel operating in burst mode. Like a selector channel it is used to transfer a block of data at very high speed. Like a multiplexer channel, it is able to poll round the devices attached to it to transfer blocks of data in turn as required. The advantage over a selector channel can be seen if the operation of transferring data from a magnetic disk file is considered. To retrieve data from a disk file the following operations are necessary:

(1) Seek for the appropriate track
(2) Search that track for the appropriate record
(3) Read the data from that record

The first two operations will involve a considerable delay in the mechanical movement of the disk heads and if a selector channel is being used it will tie up the entire channel during the whole of the above operations. With a block multiplexer channel, after the appropriate commands have been sent to the device, the channel can be released to allow it to service other devices and be reconnected when the device is ready to transfer the block of data.

10.5.4 Channel programming

As described earlier, a channel is a small processor that is responsible for carrying out input/output to and from all the peripheral devices attached to it. To examine the operation of a channel in a little more detail, let us consider the sequence of events that takes place during an I/O operation on an IBM 4300 computer. The following description is not complete (for the details refer to the appropriate IBM manual) but it illustrates the concepts, and although it relates to a specific range of machines, similar events take place on equipment from other manufacturers.

To start a transfer between a device and main store the following must be specified:

(1) The channel address
(2) The device address (there will be more than one device attached to a channel)
(3) The operation to be performed, e.g. input or output
(4) The number of bytes to be transferred
(5) The main storage address of the area from which or to which the transfer is to proceed

On the 4300 these are specified as follows. The supervisor initiates a transfer by executing an SIO (Start I/O) instruction, which has the following layout:

SIO	OP Code		Base register	Displacement
0	7		16	20 31

The sum of the displacement and the contents of the base register is formed as usual but it does not refer to a main storage location. Instead the resulting 32-bit number is treated as a channel address and a device address as follows:

	Channel address	Device address
0	15 16 24	31

The remainder of the information is specified as follows. Location 48_{16} in main store is used specially as a channel address word (CAW). When an SIO is executed the CAW must contain the address of a channel command word (CCW) set up somewhere in main store. A channel command word is actually a double word with the following format:

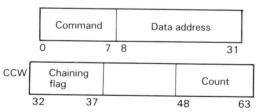

	Command	Data address
	0 7	8 31

CCW	Chaining flag		Count
	32 37		48 63

As an example, suppose that a user program issues an INPUT command referring to a device which is connected on channel 1 and has address 80_{16}. Suppose that the user program buffer is at address 5120_{16} and that 80 bytes of information is to be input. The supervisor has to:

(1) set up a CCW (say at address 42A8)
(2) set up the CAW (at address 48_{16})
(3) execute an SIO instruction (say at 4600_{16})

The contents of the various words are as follows:

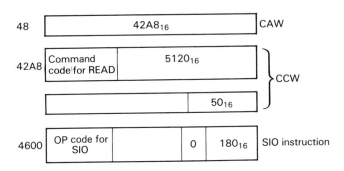

Note that immediately the SIO instruction is executed by the CPU the channel starts carrying out the I/O transfer independently of the CPU. The channel and the CPU operate autonomously. Finally the channel interrupts the CPU when the I/O transfer is complete.

Further, once the SIO instruction has been executed the CAW can be utilised by the CPU to initiate transfers through other channels. The similarity between the CPU and a channel becomes clearer when channel programming is considered. Consider the situation where it is necessary to perform a definite sequence of I/O operations, one immediately after another. For example, suppose that when a job fails the operating system:

(1) Prints a message on the line printer
(2) Ejects a page
(3) Prints a message at the top of the next page

If this was achieved by the operating system executing three SIO instructions, it would also be burdened with the task of handling the interrupt that occurs at the end of each. It is possible for this to be achieved by a sequence of CCWs, executed by the channel in sequence. This sequence of CCWs is known as a channel program. Referring back to the layout of the CCW it can be seen that bits 32–37 contain a chaining flag. This is essentially a bit pattern indicating whether this is the last CCW in a sequence or whether the next pair of words in store contain a CCW to be executed next by the channel.

A channel, once initiated by the CPU, obeys the commands until either it has completed all of the operations, or an error condition arises. It then interrupts the CPU.

For the above example, the channel program would be a sequence of three CCWs as follows:

Location	Instruction					Comments
	Command code	Data address	Flag	Unused	Count	
000300	01	000400	40	00	000B	Print line
000308	88	000000	40	00	0000	Skip page
000310	11	000500	00	00	000F	Print header line
—						
—						
—						
—						
000400 'END OF PAGE'						Data
—						
—						
000500 'TOP OF NEW PAGE'						Data

10.6 Front end processors

The task of dealing with input/output becomes even more involved in a system which provides interactive facilities to users via a large number of terminal devices attached to the CPU. The following characteristics are typical of many such systems.

● A large number of terminal devices (perhaps 150 to 200).
● The terminals may be of different speeds—perhaps low speed printing devices and high speed visual display units.
● The different types of terminals may have different communication protocols (see Chapter 13).
● There may need to be character translations to be performed.
● Every character received has to be echoed back to the terminal immediately so as to appear instantaneous.
● Characters from a terminal are collected together in a buffer assigned to that terminal, so that there is a large number of data buffers.

One of the main objectives in an interactive system is to achieve fast response to individual users. The more time that the CPU is involved in doing all of the above tasks the less time there is for it to be doing the required tasks.

Under these circumstances the concept of input/output being achieved through a channel, where a channel was a simple processor sharing the main memory with the main CPU, can be extended to the point where the channel does in fact become a processor comparable in sophistication to a CPU. That is, all the tasks relating to gathering input from terminals and routing results back to terminals are performed on a computer, this computer being linked to the main CPU and main memory in the same way that a channel is. The computer that is used in this way is said to be a 'front end processor'. It is really a logical extension of the idea of a channel, designed to take many of the tedious tasks associated with input/output off the main CPU so that it can concentrate on the required tasks. The main CPU has only to deal with one interrupt, that of the block transfer, instead of with individual interrupts from the terminals.

10.7 Summary

This chapter has dealt with the transfer of data from one device to another from the point of view of the programmer and taking into account the hardware facilities available. It has developed the techniques from the very simple arrangement of busy testing, through interrupt I/O, DMA and channel processing, to front end processors. These increasingly demand less attention from the CPU, placing more responsibility on other devices operating concurrently. Further aspects of the transmission of data, particularly over long distances, are considered in Chapter 12 in the context of data transmission within computer networks.

10.8 Problems

(1) The following question requires you to use a computer to which you have low level access (machine code or assembler).
  (a) Write and test a program to transfer a single character from a CPU register to the print device of a terminal.
  (b) Modify the program so that it repeatedly checks the CPU register for non zero contents and outputs to the print device when non zero.
  (c) Modify the program so that the character to be output is first input from the keyboard of the terminal.
  (d) Modify the program to skip round the output code. What is the difference in effect now and why?

(2) Compare and contrast the following I/O techniques:
   (a) programmed I/O;
   (b) DMA;
   (c) channel processors.
(3) (a) Describe the following methods of programming data transfers between a CPU and a peripheral device:
   (i) executing a program loop to examine a 'ready' status bit.
   (ii) using an interrupt system to interrupt the CPU when the device is ready.
   (b) If a cassette tape recorder can transfer 1500 characters per second explain why it is more efficient in terms of the CPU when the cassette recorder is used in systems (i) and (ii) above, stating any assumptions you make.
(4) Given the following choice of line speeds, 110, 300, 600 and 1200 bit/s, which line speed should an asynchronous ASCII terminal use, and which does parity checking and prints at 60 characters/s?
(5) How many ASCII characters/s can be transmitted over a 2400 bit/s line in each of the following transmission methods:
   (a) synchronous;
   (b) asynchronous?

CHAPTER 11

Computer networks

11.1 Networks and distributed systems □ 11.2 Wide area and local area networks □ 11.3 Network topologies □ 11.4 Network models □ 11.5 Summary □ 11.6 Problems

The earlier chapters of this book have been concerned with developing the concepts of the structure and mode of operation of a single computer. Chapter 10 was concerned with the techniques whereby some device (typically a peripheral) can be connected to the CPU. In fact, Chapter 10 developed the concept that the devices could become increasingly more sophisticated, from DMA, channel processors through to a front end processor. If we allow the remote device to be another computer and then link that to another one and so on, we effectively have a computer *network*. This leads to a whole new area of application for the users, and new problems for the network designers and builders, which will now be investigated.

11.1 Networks and distributed systems

A very simple definition of a network would be that it is simply a number of connected computers. However, a more precise indication of what is meant by the term computer is necessary. For example, should an intelligent terminal be included? If it is accepted that a network of computers should exclude a classical time-sharing terminal system (on the basis that there is only one computer, in full control of all the other devices) then a better definition would incorporate the notion that each device being connected should be capable of some autonomous processing. Thus a computer network is an interconnected collection of autonomous computers.

A distributed system, on the other hand, usually means that some other function, in addition to the hardware, is distributed. For example, in a simple network of computers linked together it would probably be the case that each of the computers has its own operating system and its own copy of all the communications software necessary for it to communicate. With a true distributed system, however, there would only be one copy of the operating system although the different components of that one operating system may in fact be located on different computers. In this case it may well be that when a user uses a particular operating system function he is not aware that it is being carried out by a different processor.

However, this text is principally concerned with the underlying hardware and software that allows computers to communicate, and hence it will concentrate on a study of the basic principles of computer networks.

Having established what is meant by the term 'computer network' it is important to understand the motivation behind linking computers together. Historically, early computer systems were very large (physically) devices to which all the users and their data had to come in order for some processing to be carried out. Clearly this is not the way most organisations work. In many companies, regardless of whether they are commercial in nature such as an insurance company, or an industrial manufacturer such as a car manufacturer, they often occupy many sites which may be distributed geographically.

There is usually a need for some local processing and then communication with one or more of the other sites. Rather than having one massive computer at some 'central' site which performs all of the processing for all of the sites, the developments in communications enables the computing functions to map the organisation of the company. That is, computers at each of the sites linked to the others as necessary. It is also true, of course, that the remarkable reductions in the price of computers also enables this to be more cost-effective.

On the other hand, there may be cases where there does exist a very large and powerful computer whose cost can only be justified by making it available to many users who may be geographically remote. A similar argument may apply to software. It is clearly easier to maintain one single copy of a large database on a 'central' computer and provide access to it from many places (perhaps world wide) rather than to face the problems of maintaining multiple copies of it spread over the world. An alternative solution to this database problem would be in fact to distribute the database amongst the network hosts. If the database is huge there would obviously be significant problems in keeping all the data in one location and providing many concurrent accesses to it. If the database is distributed there may be a 'natural' distribution. For example, personnel records of staff employed by a large multi-plant company could be kept at each local site with one site occasionally communicating with another. In other cases an organisation may wish to keep a copy of a database at another site for increased security, for example, a bank with its head office (and database) in an earthquake zone.

All of these examples should illustrate why there has been active interest in developing computer networks. Because there is such interest, and because such networks may span both manufacturer and international boundaries, there has also been some work involved in reaching agreements on international standards for various aspects of networking.

11.2 Wide area and local area networks

Figure 11.1 illustrates a typical terminal-based system where the terminals, or the remote computers, communicate with a central computer system.

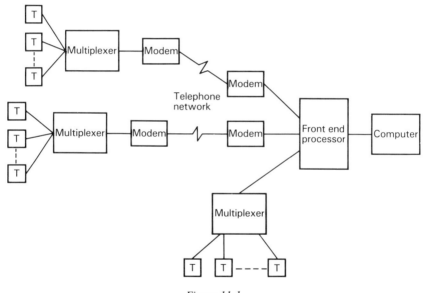

Figure 11.1

Those terminals situated some distance from the central computer communicate using the public switched telephone network.

The disadvantage of such links are those associated with the use of the analogue telephone network for data communications, namely the limited data capacity (slow speed plus significant error rates—see Chapter 12). In addition, since all the communication is between a terminal and the central computer or vice versa the communication demands are relatively straightforward. Connecting multiple computers together which are situated some considerable distance apart, and allowing any of them to communicate with any other, is a much more difficult task. It also requires a very

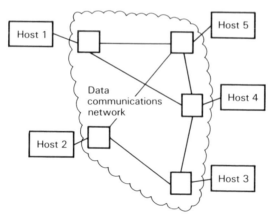

Figure 11.2

sophisticated data communications network to provide the facility for carrying data from one host computer to another, as illustrated in Figure 11.2 and discussed further in Chapter 14. Such a network, because it is physically spread over a wide geographical area, is often known as a *wide area network* (WAN).

Many of the resource-sharing arguments for computer networks might equally apply to relatively small microcomputer systems which are located close to each other, such as in the classroom or in a group of offices. Although the microcomputers themselves may be inexpensive and it is cost-effective to have one, say, in each office, some of the peripheral devices, such as disc store (particularly hard Winchester discs) or printers, are not inexpensive, and are also unlikely to be in continuous use. If all these microcomputers were linked together in a network, together with a single hard disc and a printer, each micro could use these resources as it wanted them, making their provision much more cost-effective. Clearly the network itself needs to be inexpensive also, otherwise there is no saving. Such a network of computers which are situated relatively close together is called a *local area network* (LAN).

Chapter 14 explores characteristics of WANs and LANs in much more detail.

11.3 Network topologies

There are many different topologies that are possible for a computer network, regardless of whether they are wide area or local area networks. As will be seen, some topologies are more resilient to failure of some node or communication link, but they may be more expensive. Generally the compromise to be reached when deciding on a topology is a trade-off between the reliability of the network (its resilience to failures) and the cost of the various links.

In general terms there are two types of communication channel:

● Point-to-point channels
● Broadcast channels

11.3.1 Point-to point topologies

As its name suggests a point-to-point channel is one where individual computers in the network are linked by communication channels to one or more (but not necessarily all) computers in the network. If two computers which are directly linked wish to communicate they can do so directly. If two computers which do not share a link wish to communicate they can do so but indirectly via other computers. Figure 11.3 illustrates some possible topologies for point-to-point systems.

With a *star* system the various nodes can communicate simply with the central computer (as in a terminal system), or they communicate with each other but only 'through' the central computer. The cost of adding a new node to the network is modest if the central computer has a spare port, impossible if not. If a particular node fails this does not affect the other computer communications at all, but if the central computer fails all of the network is unusable. The processing power of the central computer is also clearly a bottleneck for multi-communications and hence restricts the throughput. Many terminal systems, however, are of this type.

With a *fully connected* network every computer is linked to every other computer in the network. The effect of a failure of either a computer or a communication link is minimised since all the rest can continue communicating. There are no obvious throughput bottlenecks. However, the cost of the network is very high and since every computer has to link directly with every other the size of the network (the number of computers) is linked to the number of ports on each computer. Because of this very high cost it is generally impractical for most applications.

An *irregular* network is similar to the fully connected network except that the requirement of connecting every computer to every other is removed. That is, the connections are irregular. The cost of the network and the flexibility to add a new computer to it are very reasonable since the new computer can merely be connected to its nearest physical neighbour (it may be advantageous to connect it to some of the others as well if they are regularly to communicate, but it is not strictly necessary). The effect of a failure and likely bottlenecks depends on the exact topology of the network and may vary from serious to unimportant.

A *hierarchical* topology is a special case of an irregular network. The difficulty inherent with irregular networks is the problem of routing a message from one computer to a remote computer. There may be a

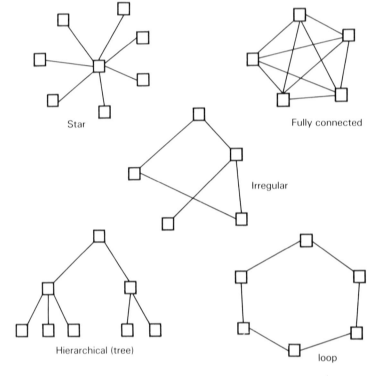

Figure 11.3

number of alternative routes and whatever algorithm is used will have to be adaptable to a changing topology in case a node fails. With a hierarchical network the routing problem is much simplified because there is only one route from a node to the next node higher up the tree (or nearer the root) (see Chapter 14 for more on routing).

In a *loop* topology (not to be confused with a ring network described in section 11.3.2) a message is passed to the next computer in the loop in its entirety before being retransmitted. It is also possible for a different message to be on each link in the loop. The cost of the network and the flexibility to add a new node is reasonable since it would merely be necessary to connect it to its two adjacent neighbours. The effect of a failure can be serious, preventing communication continuing, and the bandwidth of the loop is an obvious bottleneck.

11.3.2 Broadcast topologies

A broadcast channel is a single communication channel shared by all the communicating computers. Any message sent by one computer is received by all the other computers and hence the message must contain the address

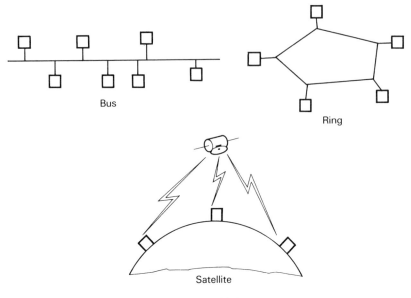

Figure 11.4

of the intended receiver so that all the other computers can ignore it. Figure 11.4 illustrates possible broadcast topologies.

With a *bus* topology all the computers are connected to a common bus and at any time one computer is allowed to transmit onto the bus, all the others being required to receive, not transmit. Since two or more computers may try to transmit simultaneously there needs to be some arbitration mechanism to resolve such conflicts. The cost of adding a new node to the network should be reasonable since it does not matter at which point it is added. The effect of the failure of a computer is unimportant, whereas the failure of the bus is serious. The bandwidth of the bus is a potential bottleneck. This topology has become a common LAN topology (see Chapter 14).

A *ring* topology involves the bits (or bytes) of a message being transmitted round the ring without waiting for the rest of the message to which they belong. Indeed it may be that consecutive groups of bits or bytes actually belong to different messages and are intended for different nodes, so that the messages are being interleaved and hence the bandwidth of the ring is shared out. Like all broadcast systems some mechanism is necessary to arbitrate simultaneous accesses. Again the effect of failure of a computer is unimportant but that of the ring is fatal. The bandwidth of the ring is also a potential bottleneck. This is another common LAN topology (see Chapter 14).

With *satellite* broadcasting each computer may be able to transmit and receive to and from the satellite (in practice it need not be all the computers in the network but only one in each locality, the other local ones being connected to it more conventionally). All the computers can hear the output from the satellite and may also be able to hear transmission to the satellite from neighbouring computers. As the cost of launching satellites comes down they will increasingly be a useful way of transmitting over large distances.

11.4 Network models

Although the processing functions of various applications which need to access a network may be very different there are only a limited number of types of network and the problems of communication from one host computer to another are in the main independent of the application process. In other words, the problems to be faced when reliably conveying a message (data) from one computer to another are not concerned with what that message is for. In addition, in order to allow for computers from different manufacturers to communicate it is clearly useful if there is some international consensus as to what the problems of communication are and how they can be resolved in a 'standard' way.

A very simple view of the communication problems may be as follows:

- There needs to be some agreement as to the form of exchange of the physical signals which allow bits to pass from one computer to another.
- Assuming that bits can be transmitted and received, can the receiver be sure the bits it is receiving are those being sent? In other words some form of error detection and recovery is necessary.
- If a message is reliably received by a computer, is the message for it or should it pass it on to another node and, if so, which one?
- If the message is for this node is there a user program here that is able and willing to receive it?

This very simplistic view introduces the concept of 'layers' into the communication process. In fact we may use the term 'higher' and 'lower' layers in much the same way that they are used with respect to programming languages, that is lower layers are nearer the fundamental machine or network. In the example just illustrated each of the different layers can be imagined to be a set of rules, or a protocol, defining how the two computers will communicate at that level (for more details of protocol see Chapter 13).

This introduces two important concepts:

(1) The protocols which are in each layer and the boundaries between layers should be sufficiently well defined so that any changes necessary

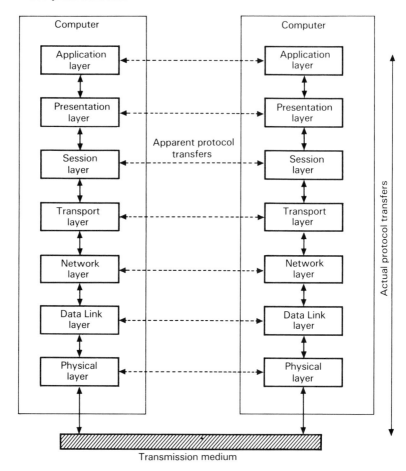

Figure 11.5

can be made to that level without affecting any of the other levels. For example, a new error detection mechanism could be introduced without the other software in other levels being aware of any change.

(2) The protocol at each level appears to communicate only with the corresponding level protocol in the remote computer (peer level processing).

In practice data is not transferred from one machine to another at any layer or level other than the 'lowest' one. Each layer only communicates with the layers above and below it, passing information down to the lowest layer or up from the lowest layer.

This concept of structuring the communication process into layers has been adopted by one of the foremost standards organisations, ISO (International Standards Organisation). This organisation has developed

and published a formal architecture of protocols for open system interconnection (connecting heterogeneous computers) known as the ISO OSI
reference model. This model is intended to be used as a framework for the
design of standard protocols and services, rather than as a definition of the
protocols. It is likely to provide the framework within which most future
protocols will be developed.

The ISO OSI reference model incorporates seven layers. Figure 11.5
illustrates the logical structure of this model incorporating the seven layers:
the physical, data link, network, transport, session, presentation and
application layers. The purpose of each of the seven layers will now be
described.

11.4.1 The physical layer

This layer is concerned with the mechanism for transmitting bit patterns
over a communication link or channel. It is concerned with the physical
aspects of things such as the voltage levels used for representing 0 and 1,
the control signals indicating the status of the physical circuit in order to be
able to synchronise the exchange of data. It also will define the mechanical
properties of connecting plugs and pin assignments. Much of the material
covered in Chapter 12 is concerned with this physical layer. There are also
some internationally agreed standards applicable to this layer, such as
RS-232-C and X21 as described in Chapter 13 (13.2.2 and 13.2.3).

11.4.2 The data link layer

This layer uses the raw transmission facility provided by the physical layer
and makes the communication channel appear free of errors. It incorporates some form of error detection mechanism and handles the problems
associated with retransmitting that information that has been corrupted.
Much of Chapter 13 is concerned with data link layer protocols (13.3, 13.4
and 13.5), HDLC being an internationally agreed one (see 13.5.2).

11.4.3 The network layer

Whereas the bottom two layers are essentially concerned with communication between two adjacent machines in a network, the network layer is
concerned with routing 'packets' across a network. It essentially takes a
message from a host machine, splits it up into packets and organises the
transmission of packets across the network to the desired destination. In
doing so it is responsible for the sequencing and flow control of the
packets. Level 3 of the X25 set of protocols (see Chapter 13—13.5.3) is an
internationally accepted standard for a network layer for a *packet switched
data network* (PSDN).

11.4.4 The transport layer

The transport layer's primary task is to hide all the network dependent characteristics from the layers above it. This means that it provides transparent data transfer. That is, a user on one host computer may communicate with a user on another host computer without having any concern at all about the underlying network structure being used to convey their messages. The implication of this is that all protocols defined for the transport layer will only need to be implemented on the host computers, not the intermediate switching computers in the network.

The services provided by the transport layer are essentially connection management and the transfer of data. The user of the transport layer (i.e. the layer above) can use the transport layer to establish and maintain a logical connection to the corresponding transport layer user in a remote computer during which time the transport layer will also transfer data between the two users over this connection.

11.4.5 The session layer

The period of time for which a pair (or more) of users remain logically connected together (even though they may not be continuously transmitting or receiving) is known as a *session*. The session layer is concerned with establishing and managing a communication path between two users. In many ways it can be seen as being analogous to the logon and logoff procedures that are necessary on a conventional time-sharing system. It may, for example, be necessary to authenticate the users to ensure they are both bona fide users and to enable the appropriate party to receive the bill for the communication session.

11.4.6 The presentation layer

The presentation layer is concerned with the format of the data being exchanged by communicating parties. It could be argued that the concern of the presentation layer is really associated with the user's application, but there are a number of common features of many applications which make a presentation layer sensible.

One area of concern is code conversion. It may be, for example, that one of the communicating parties uses the ASCII code for internal character storage, whereas the other one uses EBCDIC. The presentation layer would perform the appropriate conversion.

If in a particular system the messages being exchanged contained a lot of commonly occurring words or expressions, e.g. *credit* and *debit* in a financial system, these words or expressions could be coded to reduce the amount of information being exchanged. For example, the use of an eight bit code allows one byte to represent 256 different words or expressions. Other more sophisticated text compression mechanisms are clearly poss- ible.

On a network where data security (confidentiality) is of concern the presentation layer could perform some form of data encryption operation on the data to be transmitted, performing the reverse function on the data being received.

11.4.7 The application layer

This is the highest layer in the reference model and is the environment in which users' programs operate and communicate. It would appear that because this layer is concerned with the user, the details of such com- munication are dependent on the application and will be different for every application. For some applications this will be true and hence appropriate protocols at this level will be designed by the user. However, there are a number of common application areas where work is progressing to define standard protocols for such applications. A fairly common requirement would be that of a file transfer application, e.g. a network of relatively small single-user work-stations each with some local limited file storage facility, connected to a large multi-user system which has a very large file store. A variation on this would be a file access protocol, to access part of a file which is stored on a remote computer's file-store. Other examples might include electronic mail document transfer.

11.5 Summary

This chapter has set the scene for computer networks by introducing the concept, identifying the idea of wide area and local area networks, looking at a variety of possible topologies and finally describing an internationally agreed model within which standardised communication systems can be designed.

The remaining chapters will in fact follow this model in describing first the physical transmission of data (the physical layer), secondly the techniques of communication protocols (the data link layer) and finally a variety of network types (the network layer).

11.6 Problems

(1) (a) Summarise the main functions of the various layers of the ISO model network architecture.

(b) Explain how peer protocols in a layered architecture make possible direct virtual communication between processes in the same layer. Trace the transformations a message undergoes as it passes across the network from one application process to another.

(2) Review the various topologies that are possible for interlinked computers, paying particular attention to their advantages and disadvantages.

CHAPTER 12

Data transmission

Chapter 10 presented a developing sophistication of input/output methods to cater for the different requirements of small and large computer systems. Chapter 11 has developed these ideas to the concept of networks of communicating computers and it is now necessary to consider just how data is to be transmitted along a line, whether the line is physically short for the devices in the immediate vicinity of a CPU, or long for devices or computers situated at remote locations.

Data transmission involves the transfer of information between various pieces of computing machinery. This information is usually coded as patterns of bits. In order to transmit such data two voltage levels could be used to represent the two bits, say 0 volts and +5 volts. The use of such binary signals leads to so called square waves, since when it is displayed on an oscilloscope the signal has a characteristic square shape, as illustrated in Figure 12.1.

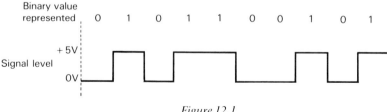

Figure 12.1

The form in which messages, consisting of sequences of bits, are conveyed falls broadly into one of two classes: parallel and serial systems. These systems are described in section 10.2.

Earlier, the term 'line' was used to refer to the medium of the transmission system. As discussed later in section 12.6 the medium could take the form of various types of cable, optical fibres, microwave links and even satellite communication. Consequently the general term channel will be used to indicate the link between a transmitter and a receiver.

One of the characteristics of the transmission of signals down a channel which is clearly of great interest is the speed at which the information can be transmitted. A major deciding factor in this is the characteristics of the channel itself. To establish these, an understanding of the major results of some information channel theory is necessary.

12.1 Simple information channel theory

Waves are used to carry information through most media, e.g. sound waves, light waves. One of the simplest waveforms is that of a sine or cosine wave, as illustrated in Figure 12.2.

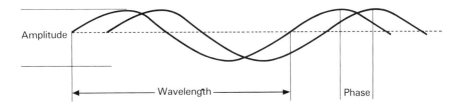

Figure 12.2

The major features of such a waveform are its amplitude, frequency and phase. The amplitude is the height of the wave measured, for example, in volts if the wave is a voltage wave, or millibars if it is a sound wave. Its frequency is the number of times the waveform repeats itself in a second (measured in Hertz (Hz) where one Hz is one cycle per second), and the phase is essentially the difference in time between two separate waves of the same frequency.

As indicated in the introduction to this chapter, a voltage applied to a wire to represent logic 1, and 0 volts to represent logic 0 produces a square wave as illustrated in Figure 12.1.

It can be shown, using a branch of mathematics called Fourier analysis, that any waveform is actually made up of a summation of simple sine and/or cosine waves. That is, any recurrent waveform of frequency F can be resolved into the sum of an infinite number of sinusoidal waveforms

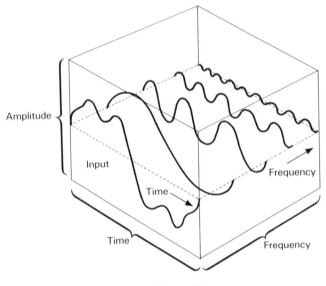

Figure 12.3

having frequencies F, $2F$, $3F$ . . . to infinity. In particular, a square wave is actually made up of the sum of a series of sine waves having frequencies:

$$F + 3F + 5F + 7F . . .$$

Although at first sight this may seem very strange, an understanding of the truth of this can be obtained graphically from Figure 12.3 which shows the resultant waveform of adding together a wave of frequency F with waves of frequency $3F$ and $5F$. It can be seen that the resulting wave is tending towards a square wave.

The first important result, then, is that in order to transmit a perfect square wave it is necessary to transmit an infinite number of frequencies. Unfortunately all transmission media (and often the sending and receiving equipment) are limited in the frequency range that they can cope with, some more than others. The range of frequencies that a particular channel can cope with is called its frequency range. The difference between the upper and lower limits is called the *bandwidth* of that channel.

Some commonly encountered frequencies are:

Human voice	100 Hz to 10 000 Hz
Human hearing	20 Hz to 15 000 Hz
The telephone	300 Hz to 3400 Hz (restricted by British Telecom for practical reasons)
Mains electricity	50 or 60 Hz

Since an infinite range of frequencies will never be transmitted the resulting waveform will be distorted. Thus, for example, a square wave will never be exactly square. The amount of distortion will clearly depend on the bandwidth of the channel and the base frequency of the waveform.

This leads to another very important result. If the bandwidth of a particular channel will only cope with frequencies up to, say, X Hz then a square wave of frequency X Hz cannot be transmitted, since it will require waveforms of frequency X, $3X$, $5X$, etc., which the channel cannot transmit.

Hence, if there is a limit on the frequency capacity of a channel (bandwidth), there is a limit on the frequency of the square wave, that is the rate of transmission of the data. Alternatively, the greater the bandwidth the faster information can be transmitted.

These arguments merely confirm the following theories developed by the mathematicians Nyquist and Shannon some years before computers were first developed. If we define the information content I as:

$$I = \log_2 (M) \text{ bits}$$

where M is the number of different symbols or characters, then, for example, with 128 ASCII characters:

$$I = \log_2 (128) \text{ bits}$$
$$= 7$$

That is, 7 bits are required to represent 128 characters.

The capacity C of a channel is the maximum rate at which information can pass through. So, if T is the minimum time to transmit one symbol, then:

$$C = \frac{1}{T} \text{symbols/sec}$$

$$C = \frac{1}{T} \log_2 (M) \text{ bits/sec}$$

It can be shown that the bandwidth W of a channel is given by:

$$W = \frac{1}{2T}$$

Thus $C = 2W \log_2 (M)$ bits/sec.

Another way of expressing this is that the channel capacity is proportional to the bandwidth.

This, unfortunately, is only true for a perfect channel. It has to be modified for noise, those random imperfections that reduce the information rate by introducing errors in the information being transmitted.

Shannon's equation modifies the above equation to:

$$C = W \log_2 (1 + S/N) \text{ bits per sec}$$

where S/N is the signal to noise ratio, and S is the power of the signal and B is the power of the noise.

Signal levels are commonly referred to in terms of decibels, where:

$$\text{decibel value} = 10 \log_{10} (S/N)$$

As an example of the application of Shannon's equation, consider the maximum information rate (channel capacity) of a channel with a frequency range 300 Hz to 3300 Hz and an approximate signal to noise ratio of 20 db (this is typical of the public telephone network):

$$
\begin{aligned}
db &= 20 \\
&= 10 \log_{10} (S/N)
\end{aligned}
$$
$$\text{Thus } S/N = 100$$
$$C = 3000 \log_2 (1 + 100)$$
$$= 3000 \log_{10} 101/\log_{10} 2$$
$$\text{Therefore } C = 19\,963 \text{ bits per second.}$$

This is in fact only an approximation since the db value of 20 is an average value. In practice transmission on telephone lines takes place at much lower speeds for a variety of reasons.

12.2 Baud rate and communication channels

A common term used in communication technology is that of *baud rate* and it often appears to be synonymous with bit rate, bits per second.

However, the term baud rate refers to the signalling rate, or the number of times the signal may change per second. If the signals are sent using a 2-bit code (0 and 1) then the signal could change after every bit (010101 . . .), so in this case the baud rate is equal to the bit rate.

If however, a four-level code is used, say 0 V, 5 V, 10 V and 15 V, then each signal could represent two bits, 00,01,10,11.

In this case with every signal level change two bits of information are being transmitted so that the bit rate is twice the baud rate. (See section 12.3.1 for another example of the bit rate being twice the baud rate.)

Types of channels can be classified as follows:

Simplex   —Communication can only take place between the sender and the receiver whose designations cannot change, i.e. transmission is in one direction only.

Half duplex   —Communication can take place in either direction, but not at the same time.

Full duplex   —Communication can be taking place in both directions simultaneously.

These definitions are the generally accepted meanings of these terms. However, in Europe an alternative meaning is applied. Here, simplex is the term used to describe a line capable of carrying data in either direction but only one direction at a time, and half duplex is used for a full duplex line to which is attached terminal equipment limited to working in half duplex fashion.

Simplex transmission is useful if the line is connected to a device which has only either input or output capability but not both, e.g. an input device (such as a transducer) used at a remote site to collect and transmit data to a computer centre could use a simplex line. The choice between half and full duplex is a compromise between cost and speed. A full duplex line requires either two simplex lines in opposite directions or a line with two non-overlapping frequency bands so that there are two independent transmission facilities, one in each direction. Half duplex requires the same sort of transmission line as simplex, but with switches at both ends to connect either the transmitter or the receiver, but not both, to the line.

Consequently, full duplex transmission is usually more expensive to provide than half duplex transmission. A large number of computer applications require the computer to receive data, perform some computation and then return the results. This is essentially half duplex operation, and many interactive terminal systems are of this nature.

There are other situations, however, such as data being transmitted over a communications network (see Chapter 11), where messages travelling in opposite directions often bear no relation to each other and can therefore be transmitted simultaneously if the line is full duplex.

12.3 Analogue transmission and modulation techniques

In the early days of computer communication when it became necessary to connect computers together which were some considerable distance apart, there was already in existence an extensive network of cables carrying information, namely the telephone system. Thus it was an obvious medium to adopt to carry data as well as speech.

In order to use lines from the public switched telephone network (PSTN) as the transmission medium, it is necessary to convert the electrical signals from the computer, or terminal, into a form acceptable to the equipment used in the PSTN. This is designed for speech communication and audio frequencies in the range 300 to 3400 Hz (see section 12.1).

A carrier wave (a sine wave within the above frequency range) is transmitted and one of its characteristics altered in order to represent the 0s and 1s of the desired binary transmission. At the receiving end is a device which converts this signal back into its binary form. The circuit to

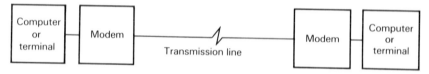

Figure 12.4

perform the transmission alteration is known as a *modulator* and that to perform the reverse function is a *demodulator*. Since each end of a transmission line usually both sends and receives data, the combined device is known as a *modem*. This is illustrated in Figure 12.4.

12.3.1 Modulation

As discussed in 12.1 above the three characteristics of a waveform are its amplitude, frequency and phase. Three possible modulation techniques are known as amplitude modulation (AM), frequency modulation (FM) and phase modulation (PM). Figure 12.5 illustrates the principle of each technique.

Amplitude modulation involves varying the amplitude or signal level of the carrier wave between two specified levels. Although a simple principle,

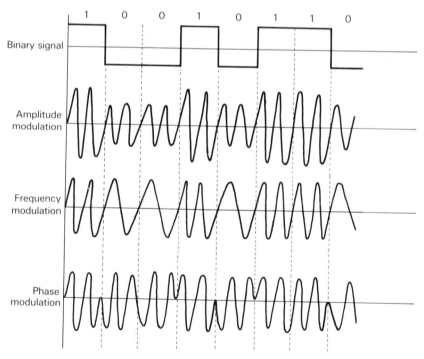

Figure 12.5

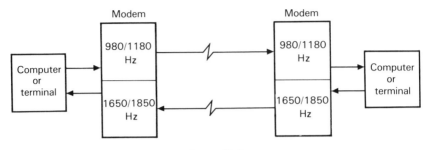

Figure 12.6

it is very prone to the effect of noise on the line and hence is not often used.

Frequency modulation involves changing the frequency of a carrier wave (which has a fixed amplitude) between two fixed frequency values. It is sometimes known as *frequency shift keying* (FSK). Since this technique is less prone to errors it is more commonly used. However, there are a number of problems.

● The chosen frequencies must be significantly (measurably) different.
● To detect the frequency at least half a wave needs to be transmitted. Thus the lowest frequency must be greater than the baud rate.
● Certain frequencies on the telephone network are used by the switching equipment and so are prohibited for general use.

The actual frequencies chosen for modems are in fact agreed internationally by the CCITT (International Consultative Committee for Telegraph and Telephones). This is a part of the United Nations and co-ordinates the activities of the telephone companies throughout the world.

For a modem to provide a full duplex link it clearly needs two channels, one for each direction. An example of the chosen frequencies for a 300 bit/second modem is shown in Figure 12.6. Data in one direction is encoded in the frequency pair 980/1180 Hz while in the opposite direction 1650/1850 Hz signals are used.

Note that the results of channel theory explained in section 12.1 indicate that there is a limit to the frequency that can be used on a PSTN line, since the bandwidth is limited to 3100 Hz. For example, a 9600 bit/sec speed cannot be used on a normal PSTN line using frequency modulation since the bandwidth is insufficient.

With phase modulation, the amplitude and frequency of the carrier wave are kept constant but the carrier is shifted in phase to represent each bit being transmitted.

In principle, the simplest phase modulation scheme—known as phase shift keying (PSK)—would use two carrier signals to represent binary 0 and binary 1 with a 180° phase change between them (see Figure 12.7 (a)). This requires a reference carrier signal at the receiving modem against

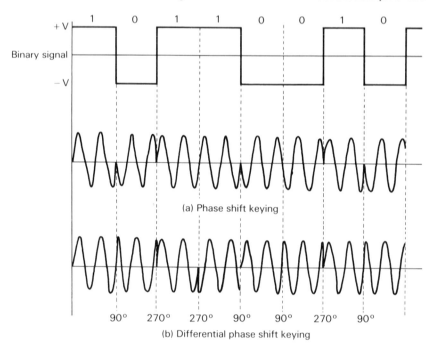

Binary signal

(a) Phase shift keying

(b) Differential phase shift keying

Figure 12.7

which the phase of the incoming signal can be compared. In practice this is very susceptible to random phase changes from noise, and the demodulation circuitry is complex. Hence an alternative phase modulation—known as differential phase shift keying—is often used (see Figure 12.7 (b)). Here a phase shift of 90° could represent a binary 0 and a shift of 270° a binary 1. The advantage is that there is a change in phase for each bit transition determined by the state of the next bit relative to the current bit. The demodulator only needs to detect the size of each phase shift rather than its absolute value.

A more complex phase change scheme can be employed to increase the transmission speed. For example, four different phase changes could be used so that each change represents two bits. A '00' results in a phase change of 0°, a '01' in a phase change of 90°, a '11' of 180° and a '10' of 270°. This means that, since for each signal change two bits are being transmitted, the bit rate is twice the baud rate (see section 12.2).

With all these different modulation techniques, it must be remembered that using the PSTN still imposes a limit on the speed of the transmission due to the limited bandwidth. This can be overcome to a large extent by the leasing of a private line bypassing the local exchange, to be used only for computer communication and therefore not subject to the same limitations. The noise levels on a private circuit are usually lower than on a dialled connection (remember Shannon's equation in section 12.1). Clearly this solution is more expensive but the volume of data transfer may be sufficient to justify it.

12.4 Digital transmission and modulation techniques

The modulation techniques discussed in section 12.3 were required to make use of the existing PSTN which was originally designed for transmission of voice (audio) signals with a limited bandwidth. If use could be made of, say, a private line, then the original signal (known as the baseband signal) could be applied directly to the line and transmitted. There is of course still a relationship between the speed at which the transmission can take place and the bandwidth of the transmission media which renders some media more suitable than others for high speed transmission lines (see section 12.6). However, even with ordinary copper cabling much higher transmission rates are possible than is the case with the old PSTN. Also, if the line is a long one, *attenuation* becomes a problem. Since all transmission media involve electrical resistance, energy from the transmitted signal is used to make the current flow against this resistance, so the energy available gradually decreases as the signal travels along the line and this loss of energy is known as attenuation.

If the line is long and the attenuation becomes large, the received signal may be very distorted, and so the signal will have to be regenerated at intermediate positions on the line. With an analogue signal involving an infinite number of signal levels (a continuously varying modulated sine wave), reconstructing the signal exactly is very difficult, whereas with a digital signal having only two discrete levels, it is easy. Hence the case of digital transmission over long distances has significant advantages for transmitting data.

As the volume of data transmitted nationally and internationally has grown and as the advantages of digital transmission have become understood, the national and international telephone companies have invested very large amounts of money into converting the existing (and often old) analogue telephone equipment into digital technology. The advantages for transmission of data are clear. If speech (audio) signals can be converted into digital form to use these digital networks (see section 12.4.1) what are the advantages for the telephone network?

● The effects of noise and attenuation are considerably reduced since the signal can be reconstructed exactly.
● Since all the signals are digital (binary) all the switching taking place in exchanges can now be done by computers and done very quickly.

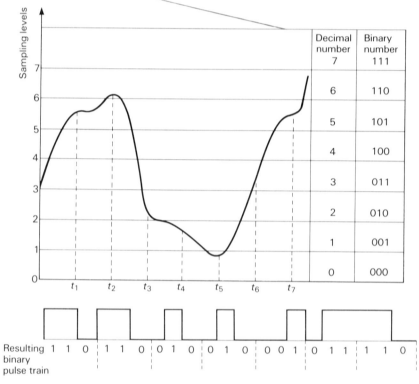

Decimal number	Binary number
7	111
6	110
5	101
4	100
3	011
2	010
1	001
0	000

Resulting binary pulse train 1 1 0 1 1 0 0 1 0 0 1 0 0 0 1 0 1 1 1 1 0

Figure 12.8

• Software can be developed for these computers which will allow considerable intelligence to be built into the telephone network.
• Multiplexing techniques can be used to make full use of very high bandwidth transmission media (see section 12.5)

Speech signals can be coded into digital form by a technique known as *pulse code modulation*.

12.4.1 Pulse code modulation (PCM)

The principle of pulse code modulation is that the analogue speech signal is sampled at regular intervals and its amplitude at that point is represented by a binary number which is then transmitted. In order to represent the waveform adequately, but not require the transmission of too much data, there is a compromise reached on the number of levels into which the waveform amplitude is divided.

Figure 12.8 illustrates this sampling process. In this diagram only eight amplitude levels are shown for clarity, each of which therefore requires three binary digits for representation. In practice, a typical sampling rate is 8000 times per second, with a total of 256 amplitude levels, giving 8 bits per sample. This generates therefore 64 000 bits per second for a single PCM channel (a number of channels may share a very high bandwidth medium as described in section 12.5).

Since the continuous analogue signal is being sampled, it can never be reconstructed exactly when received and hence the resulting signal will involve some error which distorts the speech waveform. However, with the above sampling rates the resulting noise is found to be acceptable (remember that on the old analogue telephone network the speech is distorted by restricting the bandwidth of the transmission).

12.5 Multiplexing

Since it costs roughly the same to install and maintain a high bandwidth cable as a low one (for example, the cost of digging and filling a trench), there are schemes for sharing the bandwidth of a high bandwidth channel to enable a number of users to use just one line.

There are essentially two ways of dividing the bandwidth, frequency division multiplexing (FDM) and time division multiplexing (TDM).

12.5.1 Frequency division multiplexing

This technique is mainly used by the analogue PSTN rather than by computer communications equipment. The technique consists of dividing the frequency range (bandwidth) of the high bandwidth transmission line into a number of narrower frequency range channels. Signals from different sources are then modulated onto carrier waves within their allocated frequency range. Thus the fast transmission line is simultaneously carrying a number of slower transmissions.

Because it is important that the frequencies do not overlap, the main disadvantage of FDM is that it does not utilise the full capacity of the line. Also, if a particular slow channel is not in use at any time that particular frequency range is being wasted. However, it is useful for systems where the channel is in continuous use and so is used on the PSTN to carry a number of telephone conversations on the high speed channels used to connect telephone exchanges.

12.5.2 Time division multiplexing

Time division multiplexing is achieved by transmitting blocks of characters down the line. Actually, the blocks may consist of 8-bit characters or eight bits representing something else, such as the 8-bit representation of an amplitude level in pulse code modulation (see section 12.4.1). Each sharer of the line (each subchannel) is allocated a character position in the block so that every block is made up of one character from each subchannel. The whole bandwidth of the channel is used to transmit each character in turn (and hence the block) so that it is transmitted very quickly. Each character position can be considered a time slot, so that if there are n subchannels (users) connected to the multiplexer then the time slots are allocated to each subchannel in turn, so that every nth slot contains a character from the same subchannel. There is still the potential problem of a subchannel not having a character available, particularly if the multiplexer is used with asynchronous terminal devices and the terminal user is thinking or typing slowly. In that case the multiplexer inserts a null character which reduces the use being made of the very high bandwidth. If the multiplexer is being used on a PSTN where the volume of traffic is high then this is not a problem. For use with asynchronous slow devices however, statistical time division multiplexers have been developed which insert characters into the high speed channel as they are ready, along with some address bits to identify the subchannel. Since there is then the need for address decoding to decide where the character has come from this type of multiplexer is often based on a microprocessor.

12.6 Transmission media

Transmission of data in the form of an electrical signal requires the use of some sort of transmission medium, often referred to as a 'line'. Whilst this may take the form of some sort of copper cabling it could equally be a beam of light passing through glass fibre or even radio signals.

12.6.1 Wire cabling

The simplest form of cabling is a two wire piece of cable with each wire insulated from the other. The signal (a voltage or current) is applied to one wire and the ground reference to the other. It may in fact take the form of a pair of wires, or could be a number of pairs moulded into one cable either as a flat ribbon cable or in a single protective sheath known as multicore cable (see Figure 12.9). The major problems with such cables are those of

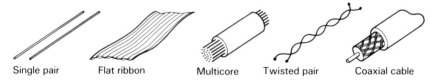

Single pair   Flat ribbon   Multicore   Twisted pair   Coaxial cable

Figure 12.9

electrical interference from nearby electrical signal sources, and of crosstalk—the cross coupling of electrical signals from one wire to another. Hence this type of cable is only used for short distances and with low bit rates.

An improvement on this in terms of immunity to noise is provided by the use of pairs of wires twisted together, known as twisted pair cable. The effect of twisting the wires together reduces the incidence of both crosstalk and extraneous noise. At higher frequencies (for faster transmission), however, an increasing loss of signal power, or attenuation, occurs due to radiation effects, so an improvement on twisted pairs is given by the use of coaxial cable (as used in the receipt of television transmission). Here the signal and ground wires occur as a solid centre conductor concentrically (coaxially) inside a braided outer conductor separated with an insulating material (see Figure 12.9). This overcomes most of the problems associated with two wire and twisted pair cables. The bandwidth of coaxial cable is such that it can carry up to the equivalent of 10 000 voice channels in a telecommunications network, whereas a twisted pair may only carry up to 100 equivalent voice channels (using TDM). With all of this wire cabling, however, the bandwidth of the wire is still limited and hence the transmission speed (or the number of lower speed channels which can be multiplexed) is limited. For improved rates, optical fibre or microwave links must be used.

12.6.2 Optical fibre

Optical fibre cable carries the transmitted information in the form of a fluctuating beam of light in a tube of glass fibre. It provides the high performance capabilities of very high bandwidth, high noise immunity and long distance spacing between signal amplifiers whilst remaining cost competitive. Because of its high noise immunity it is particularly useful for transmission through electrically noisy environments such as industrial plants employing high voltage switching equipment. Typically, the bandwidth of such optical fibre cables will be several thousand MHz giving hundreds of thousands of communication channels, although only a few thousand are possible with the current technology existing at each end of the cable. Optical fibre systems are now in service using bit rates of 140 M bits/sec, providing the equivalent of 1920 communication channels, carried on a single fibre about the same diameter as a human hair.

12.6.3 Microwaves

Microwave transmission carries the transmitted information in the form of radio waves through the atmosphere (or space) and hence requires no cabling. It has a very high bandwidth and therefore can provide many hundreds of high speed links. Because it requires no cable it is very convenient where laying cables would be difficult or expensive. However, because the signals travel through the atmosphere they are affected by weather conditions and buildings and so require line-of-sight transmission between relay towers. For further distances (intercontinental, for example) the microwave beam can be transmitted to a satellite which then retransmits to a ground station many thousands of miles away.

12.7 Error detection

As has been discussed earlier in this chapter, all transmission systems are subject to 'noise' and the effect of this is that bit patterns being transmitted may be corrupted. As a simple illustration consider the following:

Suppose only two messages are to be sent and since both ends of the communication channel know what the messages are they can be coded. For example, send a binary 1 to indicate the occurrence of something and a binary 0 to indicate its absence. This communication system could be handled thus:

(1) Simply transmit 0 or 1. However, if this bit is corrupted (so 0 becomes 1 or 1 becomes 0) the wrong message is sent but neither end knows.
(2) Send 00 for one message and 11 for the other. If 01 or 10 is received the receiver knows that an error has occurred (it has *detected* an error) but does not know what the message should have been. If both bits are corrupted this remains undetected.
(3) Use three bits 000 or 111 to represent the two messages. If 001 or 010 or 100 is received the receiver knows an error has occurred and may assume the message should have been 000 (assuming of course, only one bit has been corrupted). If 110 or 101 or 011 is received then it would assume the message should have been 111.

Hence, technique (2) illustrates a method of detecting single bit errors, whereas (3) shows a method of detecting and correcting single errors. The conclusion reached from this simple example is that if the code is made more complicated the effect of noise can be reduced. In general, recovery from transmission errors may be achieved in one of two ways:

● By including enough redundancy in the message to enable the receiver to reconstruct the message even when it is in error.
● By using an error detection scheme and requesting retransmission when an error is detected.

Because of the great overhead involved in transmission if an error correction scheme is used (particularly if the error rate of the line being used is low), most systems will merely use an error detection scheme and ask for retransmission if an error occurs, and therefore the techniques described now are error detection systems.

12.7.1 Parity checking

The technique of parity checking has already been described in sections 4.2.1 and 5.4.4, and its implementation in this context is exactly the same. Just prior to transmission an additional bit is appended to a character such that the sum of binary 1s in the character is an odd number (odd parity) or an even number (even parity). The receiver will then recompute the parity for the received characters and determine whether any transmission errors have occurred. Note that this simple mechanism will only detect errors that occur in a single bit (or 3 or 5, etc.). This mechanism is commonly used with asynchronous transmission and the generation and checking of the parity bit is often incorporated into the circuitry of the UART or USARTs (see section 10.2.2).

12.7.2 Block parity check

With a block-oriented transmission system (blocks of characters are transmitted), in addition to the parity bit being appended to each individual character, an additional character is generated and transmitted, where each of its bit positions is made up of a parity bit of that bit position down the block of characters (a column or longitudinal parity bit). Figure 12.10 illustrates this with a block of five characters to which has been appended a block check character.

								Parity bit
Character 1	0	1	1	0	1	1	0	1
2	1	0	1	0	1	1	1	0
3	0	1	1	1	0	1	0	1
4	1	1	1	0	0	0	1	1
5	0	0	0	1	0	1	1	0
Parity check character	1	0	1	1	1	1	0	0

Figure 12.10

Assume that character 1 is sent with bits 6 and 7 reversed (or both corrupted). The parity within the character is still odd and so that will not detect the error, but the parity check character would now be incorrect. This, of course, is true only if no 2-bit errors occur in the same column in the same block. Whilst this is unlikely in general, if the line is very error prone or more security is essential then the system will have to use a more effective method, such as that provided by cyclic redundancy check.

12.7.3 Cyclic redundancy check

This method is based on treating a string of bits as the coefficients of a polynomial, i.e. a k bit message is the coefficient list for a polynomial with k terms:

$$x^{k-1} \text{ to } x^0$$

For example 110001 represents the polynomial:

$$x^5 + x^4 + x^0$$

The mathematical theory of polynomial codes and their manipulation is

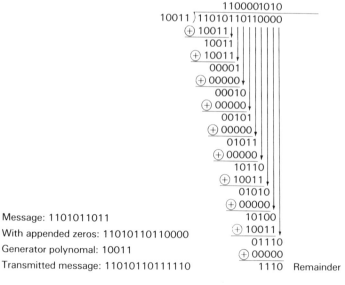

Message: 1101011011

With appended zeros: 11010110110000

Generator polynomal: 10011

Transmitted message: 11010110111110

Figure 12.11

beyond the scope of this book but is used in error checking as follows.

● Both the sender and the receiver must agree on a *generator* polynomial, $G(x)$, in advance.

● The idea is to append a checksum to the end of a message prior to transmission in such a way that the polynomial represented by the checksummed message is exactly divisible by $G(x)$.

● When the receiver gets the transmission it tries dividing it by $G(x)$. If it has been transmitted correctly it should still be exactly divisible by $G(x)$ and hence the remainder will be zero. If the remainder is not zero there has been a transmission error.

- All polynomial arithmetic is performed modulo 2. This means that there are no carries for additions or borrows for subtraction and hence plus and minus are the same as Exclusive OR (see section 2.1).
- To compute the checksum:
  (1) Let r be the degree of the generator polynomial G(x). Append r zero bits to the low order end of the message so that it now contains $m + r$ bits, and corresponds to $x^r M(x)$ (where $M(x)$ is the message polynomial of order M).
  (2) Divide G(x) into the message with the zero bits appended ($x^r M(x)$) using modulo 2 division.
  (3) Subtract the remainder (modulo 2) from $x^r M(x)$. The result is a message to be transmitted. The principle of this is that, in a division problem, if you diminish the dividend by the remainder what is left is divisible by the divisor, e.g. 35/6 leaves a remainder of 5; 35−5=30 which is divisible by 6.

Figure 12.11 illustrates the technique.

Clearly, if this method is to be effective the choice of generator polynomial is crucial. A lot of investigatory work has been done on possible generator polynomials and there are internationally agreed ones which have been found to be particularly effective.

An example is the polynomial defined by the CCITT for use on the switched telephone network:

$$x^{16} + x^{12} + x^5 + x^0$$

This would have a 16-bit remainder appended to the message. It has been found that it will detect:

- all single and double errors
- all errors with an odd number of bits
- all burst errors of length 16 bits or less
- 99.998% of 18-bit and longer bursts.

A burst error is when a string of bits are corrupted due to, for example, a burst of electrical interference, or to electrical noise caused within a switching exchange. Since the arithmetic which is carried out in this technique is done modulo 2 which is equivalent to Exclusive OR, the method is not difficult to implement in hardware and it is commonly found in data communication integrated circuit chips.

12.8 Summary

This chapter has presented the basic physical characteristics of the transmission of information between two points. The material contained here corresponds to the physical layer 1 of the ISO OSI reference model (see Chapter 11).

The most important result is that the rate of transmission of information is limited by the bandwidth and noise of the communication channel.

12.9 Problems

(1) Draw a block diagram of a link between two microcomputers using a telephone network as a transmission medium. Describe how the data is transferred down the link, explaining all the technical terminology commonly used.

(2) Explain the relationship between bandwidth and the rate of information transfer through a transmission medium. Describe two schemes for sharing the bandwidth of a single channel and indicate the advantages of using optical fibres as a transmission medium.

(3) (a) In an attempt to reduce the effect of error on a certain link it has been decided to 'echo back' every character from the sender to the receiver.

How would you detect and correct errors using such an arrangement? Under what circumstances would it be difficult or impossible to detect and correct errors using such arrangements? Outline the algorithms that might be used by the sender and the receiver.

   (b) Assuming:
   (i)   a line speed of 9600 baud;
   (ii) asynchronous transmission with single start and stop bits and eight data bits;
   (iii) a receiver delay of 2 ms between the receipt of a character and the start of the 'echo block';
   (iv) a transmitter delay of 1 ms between the receipt of an echoed back character and the transmission of the next character;
   (v)   instantaneous transmission, i.e. no delay between either end placing a bit on the link and the other end seeing it;
   (vi) there are no errors;
   calculate the effective data transmission speed for such an 'echo-back' arrangement.

   (c) In order to improve the speed of such an arrangement it is proposed to transmit blocks of 100 characters with a 0.3 ms delay between each character and then wait for an 'echo-back' of the block. Estimate the effective data transmission speed of this arrangement and discuss its susceptibility to errors compared with the basic arrangement.

   In each case calculate the effective data transmission speed in the presence of a 0.001 character error probability. You may ignore 'error-on-error' conditions.

(Note: $0.999^{100} = 0.905$)

(4) (a) Describe the factors which limit the channel capacity of a telephone line, illustrating your answer with any relevant equations.

(b) Define the terms 'frequency shift keying' and 'differential phase shift keying', and show how the latter technique may be used to increase channel capacity.

CHAPTER 13

Communication protocols

When two parties wish to exchange information it is clearly necessary to establish some rules by which that exchange can take place sensibly and ensure it is received correctly. With a telephone conversation, for example, the principal requirement is that both parties do not speak at the same time, otherwise the transmissions interfere with each other and neither party knows what the other was saying. Also, before the messages are exchanged, some initial information is exchanged to establish that the correct parties are in fact present and in a position to receive the messages. If the receiving party is writing down the message it could be that the information is being spoken too quickly so that the caller (transmitter) will have to stop for a while and then recontinue. All of these 'rules' are essentially a communications protocol. With human communication the 'rules' are often imprecise with the result that misunderstandings or even gross errors are commonplace. With computer communication it is obviously important to try to establish more precise protocols to reduce the effect of errors.

A communications protocol, then, is a set of rules, adhered to by the communicating parties in order to ensure that the information being exchanged is received correctly. Section 12.7 described some error detection techniques, and clearly the detection of errors is of prime importance in a protocol. However, there are many other potential problems to be solved by the protocol. These will be introduced in section 13.1 and the major ones explored further in some detail in section 13.3.

13.1 Functional tasks of a protocol

There are many different types of protocol, some concerned with a simple exchange of messages between two parties connected by a single link, and others concerned with communicating computers connected in a network. Clearly there will be different requirements of these differing protocols, but all of them will incorporate the following protocol elements in some way or other.

13.1.1 Error control

Section 12.7 described some error detection mechanisms to allow a receiver to detect if any transmission errors have occurred. Clearly, if an error is detected some action is necessary so that the receiver obtains a correct copy of the transmitted information. This action is termed 'error control'. A very simple example is that of a user at a terminal which is connected to the computer using asynchronous transmission. When a character is received by the computer it will echo back the bit stream to be displayed on the screen of the terminal. If that is not in fact the character the user intended, the user can then send a special character (a delete, for example) to inform the computer to ignore the last character received. However, most communication systems require this mechanism to be built in rather than provided by an 'intelligent user'.

13.1.2 Sequence control

Most communication systems do not involve the exchange of just a single message, but a whole series of messages, usually in a particular sequence. In addition, the message may be split into a number of smaller blocks or packets (see section 14.1.3) and these packets need to be in a particular sequence to make up the required message. If a particular message or packet gets 'lost' or is sent on a 'long route' over a network it could be that it will be received out of sequence. Therefore the protocol must include some sort of sequence identification which designates the order in which the message or packets should be processed at the destination, as the order in which they were received might be different.

13.1.3 Flow control

If in a communication system the source generates information faster than the receiver can accept it then some means of controlling the production or flow of the information is necessary. Flow control is the management of the flow of information from the source to the destination. This can be particularly important when two computers are communicating over an intermediary communications network. The network will only buffer a limited amount of information (see section 14.1.2) and so it becomes necessary to control the output of the faster computer to prevent the network becoming congested.

13.1.4 Time-out control

Time-out control is essentially concerned with the action to be taken if the flow of messages stops. Some protocols, for example, require that after sending a message, the sender receives an acknowledgement that the message was received correctly or not before sending the next message. If that acknowledgement never came (e.g. the line had been disconnected or the receiving node had failed), the sender may wait forever and hence be deadlocked. A time-out is a mechanism whereby, on transmission of a message which requires a reply, a clock is started. If no reply is received within a certain period the communication is 'timed-out'. The message could either be retransmitted or the communication abandoned.

Clearly the time-out time must be appropriate for the communication system. In a simple point-to-point system connecting two computers the time-out time could be quite small. On a large communications network, however, if particular nodes become congested the reply might simply be delayed, and if the time-out was too small the sender could be retransmitting unnecessarily, adding to the congestion of the network.

13.1.5 Start-up control

Start-up control is responsible for getting transmission started in a system that has been idle. As with a telephone conversation it is necessary first to establish the physical link and then to exchange control information to verify that the correct parties are at each end.

With a very short link between, say, a terminal and a computer these functions can be achieved by an exchange of signals on control lines, known as a *handshake* (see 13.2).

When the communicating devices are computers the start-up control is achieved by the exchange of a set of control or supervisory messages or packets of information. With a half duplex link this process will also establish which is the master and which is the slave, and there must then be an additional mechanism to reverse their roles during the communication process.

13.2 Levels of protocol

Chapter 11 introduced the concept of structuring the communication software and hardware into a series of levels in order to provide a reliable communication system independent of any particular manufacturer's equipment. This is typified by the ISO reference model discussed in section 11.4. Each of these levels or layers is concerned with a protocol defining a set of rules which are used by that layer in order to communicate with a similar layer in the remote system. Most of this chapter is concerned with protocols in the non-physical layer of the ISO reference model, but it will be useful to examine first some examples of physical level protocols.

13.2.1 Input/output bus handshaking

A typical I/O bus consists of three sets of lines: data lines, address lines and control lines (see section 10.1). Some of the control lines are used to co-ordinate data transfers over the bus and these are the ones discussed here. With asynchronous transmission, the fact that there is no common clock to which activities can be related means that there needs to be an exchange of signals which are referred to as a handshake. There are two timing control lines named 'Ready' and 'Accept'. The handshake protocol proceeds as follows.

The CPU places the address and mode (input or output) information on the appropriate lines. It then indicates that it has done so by a signal on the Ready line. When the addressed device receives the ready signal it performs the required operation and indicates the completion of this by a signal on the Accept line. On receipt of the Accept signal the CPU will remove the address, mode and ready signals and, in the case of an input operation, strobe the data into its input buffer. The timing of these operations for an output transfer are illustrated in Figure 13.1.

Because this is an output operation the CPU places the output data on the data lines at the same time as the address and mode information. The addressed device strobes the data into its buffer when it receives the Ready signal. The delay t_1-t_0 is to allow for both the possibility of skew (see section 10.2.1) and for the devices to perform address decoding. It also sets the Accept signal to indicate its acceptance of the data. On receipt of the Accept signal the CPU drops the Ready signal. After that the CPU will remove the data, address and mode signals from the bus and when the device interface detects the transition of the Ready signal it will then remove the Accept signal. An error detection scheme is provided by the interlocking of the Ready and Accept signals. If the Accept signal is not received within a specified time after setting the Ready signal, the CPU assumes that an error has occurred. This could cause an interrupt to an error routine.

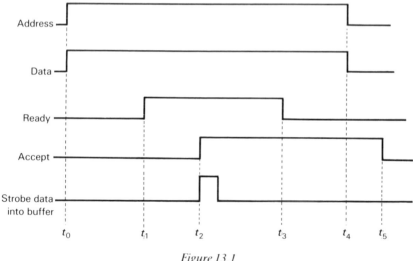

Figure 13.1

13.2.2 RS232-C interface protocol

As was discussed earlier in section 10.2.4 the RS232-C (V24) interface can be used very simply as an interface for connecting a terminal to a computer using just three of its pins. However, it was intended as a standard completely specifying the interface between data communication equipment (DCE—modems) and data terminal equipment (DTE—computers or terminals). It involves a comprehensive protocol to establish connections before data transmission takes place. As an example of this consider the link illustrated in Figure 13.2 and using the same frequency pairs for

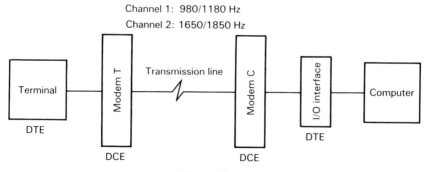

Figure 13.2

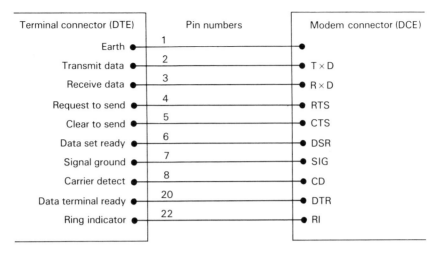

Figure 13.3

transmission as illustrated in Figure 12.6. Figure 13.3 indicates the interface pins required in this example. The sequence of signals required to establish a connection, transmit data and terminate the connection are now described.

● When the computer is ready to accept a call it sets the data terminal ready signal (DTR) to 1.
● Modem C monitors the telephone line and when it detects the ringing current, indicating an incoming'call, it signals the computer by setting the ring indicator (RI) to 1. If DTR is 1 at the time the ringing current is detected, the modem automatically answers the call by going 'off-hook'. Then it sets the data set ready (DSR) signal to 1.
● The computer directs modem C to start transmitting the frequency 1850 Hz by setting request to send (RTS) to 1. Then modem C will set clear to send (CTS) to 1. The detection of the 1850 Hz frequency at modem T causes it to set the carrier detect (CD) signal to 1, and turn on a front panel indicator light.
● The user responds by pressing a button on the front panel of the modem, equivalent to setting request to send (RTS) to 1, causing transmission of a 1180 Hz signal. Modem T then sets CTS and DSR to 1. When modem C detects the 1180 Hz frequency it sets CD to 1.
● A full duplex link is now established between the computer and the terminal. The computer can now transfer data to and from the terminal as if it were a local terminal using the transmit data (TxD) and receive data (RxD) pins.
● When the user finishes, the computer sets the RTS and DTR signals to

0, causing modem C to disconnect from the line. Signals CTS, DSR and CD are also set to 0. When modem T senses the disappearance of the 1850 Hz frequency it sets the CD signal to 0.

● Modem T then removes its 1180 Hz frequency from the line and sets CTS and DSR to 0.

● The computer sets DTR to 1 to prepare for a new call.

13.2.3 X21 interface protocol

Section 12.4 discussed the concept of digital transmission. As public data networks (PDNs)—networks established and operated by a national network administration authority specifically for the transmission of data—began to appear, and since they often required equipment from different manufacturers to be connected to them, it was clear that there needed to be some national and international agreements on interface (and use) standards. Eventually a set of internationally agreed standards were accepted by the CCITT for use with public data networks known as the X-series recommendations. As explained later (in section 13.5.3) there are a series of protocols known as X25 which have been defined to facilitate the interface of data terminal equipment with a packet switched data network. At the lowest layer of X25 is an interface standard defining the physical interface to an all-digital network, called X21. Because there are still many analogue networks in use, a second interface standard, known as X21 (bis), for use with analogue networks has been defined.

13.3 Principles of data link protocols

Section 13.1 introduced the major functional tasks of a protocol. These will now be examined in more detail.

13.3.1 Error control

The various error detection schemes discussed in section 12.7 allow a receiver to detect when an error has occurred but do not provide any mechanism for correcting the error. The combination of an error detection mechanism and some means of correcting such errors is known as error control. There are two basic mechanisms in common use for handling the correction of errors: echo checking and automatic repeat request (ARQ).

Echo checking

Echo checking simply involves the receiver in sending back (echoing) the data it received to the transmitter. If the transmitter receives the same data as it sent, it assumes it was received correctly. Although a simple concept it is very expensive in bandwidth since everything is transmitted twice. The major use of such a system is in an asynchronous terminal-computer time-sharing system. When the user types a character at the terminal that character is not displayed by the terminal. Instead it is transmitted to the computer, which then echoes it back for it to be displayed to the user. If the displayed character is not the one it was intended to send, a special character can be sent to the computer by the user indicating that it should ignore the last character sent.

Clearly this mechanism is simple as far as the computer is concerned. All of the error checking and error correcting is in fact being done by an intelligent user at the terminal. If the correcting mechanism needs to be automatic then another system, such as ARQ, should be used.

Automatic repeat request—ARQ

As has just been discussed, echo checking depends on the intelligent user checking the received character against the transmitted character and retransmitting it if in error. Clearly, this same function could be programmed into the transmitter in computer–computer communication, but the method is still very wasteful of bandwidth since everything is transmitted twice.

Section 12.7 introduced techniques whereby the receiver could detect the occurrence of an error, and an obvious improvement on transmitting everything twice is for the receiver to inform the transmitter when an error has been detected and ask it to retransmit that data again, hence the name—automatic repeat request. Because the block of data in error is being discarded and retransmitted it would seem to work best with as small a block as possible. However, in order to utilise the transmission channel efficiently a high ratio of data to check bits is required, indicating a large block size. Hence, the solution is always a compromise, although the amount of storage available at the receiver can also play a significant part.

There are two ARQ mechanisms in common use: idle RQ and continuous RQ. Figure 13.4 illustrates their principles.

Idle RQ

The transmitter will send a single block of data (including appropriate check bits) and then wait for an acknowledgement (hence the name idle RQ because the transmitter is idle whilst the receiver is checking the data received and sending back an acknowledgement).

The receiver will check the block of data on receipt and, if there are no errors, return a positive acknowledgement (e.g. an ACK character from the ASCII character set—see section 13.5.1). If an error is detected the receiver will ignore that block and return a negative acknowledgement. If the block never arrives (or its format is corrupted so the receiver does not recognise it) no acknowledgement is returned.

If the transmitter receives a positive acknowledgement it will then transmit the next data block. If it receives a negative acknowledgement it will retransmit the same data block. If it receives no acknowledgement within a specified time-out period (see section 13.1.4) it will also retransmit

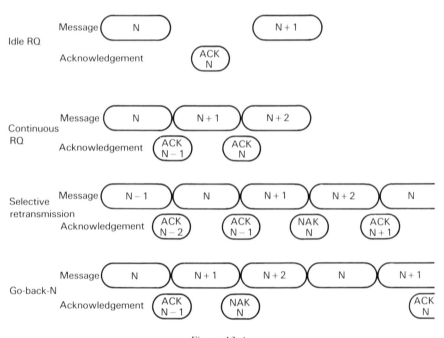

Figure 13.4

the same block. After a specified number of consecutive time-outs for the same block the transmitter will assume the receiver is unable to continue and will abort the communication. There may be occasions when the transmitter will time-out before the receiver has had chance to return an acknowledgement, in which case a duplicate copy of the same data block is transmitted. In order to allow the receiver to detect such duplicate data, a data block will usually contain some sort of sequence number.

The advantage of idle RQ is that both the transmitter and the receiver only need sufficient storage for one block, so storage requirements at each end are minimised. The system is also relatively simple. Its disadvantage is the wasting of bandwidth, since the transmitter is idle for the following time:

Propagation delay for one block + Time for receiver
to process block + Time for receiver to send acknowledgement
+ Time for transmitter to process acknowledgement

If this idle time is small compared with the transmission time of a block, then its efficiency is increased and the simplicity of the system may make it attractive. In many cases, however, its inherent waste of time (idleness) renders it very inefficient.

Continuous RQ

The problem with idle RQ is that of the transmitter wasting time waiting for receipt of an acknowledgement from the receiver. An obvious improvement is for the transmitter to continuously send data blocks without waiting for an acknowledgement. As the receiver receives blocks it will perform appropriate error checks and acknowledge their receipt as in the idle RQ scheme. The essential difference is that by the time the transmitter receives an acknowledgement for a block, it will already have transmitted a number of others. This has two implications for the sender:

● Each block clearly needs a sequence number and each acknowledgement needs to include the sequence number of that block that is being acknowledged, so that if it does need retransmission the transmitter knows which one to send.
● The transmitter needs to store a copy of every block it transmits in case it needs retransmitting. The receipt of a positive acknowledgement (with its sequence number) can be used to remove that particular data block from this storage area.

From the receiver's point of view the occurrence of an error, resulting in the retransmission of a data block, means that blocks are going to be received out of sequence, since the transmitter will have continued to send more blocks up to the time a negative acknowledgement was received.

There are two ways of handling this situation, again illustrated in Figure 13.4. The first of these is *selective retransmission*. With this procedure only the single block that was corrupted is retransmitted. Its operation can be described as follows:

(1) Assume block with sequence number N is corrupted.
(2) The receiver returns an acknowledgement block (an ACK + sequence number) for each correctly received block.
(3) Hence the transmitter receives acknowledgement blocks for blocks N−2, N−1, N+1, N+2. . . .
(4) On receipt of the acknowledgement block for block N+1, the transmitter will detect that this is not the correct sequence and that therefore block N has not been acknowledged. It will therefore retransmit block N before transmitting the next block in the original sequence. (Note that we have already identified the need for the transmitter to store each block sent until it receives an acknowledgement.)

Note that there is no need for a negative acknowledgement. The transmitter knows a block was not received correctly by detecting an out of sequence acknowledgement. It will still be necessary to have a time-out mechanism in case the flow of acknowledgements stops altogether, or in case the transmitter has no further blocks to send at this time so that there will be no acknowledgements coming back.

The receiver does need to store the received blocks for two reasons:

(1) In order to be able to pass a complete message (which may have been broken down into blocks or packets) in the correct sequence, since some blocks may be out of sequence.
(2) If the acknowledgement block gets corrupted and hence not recognised, the effect is that the transmitter will retransmit that block. As the receiver can detect that this is a duplicate (from the sequence number) it will discard it (but it does need to return an acknowledgement to satisfy the transmitter).

The major problem associated with selective retransmission is the receipt of out of sequence blocks. The number of blocks the receiver has to buffer is not known, and if the receiver is doing this for a number of messages the store requirement might be quite large. For this reason, if messages do have to be passed on with their blocks in sequence, the other method, *go–back–N*, is more common.

With this mechanism when the transmitter is informed of a block being received incorrectly, it retransmits it and continues transmission from that point even though it may already have transmitted some of the blocks.

Its operation is as follows:

(1) Assume block with sequence number N is corrupted.
(2) The receiver returns an acknowledgement block for each correctly received block.
(3) On receipt of a block in error, the receiver will return a negative acknowledgement (NACK), plus the sequence number of the last block received correctly (N−1). It will also ignore all blocks it has received since block N−1.
(4) The transmitter, on receipt of a NACK, will retransmit from block N and continue.

Note that if acknowledgement (ACK) blocks are corrupted, the effect is that the transmitter suddenly receives an ACK block out of sequence. Since it is an ACK block, it assumes that those acknowledgements which did not arrive were simply corrupted and so will use this acknowledge block to acknowledge the others also.

In contrast with selective retransmission, this mechanism does not require a lot of buffer store at the receiver but does occasionally cause the retransmission of blocks which had in fact been received correctly. That is, it occasionally wastes bandwidth. However, because of the minimum storage requirements it is a common method where it is essential that the blocks are passed on in sequence.

13.3.2 Sequence control

As has just been discussed blocks being transmitted need sequence numbers in order to ensure both the correct sequence of received blocks and, in some cases, detect corrupted or 'lost' blocks. It has been assumed that the sequence numbers are integers starting at, say, 0. However, if a large number of messages, consisting of a large number of blocks is to be transmitted these sequence numbers could potentially get very large and hence require a large number of bits in the blocks being transmitted. Therefore, in order to limit the size of such sequence numbers they could be computed (incremented) using modulo n arithmetic, so that they cycle round a limited number of integers. For example, HDLC and X25 both use modulo 8 arithmetic for incrementing the sequence number so that they cycle round the digits 0 to 7. However, it is important to make sure that a new block is not given the same sequence number as a previous block which has not been acknowledged. Since this also implies a limit on the storage requirement for blocks (it means the receiver cannot store more than eight blocks), this restriction is handled by an appropriate flow control mechanism (see section 13.3.3).

In addition to the sequence number sent with a block or an acknow-ledgement, both the transmitter and receiver need to maintain an integer variable which, in the case of the transmitter is the sequence number of the next block to be transmitted, and in the case of the receiver is the sequence number of the next block it should receive.

In order to introduce the principles simply, all of the previous discussion about ARQ mechanisms assumed that blocks flow in one direction only, and that therefore the acknowledgements flow in the reverse direction. Typically, however, messages are being transmitted in both directions across a link, and hence both ends are both receivers and transmitters. Therefore, each end of a link needs to maintain both of these sequence number variables, one for receiving and one for transmitting.

Also, if messages are being transmitted in both directions, then rather than sending a special acknowledge block, the appropriate acknowledge sequence number could be included in a block being transmitted in that direction. In this case, a block contains two sequence numbers. One is that of the block of data being transmitted and one being that of a previously transmitted block that is being acknowledged. This technique is known as *piggy-backing* and is intended to improve the efficiency of use of the link. The protocol HDLC uses such a technique (see section 13.5.2).

13.3.3 Flow control

When two parties are communicating, the receiver clearly has to do something with the data blocks it is receiving. There may be occasions when it has not completed its tasks before the next data block arrives. For example, a printer receiving records into its print buffer will not be able to print the records as fast as they are arriving. Once its buffer is full it cannot accept any more. With the selective retransmission scheme described in section 13.3.1 the receiver has a fixed number of blocks which might become full before the out of sequence block is received. In both these cases the receiver will have to inform the transmitter that it cannot cope with more blocks and that it should therefore temporarily stop sending them. There are two common ways this can be achieved.

X-on/X-off

Consider the example of a printer, printing records sent to it by a computer. Clearly the computer may be able to supply records faster than the printer can print them even if the printer has a print buffer capable of storing a number of records. When the print buffer becomes full the printer will return a special character, X-off, to the computer indicating that the computer should stop transmission of records. When the buffer is emptied, the printer will then return another special character, X-on, indicating that the computer should recommence sending records.

The window mechanism

With the ARQ mechanisms described, there was a requirement for the receiver to store the received data blocks in order to allow the forwarding of the correct sequence of blocks if a block has been transmitted in error. Assuming that there is a fixed amount of buffer storage at the receiver for this purpose this imposes a limit on the number of blocks the transmitter can transmit without receiving an acknowledgement for any of them. This limit is also associated with the range of sequence numbers allowed (see

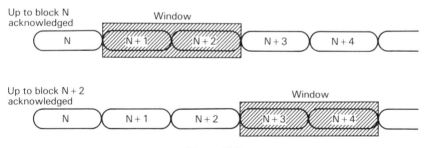

Figure 13.5

section 13.3.2). The name given to this group of blocks is a *window* and the number of blocks is the *window size*. Figure 13.5 represents a window and how the window progresses along the blocks being transmitted as blocks are acknowledged.

The mechanism is implemented as follows:

(1) The transmitter and receiver must agree on the window size for the link.
(2) As the transmitter sends blocks it monitors the number of blocks it is storing in case they need retransmitting. (Remember that acknowledged blocks are removed from this store.)
(3) When the number of blocks builds up to the window size the transmitter will cease to transmit blocks.
(4) As acknowledgements are received and the blocks stored are reduced the transmitter can recommence transmission.

Note that if the window size is 1, the mechanism then becomes identical to the idle RQ method, since each block needs to be acknowledged before the next one is sent.

As mentioned above the window size is associated with the range of sequence numbers allowed.

If the protocol uses the go–back–N mechanism and a window size of W then the number of identifiers should be W+1. To confirm this, imagine a link with a window size of 4. The transmitter sends blocks 0, 1, 2, 3. They are received correctly and the receiver returns acknowledgements for all these four. If the range of sequence numbers allowed was also 4 then the next sequence number the receiver is expecting is 0 (using modulo 4 arithmetic). Unfortunately, all the four acknowledgements are 'lost' (corrupted) and so on the occurrence of the time-out the transmitter retransmits the original block 0. The receiver, on receipt of block 0 has no way of distinguishing between this repeated block 0 and the next block it was expecting (with sequence number 0). If, however, the range of sequence numbers was 5 (one more than the window size) it would be expecting sequence number 4 and so would know that block 0 was a repeat of the previous block 0.

If the protocol uses the selective retransmission mechanism and a window size of W then the range of identifiers should be 2W. This can be seen by a similar situation to the last example. Suppose the window size is 4 and all four blocks are sent but their acknowledgements are corrupted. All four blocks will then be retransmitted but the only way the receiver has of distinguishing these from the next four in sequence is if the next four in sequence had a completely different set of sequence numbers. Hence the sequence numbers must be 0, 1, 2, 3, 4, 5, 6, 7.

13.4 Protocol types

As has been discussed, data link protocols must be capable of detecting errors in strings of bits the contents of which, or meaning of, is unknown. No method can be devised which can detect errors in a continuous arbitrary bit stream. In order to be able to detect errors the data is broken up into blocks and, typically, the block of data is transmitted together with some error control character(s) (for example, a CRC checksum). Another common term for such data blocks is a *frame*.

A number of schemes have been devised for separating data into frames ready for transmission. The aim of all of them is to preserve the transparency of user data. This means that if special characters or bit patterns are used to convey protocol meaning, some other mechanism is incorporated to allow that same bit pattern to be transmitted as part of the user data without causing confusion.

Three types of protocol, that is three types of frame format, are now described and illustrated in Figure 13.6.

13.4.1 Character oriented

This type of frame format assumes that the data being sent is a sequence of characters (groups of 8 bits) and it uses special characters to indicate the start of frame, the end of frame and other protocol information. Transparency is achieved as follows: the start of frame sequence is the pair of characters DLE and STX (see ASCII character set), the end of frame is indicated by DLE ETX. To avoid the possible occurrence of this bit pattern in the user data the transmitter will insert another DLE character after every occurrence of DLE in the user data. The receiver will recognise the end of frame by the occurrence of DLE ETX. Every other occurrence of a DLE (after the start of the frame) will be followed by another DLE which the receiver will remove.

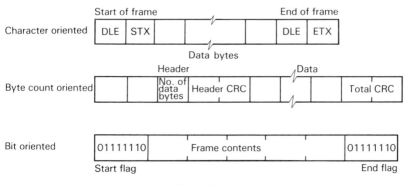

Figure 13.6

13.4.2 Byte count oriented

This frame format precedes the data bytes with a header containing, amongst other information, a count of how many characters (bytes) are in the data field of the frame. The receiver then merely has to count the number of data bytes, continually comparing the count with this header field in order to determine the end of the frame. Because the header information has to be used correctly before the end of the frame is found, the header is usually terminated by its own CRC checksum which is validated by the receiver before beginning to read the rest of the frame.

13.4.3 Bit oriented (bit stuffing)

With a bit oriented frame format the data field does not have to be an integral number of bytes (although it often is). The start and end of the frame are delineated by a special eight bit flag, consisting of the following bit pattern:

$$0\ 1\ 1\ 1\ 1\ 1\ 1\ 0$$

Transparency (making sure this bit pattern cannot occur in the data) is achieved by the transmitter inserting a zero bit after any contiguous group of five one bits (apart from the final flag which it transmits after all the data bits have been transmitted). The receiver will remove any zero occurring after five contiguous ones. This technique is known as bit stuffing.

13.5 Examples of protocols

Some common examples of real protocols will now be described. The first example (BSC) is one in common use on terminal networks. If the terminal system transfers single characters at a time, then the protocol could consist of an echo checking mechanism for error control, and the use of X-on/X-off for flow control. If, however, it transfers blocks of characters then a more sophisticated protocol is required.

The other two examples (HDLC and X25) are both commonly used protocols within computer networks although HDLC is sometimes used with terminal based networks.

13.5.1 Binary synchronous communication (BSC)

This is a character oriented protocol using special characters to control the protocol functions. The special characters used are as follows (see the ASCII character set for their codes):

SOH   The start of the header (optional)
STX   The start of the text (data)
ETB   The end of a data block (but there are more blocks before the
       message is complete)
ETX   The end of the message started with an STX
ACK   A positive acknowledgement
NAK   A negative acknowledgement
DLE   Used to achieve data transparency
ENQ   Used in connection with setting up the link (bidding for a line)
EOT   End of transmission—closes down the link

Possible message formats are shown in Figure 13.7. A message may be
preceded by a header. This is optional, but if a sequence number is needed
for error control and/or the address of the destination of this message is
required, these are contained in the header.

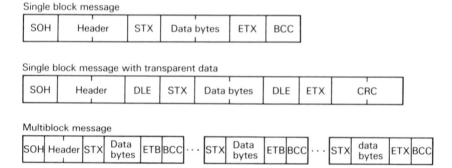

Figure 13.7

A single frame message is preceded by STX and terminated by ETX,
followed by a block check character (BCC) (a block parity check—see
section 12.7.2). A longer message composed of a number of blocks or
frames would have each intermediate block preceded by STX and terminated by ETB (followed by a BCC) with the last block terminated by ETX.
As discussed in 13.4.1, if the data consists of transparent 8-bit binary
values rather than characters from the ASCII character set, then the
control characters are all preceded by a DLE character. Also, since a
normal parity check cannot be carried out on each character, the BCC is
often replaced by a 16-bit CRC check.
The protocol operates as follows. The controlling end of the link (in a
terminal-based system this would typically be the computer) would send an
ENQ character and an indicator that it wishes to send data to the receiving
end. If the receiver is able to receive the data it will respond with an ACK
frame, whereupon the transmitter will send the appropriate data frame(s).

On successful receipt of the message the receiver will send back an ACK frame and the transmitter will return an EOT character to signal the end of the transmission.

The other mode of operation is the computer polling a terminal to see if the terminal has any data to send. In this case the computer will transmit an ENQ and a polling indicator. The terminal will then respond by transmitting its message frame(s) to the computer. The computer will then return an ACK to the terminal which will respond with EOT. If, in fact, a message is made up of a series of frames (rather than just one) an ACK or NAK is returned after each frame. Thus the system is an example of an idle RQ mechanism.

13.5.2 High level data link control—HDLC

HDLC is a protocol which has been defined by the International Standards Organisation (ISO) for use on both point-to-point and multi-point data links. Historically it was developed for links having one master station on the link controlling one slave or a number of slaves. The master station is responsible for initiating all data transfers and for initialising and controlling the link. The master station in HDLC is called a *primary* and the slave a *secondary*. Figure 13.8 shows examples of such links. In a distributed network each node is of equal status to all other nodes and hence a balanced configuration with a combined station at each end of the link is possible. The combined station has the capabilities of both primary and secondary stations.

HDLC uses bit stuffing techniques for delimiting frames (see section 13.4.3). Many types of frames can be sent and received by stations and

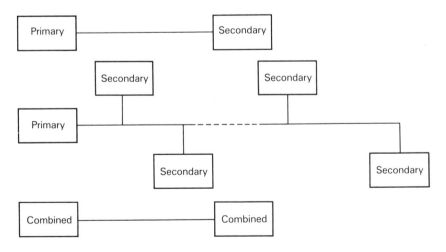

Figure 13.8

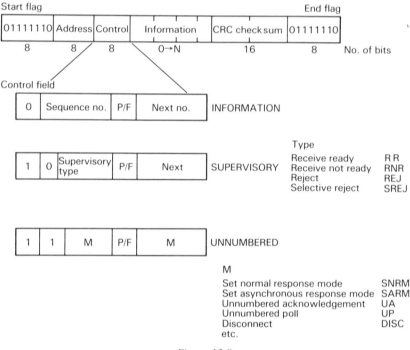

Start flag

End flag

01111110	Address	Control	Information	CRC check sum	01111110	
8	8	8	0→N	16	8	No. of bits

Control field

0	Sequence no.	P/F	Next no.	INFORMATION

1	0	Supervisory type	P/F	Next	SUPERVISORY

Type
Receive ready   RR
Receive not ready   RNR
Reject   REJ
Selective reject   SREJ

1	1	M	P/F	M	UNNUMBERED

M
Set normal response mode   SNRM
Set asynchronous response mode   SARM
Unnumbered acknowledgement   UA
Unnumbered poll   UP
Disconnect   DISC
etc.

Figure 13.9

these are divided into *commands* and *responses*. Commands are sent by primary stations to secondary stations and responses are replies to commands returned by a secondary to a primary station. Figure 13.9 illustrates the frame format and the control byte layout for the three kinds of frame. The address field is used for addressing on multi-point lines (links connecting more than two devices). The control field is different for each of the three kinds of frame.

In *information* frames (the actual data being sent) the sequence and next fields contain the sequence number of the current frame and of the next frame expected respectively. In other words the *next* field is an acknowledge being piggy-backed on a data frame (see section 13.3.2). Note also that the sequence number is three bits long, indicating that HDLC uses modulo 8 sequence numbers. The window size depends on whether go-back-N or selective retransmission is being used (it will support either depending on the supervisory frame). The checksum is a 16-bit CRC for the complete frame contents enclosed between the two flag delimiters. It uses the CCITT polynomial defined in section 12.7.3.

Supervisory frames are used for error and flow control purposes. When no reverse traffic is present on which to piggy-back acknowledgements a receive ready (RR) supervisory frame is used (as an acknowledgement).

The RNR frame is used to indicate that the transmitter should not send any more frames for the time being (flow control). Whether the receiver has just accepted the last one or not will depend on the sequence number returned with the RNR. REJ and SREJ are used as negative acknowledgements with Go-back-N and selective retransmission error control mechanisms respectively.

The *unnumbered* frames (so called because they do not contain any sequence numbers) are used for such functions as link setup and disconnection.

The P/F bit in the control field is known as the *poll/final* bit. If a frame is sent by a primary station (a command frame) and the P/F bit is set to 1 it is called the *poll* bit and indicates that the receiver must acknowledge this frame at its earliest opportunity. The secondary station will respond by returning an appropriate response frame with the *final* bit (the P/F bit) set to 1.

As was indicated the origins of HDLC are with protocols for multi-point configurations. Thus, what is referred to as the *normal response mode* (NRM) of operation is that the secondary only transmits in response to a poll from the primary. A secondary gets permission to transmit frames when it receives a command from its primary with the poll bit set. It will then transmit a series of frames and indicate completion of this by setting the final bit to 1 in the last frame. The secondary must wait for another poll before it can transmit again. If the secondary has no data to transmit it returns an acknowledgement (RR) with the final bit set to 1.

There also exists an *asynchronous response mode* (ARM). In this mode a secondary can transmit at will without having to wait for a poll.

As an example of the operation of HDLC consider a multi-point link operating using NRM and with a Go-back-N mechanism for error control. A logical connection between the two communicating parties needs to be set up first, then the data transferred and finally the link closed down. It would operate as follows.

(1) The primary station sends an SNRM frame with the poll bit set to 1 and an appropriate secondary address in the address field.

(2) The secondary station will respond with a UA frame (an unnumbered acknowledgement) with the final bit set and its own address in the address field.

(3) This exchange also causes both the primary and the secondary station to initialise to zero their sequence variables.

(4) The primary station then sends an UP frame (unnumbered poll) with the poll bit set to 1.

(5) If the secondary has no data to transmit, it returns an RNR frame with the F-bit set.

(6) If it has data waiting, it transmits the data as a sequence of information

frames with the F-bit set to 1 in the last frame of the sequence.

(7) Each frame is eventually acknowledged and the sequence number can be used for detection of errors, with subsequent Go-back-N request (REJ) as described in sections 13.3.1 and 13.3.2.

(8) When the primary receives the last frame (with F set to 1) the link is cleared by the primary sending a disconnect frame (DISC) and the secondary acknowledging that with a UA.

Whilst the above mechanism may be satisfactory for a terminal network, in a network of communicating computers each station has equal status and needs to act in combined mode. This is known in HDLC as *asynchronous balanced mode* (ABM). In this case information frames can be flowing in both directions and so the acknowledgement information can be piggy-backed onto information frames which are going in the opposite direction.

13.5.3 X25

Because of the growth in public data networks (particularly PSDNs—packet switched data networks) there has been international agreement on a network access protocol to interface to a PSDN, and this is known as X25. X25 is in fact a set of three protocols each of which builds on the lower level protocol and they are directly comparable with the first three layers of the ISO OSI reference model (see Chapter 11).

In order to understand the principles of X25 it is necessary to have understood the concepts of packet switching (Chapter 14) and of layered protocols (Chapter 11). Figure 13.10 illustrates the scope of the three layers of X25 when connecting a device to a PSDN via some local data communication equipment.

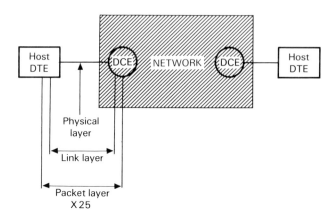

Figure 13.10

The *physical* layer used is X21 (or X21(bis) if the network is not an all digital network). Section 13.2.3 has already discussed this.

The *data link* layer used is based on HDLC using the asynchronous balanced mode of operation since information can flow in either direction at any time. The protocol is known as LAPB (link access protocol B) and varies from the original HDLC only in the way that the link is set up. LAPB allows both ends of the link to be initialised as both primary and secondary with only one exchange of SABM and UA frames. An HDLC data frame carries a single packet across the X25 interface.

The *packet* layer (corresponding to the network layer in the OSI model) is virtual circuit oriented. To set up a virtual circuit, a host DTE sends a CALL REQUEST packet into the network. (Some packet structures are illustrated in Figure 13.11). The remote host can then either accept or reject the incoming call. If it accepts it the virtual circuit is set up, otherwise it is cleared.

The first four bits of the call request packet are 0001. The next twelve bits are the virtual circuit number chosen by the originating host. The third byte is the type code of CALL REQUEST. The next byte defines the length of both the calling DTE and called DTE's addresses, the addresses themselves following in up to the next thirty bytes. The facilities field (of variable length and hence the need for the facilities length field) is used for items such as 'reverse charging'. Finally, the user data field can be used in any way the user chooses.

When the CALL REQUEST packet arrives at the destination, that station accepts the call by returning a CALL ACCEPTED packet or rejects the call by returning a CLEAR REQUEST packet. Note that the sender sends packets to the network and the network then sends the packet to the destination station with a different name but the same bit pattern.

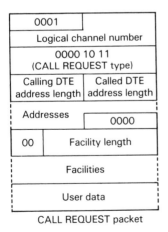

CALL REQUEST packet

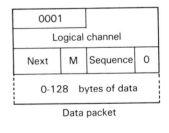

Data packet

Figure 13.11

Calling host   Called host

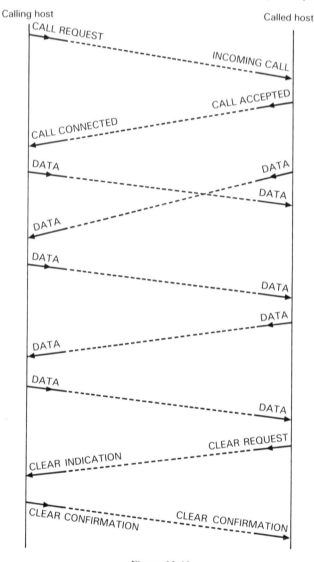

Figure 13.12

For example the CALL REQUEST and INCOMING CALL packets are the same bit patterns. Figure 13.12 illustrates the complete process of call establishment, data and call clear phases of a communication, and Table 13.1 lists the various packet types and their usage.

An ordinary data packet is as shown in Figure 13.11. The preferred maximum data field length in X25 is 128 bytes, although any number which is a power of 2 between 16 and 1024 can be chosen to define the maximum data field length. The sequence and next fields are analogous to those in

Table 13.1

Packet type		Usage
Host→ network	*Network→ host*	
Call request	Incoming call	
Call accepted	Call confirmation	Call set up and
Clear request	Clear indication	clearing
DTE clear confirm	DCE clear confirm	
DTE data	DCE data	
DTE interrupt	DCE interrupt	Data transfer
DTE interrupt	DCE interrupt	
confirm	confirm	
DTE RR	DCE RR	
DTE RNR	DCE RNR	Flow control
DTE REJ		
Reset request	Reset indication	
DTE reset confirm	DCE reset confirm	Reset and restart
Restart request	Restart indication	
DTE restart confirm	DCE restart confirm	

HDLC. This allows both the DCE and the DTE to detect the loss of data packets as well as to control the flow of data packets across the DTE/DCE interface. Acknowledgements are piggy-backed on data frames sent in the other direction (the next field) although if there is no data flow in this reverse direction in which to carry this information, it can transmit a RECEIVE READY (RR) packet. If temporarily the receiver cannot accept data packets on a logical channel it can transmit a RECEIVE NOT READY (RNR) packet, which can then be cleared by a RR packet. The M bit in the packet can be used to indicate that more data follows in the next packet, thus partitioning the packet stream into multi-packet units.

The maximum number of sequentially numbered data packets that a DTE is authorised to transmit and have outstanding (that is, unacknowledged) at any given time may never exceed the window size. The value (between 1 and 7) of the window size is a constant, agreed with the network authority at subscription time.

The data phase of the virtual call can be terminated (the link closed down) by either end sending a CLEAR REQUEST. That end will then receive a CLEAR CONFIRMATION packet, terminating the exchange. This is illustrated in Figure 13.12.

Because layers 2 and 3 in X25 have so much overlap, it must be remembered that the layer 2 sequence numbers and acknowledgements refer to the traffic between a host and the network for all the virtual circuits combined. If a host sends seven packets, each one for a different virtual circuit, the host must stop sending until an acknowledgement comes back. The layer 2 protocol is required to prevent the host from flooding the network. In contrast, with layer 3 the sequence numbers are per virtual circuit and therefore flow-control each connection separately.

There are additionally some other control packets: RESET and RESET CONFIRMATION are used to reset a virtual circuit whereas RESTART and RESTART CONFIRMATION are used to reset all virtual circuits after a host or network crash. Provision is also made for a host DTE to send a single high priority data packet, independent of the normal flow control. This sort of packet is an INTERRUPT packet and is acknowledged by an INTERRUPT CONFIRMATION packet.

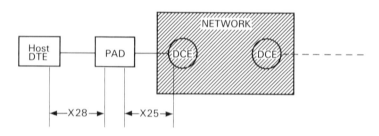

Figure 13.13

Finally, all this assumes that the host DTE is a device with sufficient intelligence to carry out all these protocol functions. To enable a more limited DTE (for example, a simple asynchronous character mode terminal such as a VDU) to interface to an X25 network an additional piece of hardware is required, situated between the user DTE and the network, which provides the necessary assembly of character strings from the terminal into packets and vice versa. This piece of hardware is known as a packet assembler–disassembler (PAD). The protocol then used between the terminal (DTE) and the PAD is defined by standard X28. Such a link is illustrated in Figure 13.13.

13.6 Summary

This chapter has introduced the need for protocols, their various functional tasks and the concepts of protocol levels. It has then looked in some detail at major protocol functions. A number of examples of real protocols have been studied, although it must be recognised that since protocols are becoming very complex only the major features of the examples have been introduced.

Nowadays there are several large scale integrated chips available which perform all the framing functions of link level protocols including insertion and removal of characters or bits for transparency and calculation of the CRC. In packet switched networks where the information is transported in discrete units, the use of these link level protocols does not require any additional processing to divide the data into blocks for transmission.

13.7 Problems

(1) Explain the difference between data terminating equipment (DTE) and data communications equipment (DCE).

A DTE computer is to be connected to a public switched telephone network via an RS232-C modem which provides the following inter-face circuits: GND, TXD, RXD, DSR, DTR, CD, RI.

Explain the functions of the circuits indicating whether they are from the DCE to the DTE or from the DTE to the DCE. Outline the software you would write to enable the computer to detect an incoming call and respond suitably.

How would you detect and respond to call termination by
(a) the remote party hanging up?
(b) the computer terminating the call?

What problems might arise if the incoming call were a wrong number? How would your software cope?

(2) (a) Indicate why protocols are necessary in data communications and name the main functions a protocol must embody, giving a brief definition of each.

(b) Explain why transparency may be a problem within a protocol and give two examples of how this problem may be overcome.

(3) Describe the frame format specified in the binary synchronous pro-tocol. What is the function and form of the BCC and CRC fields?

Describe the significance of flow control for a link level protocol. What procedures are available within the binary synchronous protocol to enable the receiver to indicate that it is congested and to enable recovery from transmission errors? What problems are avoided by the use of a bit-oriented protocol?

(4) In the HDLC (X25 level 2) communications protocol explain:
(a) the difference between the normal response mode (NRM), asyn-chronous response mode (ARM) and asynchronous balanced mode (ABM) of operation. When might they be used?

(b) how software would distinguish between the I, S and U classes of frame;

(c) how data transparency is achieved;

(d) how the SREJ mechanism may be used to improve the efficiency of flow control error recovery.

(5) Using available microcomputers which have a serial I/O port and a suitable programming language (e.g. assembler or Pascal) develop the software for a file transfer utility to transfer files from one machine to another over the serial link. Incorporate a robust protocol which exhibits all the major features described in this chapter. Investigate methods of introducing burst errors into the transmission in order that its robustness can be demonstrated.

CHAPTER 14

Network types

The previous two chapters have looked in some detail at the lowest two levels of the ISO reference model. The physical aspects of the transmission of data were explored in Chapter 12 and the concepts and techniques of the data link layer protocols were discussed in Chapter 13. The internationally agreed standard set of protocols known as X25 have been introduced and were seen to be, in fact, three protocols. The third level protocol of X25 is known as the *packet* layer and corresponds to the ISO network layer. However, the principles of packet networks (and other types) has not yet been introduced.

Chapter 11 also introduced the two types of communication channel, point-to-point and broadcast. This chapter will look at some of the remaining issues of the network layer of point-to-point networks and will then study further different types of broadcast networks, some of which have had significant impacts as local area networks.

14.1 Point-to-point networks

Section 11.3.1 discussed a number of possible topologies for point-to-point networks (star, fully connected, irregular, hierarchical, loop). Particularly with wide area networks, the use of an irregular topology is most common since it has the considerable advantages of ease and cheapness of adding a new computer to the network. It may also be fairly resilient to a node or communication path failure, depending on the precise topology. However, because there is not a direct path between every pair of computers that may wish to communicate, some form of switching within the network is necessary. This raises a number of issues such as what type of switching, how is the route worked out and what about congestion? These issues will now be examined.

There are essentially three forms of switching which can be used:

- circuit switching
- message switching
- packet switching

14.1.1 Circuit switching

When you (or your computer if its modem has auto dial facilities) use the telephone network by dialling the number of another subscriber there is usually a delay before the ringing tone is heard. This delay might be quite considerable if the call is over a long distance, international for example. The reason for this is that the intervening telephone network is searching for a continuous physical path between the two local exchanges. Although the concept of a 'physically continuous' circuit conjures up an image of a continuous copper path, it may be that part of that path is one channel on a multi-channel fibre optic cable or even a microwave link. However, there does exist a physical communication channel from the calling to the called subscriber which remains in force for the whole duration of the call. The principle of forming a continuous circuit by appropriate switching at the intermediate switching centres is called *circuit switching*.

This is the principle on which public switched telephone networks (PSTN) operate and which has often in the past been used for the transmission of data from one computer to another. However, when used for the transmission of data there are a number of disadvantages.

(1) The time required to set up the call (for all the switching to be completed) is relatively long (measured in seconds). However, as more and more digital exchanges (computerised switching) are introduced and digital transmission between exchanges increases, the set-up time will be significantly reduced (measured in milliseconds).
(2) The two communicating computers have to communicate at exactly the same speed (data rate).
(3) There is no error or flow control provided by the network on the transmitted data. Such control has to be provided by the two users.
(4) The line utilisation is often low. With most computer communications the network traffic often consists of short bursts of data separated by relatively long periods of inactivity during which time the dedicated circuit is not being used. A possible alternative might be to place a separate call for each burst of data, but this is likely to be inefficient due to the relatively long call set-up time.

14.1.2 Message switching

Message switching is a technique which overcomes most of the disadvantages of circuit switching when a network is being used to carry data. Instead of switching the circuit the circuits are permanently set up and the message is switched around the network. That is, for a network with an irregular topology the message is passed from node to node until it reaches its destination.

In particular, it operates as follows.

● The message incorporates some sort of header which includes the address of the remote destination for which the message is intended. Clearly some sort of routing algorithm is necessary.

● The message is transferred from node to node as a whole, i.e. all of the message is received at a node and stored before being sent on to the next node on its route. Error checks will be performed at each node to ensure the accurate receipt of the message. This mechanism is known as *store and forward*.

This technique overcomes the disadvantages of circuit switching in the following ways.

(1) There is no call set up delay, although there will be delays as the message may go via a circuitous route rather than by a direct connection and the various node to node protocols will introduce delays.

(2) The two user computers do not have to communicate at the same speed because they do not communicate directly. A message may be received at a particular node at a different speed to that which it is then subsequently transmitted on to the next node. In this case the network is effectively acting as a buffer. In fact, the message may be sent by the sender when it is ready, even if the receiver is not ready, since the network will store the message ready for delivery when the receiver is ready.

The disadvantage of this technique lies in the fact that the message is treated as a whole unit. For some applications the message may be quite short, such as a database query. In other applications the message may be very long, such as a complete file or even a whole database. Because of this a long message being transmitted may monopolise a particular network link, preventing other (perhaps more urgent) messages being transmitted over that particular link. Since the store and forward concept requires *all* of the message to be stored at an intermediate node before being forwarded, it is possible for an intermediate node to have insufficient memory to store all of the message, or at least prevent this node handling other messages till this one is sent.

14.1.3 Packet switching

Because the transmission of long messages requires a large amount of buffer storage and a long transmission time leading to slower response times for other users, it would seem that the answer would be to insist on only very short messages. However, these short messages may lead to inefficient operation because of the overheads associated with such things as addressing, routing and acknowledgements. Thus there must be some optimal length that provides an acceptable compromise between efficiency and response time.

Clearly, however, it is not convenient to force a user to limit all the messages to this optimal length and therefore organising this must be a function of the network. Variable length messages will be supplied by an application for transmission across the network to a remote destination. The source node will break that message down into a number of smaller messages each corresponding to that optimal length. The name of this smaller transmission unit is a *packet*. The packets can then be sent across the network separately, and when they have all reached the destination reassembled into the original message. Since these packets are being switched across the network the technique is known as *packet switching*.

Clearly the storage requirement and management at each intermediate node is easier than for message switching because of the small maximum packet size. Also, the small packets may be interleaved on the network links, thus reducing delays as seen by the host computers.

Because of these advantages most computer networks are packet switching networks (there are, however, a few circuit switched networks). The basis of the set of protocols known as X25 is that of packet switching. Indeed, the level three protocol in X25 is known as the packet layer (see section 13.5.3). Data networks based on packet switching are known as packet switched data networks (PSDNs).

14.1.4 Datagrams and virtual circuits

Chapter 11 (section 11.2) introduced the principle of a data communication network to which host computers can be attached. The purpose of such a data communications network is to provide a means of carrying data from one host computer to another. All the host computers have to do is become connected to the nearest node on the network and supply information to the network using the appropriate protocol (probably X25—see Figure 11.2). As explained in section 14.1.3 most communication networks are packet switched data networks (PSDNs) and with a PSDN two major types of service are offered: datagram and virtual circuits.

With a datagram service, each packet is treated as a separate unit.

Therefore the packet must include a destination address to ensure it is delivered to the correct destination. Because the packets are treated separately, each packet may travel across the network by a different route and hence they may arrive in a different order to that in which they were sent. Of course, they may not arrive at all! Any error and flow control necessary to detect lost or duplicate packets must be implemented by the users in the host machine (within layer 4—the transport protocol). Clearly this service is advantageous to the network nodes since routing can be flexible and sequencing and flow control is not necessary, but it places more requirements on the user of the network. It is called a datagram service since it bears some resemblance to the service offered by the Post Office. You can send a series of letters but they may arrive in a different order (or not at all!).

If it is accepted that the network itself should provide a higher level of service to the users, then a virtual circuit service can be used. In this case the network service appears to the user very much like that provided by a telephone network. After establishing a logical connection between two users of the network that logical connection remains open till the users disconnect it. Packets are routed across the network via the same route established when the virtual circuit was established. Because they go via the same route they will be delivered in the same sequence that they are sent and hence the network itself will provide end-to-end flow control. This logical connection, or virtual circuit, is identified by a virtual circuit number field contained within each packet transmitted. This was described in section 13.5.3, and illustrated in Figure 13.11. Note that this connection is only 'logical'. Actual physical transmission links are only allocated while a packet is being transmitted, hence the name *virtual* circuit.

This sort of service provided by a network is of very high quality. Because there are error and flow control procedures implemented at level 2 for every link, and error and flow control procedures at level 3 from end-to-end, the chance of a message, consisting of a number of packets, being delivered error-free is very high.

14.1.5 Simple routing techniques

Most wide area, point-to-point networks are of the irregular topology type. The major characteristic of this topology is, of course, that there is not a direct path between every pair of computers that may wish to communicate. Because of this, the messages, or more commonly the packets, are switched around the network. Hence there is a need for routing decisions to be made, to decide on the precise route the packet will take.

Consider the network illustrated in Figure 14.1. Suppose Host 1 wishes to communicate with Host 2. Packets could take the following routes:

1	2	3			
1	2	8	4		
1	7	4			
1	7	8	3		
6	5	4			
6	5	8	3		
6	5	7	2	3	
6	5	8	2	7	4

Some of these routes may appear preferable to others. For example, some involve only three links, whereas others involve four, five or six links. Of course, for a wide area network some of the links may be a very great distance so that a route involving four links may turn out to be shorter in distance than one involving three links. The routing decision may involve the fact that of two alternative links, the next node on one of the links is very busy, so it may be quicker to send the packet down the other link.

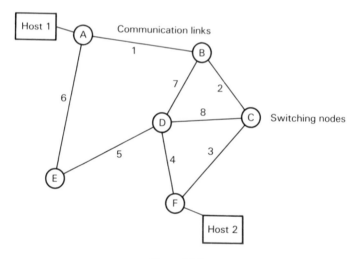

Figure 14.1

Whatever method is chosen, it is important that the following situations do not arise:

Looping —where, for example, the message is sent along
        1 7 8 2 7 8 2 7 8 2 . . .

Oscillating—e.g. 1 7 7 7 7 . . .,
        that is the message continually bounces back and forth
        between two nodes.

Clearly, the routing algorithm used could have a significant effect on the performance of the network. Some alternative strategies will now be examined.

Fixed routing

Each node in the network will contain a *routing table* or route directory. This contains one entry for each node in the network, including itself, and that entry indicates which link a packet should be transmitted on if the packet is for that ultimate node address. Table 14.1 illustrates such a table for node D of the network shown in Figure 14.1. Notice that there is, in fact, more than one entry for some nodes. These are in case there is a failure at the next node on a particular link, or a failure in the link itself. Consider, for example, node D receiving a packet which is intended for node A. The route table suggests that it should be transmitted on link 5. However, if it is unable to do this because link 5 or node E has failed, there is an alternative route via link 7 (or even link 4, though this would be a tortuous route to node A).

Table 14.1 Routing table for node D

Destination node	Link to transmit on	Alternatives	
A	5	7	4
B	7	8	5
C	8	7	4
D	*	*	*
E	5	7	8
F	4	8	–

If on receipt of a packet the node inspects the route table to see which link to retransmit it on and discovers a * entry, then clearly that packet is intended for the host attached to that node.

The route tables are organised manually, taking into account the lengths of the various links and the projected traffic on the links. The tables will then be loaded into each node just prior to the network being brought into operation. With the exception of alternative routes in case of failures, once the tables are loaded into each node the routing is fixed until there is some further manual intervention in the form of loading new route tables at each (or some) nodes. New tables can be introduced as new nodes are added to the network, nodes are removed, or some significant change in the traffic pattern becomes apparent. It is a relatively simple mechanism and can give good performance if the topology and traffic patterns do not change very much. If the traffic is very dynamic, however, then clearly this fixed routing mechanism is unable to adapt.

Adaptive routing—centralised

In order for the network to adapt to changes in traffic fairly rapidly, a mechanism for updating the route tables quickly is necessary. With a centralised system there will be one node somewhere in the network called the network control centre or the routing control centre. Each node in the network will periodically send some status information to this centre. The status information may include items such as a list of those adjacent nodes which appear to be working and to which its link is working, the size of queues of packets waiting to be transmitted on each link, the amount of traffic on each link since the last report. From all this information, the routing control centre will recompute the appropriate routes and generate and transmit new route tables to every node. Whilst this sounds as if it overcomes the problems inherent in fixed routing there are some significant disadvantages.

● To enable the network to adapt to changes in *topology* the process of updating the tables does not need to occur very often, in which case it may be an acceptable solution.

● However, to enable it to adapt to changes in *traffic* it will need to occur very often, particularly since overload conditions are likely to occur in bursts. For a large network, the time taken for all the information to reach the RCC, and for it to perform its calculations and return new route tables, may be such that the overload condition has cleared, i.e. the traffic pattern has changed completely.

● The transfer of status information from all nodes and the transmission of new route tables to all nodes is adding a considerable amount of extra traffic. Since the purpose of this mechanism is to reduce the effect of heavy traffic, the solution is in fact adding to the problems.

● If the RCC node fails then clearly the network is unable to adapt at all and will revert to a fixed route system with the existing route tables. However, those tables will be as a result of the last update, satisfying a particular set of traffic conditions, which may be less appropriate, generally, than the tables created in a genuine fixed routing system.

Adaptive routing—distributed

The problem with a centralised system is the considerable extra traffic generated, particularly in the vicinity of the RCC, and the significant delay in the updated routing tables arriving back at each node by which time the overload problems may have cleared.

A distributed system is one where a node updates its own table to reflect its own knowledge of its local traffic, queue sizes and failed links, and then sends a copy of this to each of its immediate neighbours, that is, those that

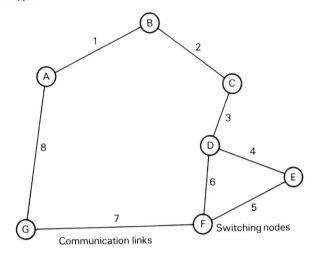

Figure 14.2

Table 14.2 Route table for node E

Destination node	Number of links	Via link
A	3	5
B	3	4
C	2	4
D	1	4
E	*	*
F	1	5
G	2	5

are only one link away. On receipt of a neighbour's table, a node will compare it with its own and for each entry retain the lower of the two values for each destination and update the transmit link entry. As this process is repeated by all the nodes in the network the current state of the network is propagated throughout.

As an example, consider the network in Figure 14.2 with the route table for node E shown in Table 14.2. This route table is based on recording simply the number of links to a destination node, in order to keep the example simple. Assume that node G fails. This will mean that shortly after, node E will receive a route table from node F as shown in Table 14.3(a) and from node D as shown in Table 14.3(b). Note that node D's table does not yet reflect the fact that G has failed. D is only just receiving the table from F that node E is just receiving.

Table 14.3(a) From node F

Destination node	Number of links	Via link
A	4	6
B	3	6
C	2	6
D	1	6
E	1	5
F	*	*
G	∞	–

Table 14.3(b) From node D

Destination node	Number of links	Via link
A	3	3
B	2	3
C	1	3
D	*	*
E	1	4
F	1	6
G	2	6

Node E can now compute an entry for each destination node. Considering just node A as an example, to go via link 5 (which is to node F) will now require a total of 5 links (1 to F plus the 4 that F now says it requires to get to A). However, the table from node D indicates that from D to A will only require 3 links, so node E computes it will only require 4 links from E to A via node D (link 4) and hence its entry for node A will now read:

Destination	No. of links	Via
A	4	4

This same calculation would of course be performed for all the other destination nodes.

Compared with the other routing methods discussed, this is certainly advantageous in that it is responsive to network changes and yet each node only communicates with its immediate neighbours. However, as a network grows in size, the routing tables become bigger and hence require more local memory, more bandwidth is used in order to send them to each other and more CPU time is consumed in calculating new tables. Eventually it will become too expensive for each node to have an entry for every other node and so the routing may be done in a hierarchical fashion as with the telephone network. Each group of nodes will only know the topology of that area. A routing table for a node in a particular area will have an entry for all nodes in that area but all nodes outside that area will be represented by one particular node so that all packets for the other areas are routed via that one node. For networks with a lot of communication within an area and occasional communication to other areas this is a very good compromise solution.

14.1.6 Congestion

Congestion is the situation where there is simply too much traffic for the network to cope. It may be caused for a variety of reasons, e.g. the buffer space may become full at a node, or packets arrive at a node much faster than it can transmit them on because an incoming line is faster than the outgoing line. Failures of nodes may also cause congestion. If a node goes down completely then this places a heavier burden on other parts of the network. It may fail, however, in a not so obvious way. Imagine, for example, that as a result of some error condition, a node suddenly decides that it can communicate with all other nodes in the network over zero links because the links column in its route table has become zeros. As this route table propagates throughout the network all other nodes will begin to direct their packets towards this particular node that is not, in fact, working properly.

At first sight, it may appear that the techniques of flow control, particularly the sliding window mechanism (section 13.3.3) will solve congestion. Remember that the window size is related to the amount of buffer storage available at a node. Although it has a contribution to make it does not solve the problem. Remember that a node in a network will be receiving packets from a number of other nodes. If the window size for each incoming link was such that there was always buffer space for a full window for every link, then although congestion could not occur, it will be at the expense of throughput because most of the time much of the buffer space will be empty. In order to give good performance most of the time, networks are designed for average traffic. This is analogous to the banking system which will allow you to withdraw your cash at any time, but if everyone went to the bank on the same day to withdraw all their cash, the bank would be unable to meet the demand.

There have been techniques suggested to handle the problem of congestion although they will not be discussed here. Suffice it to indicate that if congestion occurs the performance (throughput) of the network drops considerably until the congestion eases.

14.1.7 Point-to-point local area networks

Although most local area networks are based on the broadcast principle (see sections 14.2.2 and 14.2.3) there is one type of LAN based on a point-to-point *star* topology. This usually uses a private automatic branch exchange (PABX). A PABX system is the private switching centre installed in an organisation to provide telephone switching between the various telephone extensions around that organisation. It is now very common for that PABX system to be a computer and to use digital switching and transmission throughout that telephone network, sometimes called a PDX (private digital exchange). This means that the communication paths can be used to carry both voice and data so that a workstation might incorporate a local processor, a data communication facility (allowing electronic mail, for example) and voice communication. Since the voice communication will be digitised it could be stored for the receiver to retrieve it at a later time.

This is an attractive solution for a local area network within an organisation since it does not mean additional cabling. It does, of course, suffer the usual drawbacks of star networks: if the exchange fails so does the network, and the exchange may be a bottleneck if the volume of traffic becomes very large.

14.2 Broadcast networks

Chapter 11 (section 11.3.2) introduced the concept of broadcast networks and the most common topologies. Remember that broadcast networks use a channel to which all the users are connected, so all the users receive any transmission made on the channel. The only wide area broadcast networks all use radio broadcast, either relatively local up to a few hundred kilometres or much further distances using satellite transmission. Section 14.2.1 will examine this further. The most common examples of broadcast networks are local area networks. These may use twisted pair cables, coaxial cable or optical fibre cable as their transmission medium (see section 12.6). Comparison between twisted pair and coaxial cable is not helpful because there are many variants of each to meet the different requirements of bandwidth, loss, noise immunity, etc. In general, coaxial cable has higher noise immunity and bandwidth, but the cable is stiffer (which may or may not be helpful depending on whether it is being surface mounted or pushed through ducts). However, both types can adequately serve most LAN environments. Optical fibres are particularly suited to environments which have high levels of electromagnetic radiation, or to meet demands for very high speeds of transmission. However, it is more difficult to tap into, which makes it more difficult and expensive for the installation of a LAN. The most common forms of LAN will be also discussed further.

14.2.1 Radio and satellite broadcasting

Radio and satellite broadcast networks have one thing in common: a fairly high bandwidth communication channel which is shared between all the users.

This channel could be shared by using similar techniques for sharing a line (see section 12.5). Frequency division multiple access divides the bandwidth of the channel into non-overlapping subchannels. Each station is assigned a separate subchannel. Thus, each station uses a dedicated portion of the whole channel at all times. The difficulty with this is twofold.

First the limit on the number of stations determined by the number of subchannels that the channel can be divided into, and secondly the wasted bandwidth when some channel may not be transmitting. Time division multiple access permits each station to transmit in non-overlapping time slots. Each station is assigned a time slot, so that at any time only one station is transmitting. Again, if a station is not wishing to transmit, that bandwidth is wasted. In both these cases stations are penalised if there is only light loading on the network, because large parts of the bandwidth are unused.

A different approach would be to assume it is a single channel and allow any station to transmit at any time. However, if two or more stations transmit simultaneously their transmissions will interfere with each other so some mechanism is necessary for handling this.

The simplest technique is called *pure aloha*. The name *aloha* is used because it is based on a technique first developed at the University of Hawaii for a broadcast network using local radio transmission. With this technique, if a node has a packet to transmit, it does so immediately. It is then required to wait for an acknowledgement. If such an acknowledgement is not received within a time-out period, the packet is assumed lost and the packet is retransmitted after a random time. The packet will probably have been lost due to a collision with transmission from another node and hence they must retransmit after a random time to prevent exactly the same thing happening again. The system is simple but as the volume of traffic increases, so does the number of collisions and hence the productive use of the bandwidth decreases.

Slotted aloha is where the transmission channel time is divided into time slots of equal length. Each node is only allowed to transmit a packet at the start of a time slot, so that if a collision occurs only that time slot of the bandwidth is wasted. This will increase the usage of the overall bandwidth.

Clearly, the problem that the above schemes are trying to overcome is that of collisions. An improvement which avoids many (but not all) possible collisions is known as carrier sense multiple access (CSMA). Here, each node will listen to the channel and detect a carrier signal indicating that a transmission is taking place. A node is only allowed to transmit if nothing is being transmitted currently. This does not completely solve the problem since in the time between deciding there is nothing being transmitted, and starting to transmit, another node may do exactly the same, so that these will then subsequently collide, although it is a big improvement on the *aloha* techniques. The CSMA technique, however, can only be used with a radio network, not a satellite, because of the considerable delay with the latter between transmitting and receiving due to the very long transmission distances involved.

There are a number of mechanisms that have been proposed and used for satellite communication, the most successful of which are schemes that use an *aloha* mechanism for low channel utilisation (little traffic) and move gradually over to some kind of time division mechanism as the channel traffic increases.

14.2.2 Bus-based LANs

With a bus-based local area network the nodes are attached to a continuous bus and contend with each other for the use of this bus to transfer messages. The best known example of such a network is known as *Ethernet* and was originally developed by Xerox. Figure 14.3 shows an Ethernet network. The bus itself is usually coaxial cable. A computer is attached to the bus by a device known as a transceiver, which is responsible for transmitting and receiving to and from the bus. As a message is transmitted onto the bus it will propagate in both directions along the bus and every other node will receive it. By examining the contents of a header included within the message the transceiver can either pass the message to the attached computer or ignore it, depending on the destination address.

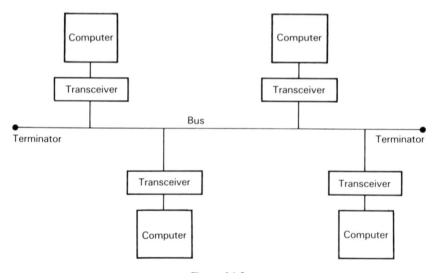

Figure 14.3

Both ends of the bus are terminated by a special terminator, which prevents the signals being reflected back down the cable causing interference.

Because any computer can transmit to any other at any time there needs to be a mechanism to control the contention for the line. In Ethernet this mechanism is known as CSMA/CD – carrier sense multiple access with collision detection—and is carried out by the transceiver. Basically, this means that before a node can begin to transmit, it has to 'listen' to the bus to see if anything is already being transmitted. It can detect this by the presence of a carrier signal (hence the name carrier sense—multiple access simply means that there are a number of nodes attached to this bus). If there is something already being transmitted it will wait for a period of time and try again. If, however, nothing is currently being transmitted, the transceiver will send its message onto the bus. However, there may be a pair (or more) of nodes which, at more or less the same time, decide nothing is being transmitted and so begin to transmit. Clearly these simultaneous transmissions will corrupt each other, and a 'collision' is said to have occurred. In order to recover from such a situation the transceivers operate as follows. As a transceiver is transmitting a message onto the bus, it will also receive what is propagating along the bus. If it is the same as it is transmitting there is no problem. If, however, it is not the same then it has detected a collision. In this case it will stop transmitting (it is said to 'backoff') and will try again after a random time period. This time period is random so that the colliding stations do not simply try again at the same time.

Figure 14.4 illustrates the layout of a message in Ethernet. The preamble consists of eight bytes of alternating bits, 010101 . . ., which allows the receiver to synchronise. The start frame delimiter indicates the start of a frame. The destination and source addresses indicate the node for which the message is intended and the node from which the message has come respectively. In Ethernet these address fields may be either 16, or 48 bits long. One particular address, say all 1s, may be used to indicate that the message is intended for *all* nodes, so that a message can be truly broadcast to all nodes. The length field identifies the length of the following data field, since this is allowed to be of variable length. The checksum is a 32-bit CRC check value based on all fields including the addresses.

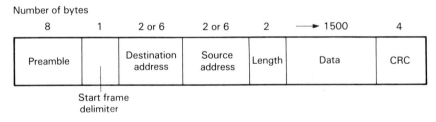

Figure 14.4

Although the CRC check allows a receiver to check receipt of a valid message there is no confirmation to the sender (an acknowledgement) of receipt and so this and other protocol features must be built into a higher level protocol. These higher level software protocols will be implemented in the nodes and will use the data portion of the Ethernet message or packet for fields appropriate to these protocols. Note that the data field of a message may be up to 1500 bytes long. This would make Ethernet well suited to the transmission of long files between nodes. With long messages, the utilisation of the bus can be quite high because there will be few collisions (remember the carrier sense mechanism avoids many collisions which might otherwise occur). However, long messages prevent other communication between nodes taking place (it is therefore difficult to guarantee any sort of message delivery time, or response to message time) and also require large buffers for sending and receiving.

Ethernet, although originating from Xerox, has since been promoted by a consortium consisting of DEC, Intel and Xerox. It transmits at a speed of 10 M bits per second, and interfaces are available for many different computers.

There are many other commercially available bus networks based on the Ethernet principle. Many are available more cheaply than Ethernet due to their lower transmission speed, the omission of the collision detection mechanism so that they rely on the higher level protocol to notice the non-delivery of messages, or because the transceiver/interface is dedicated to one particular model of computer making it much simpler.

14.2.3 Ring based LANs

A ring based LAN consists of a number of nodes each connected to its own repeater. The repeaters are then linked together by the communication medium (typically twisted pair cables or coaxial cable, although fibre optics are being developed) in the form of a complete ring. The repeaters pass on serial data from one link to the next and also allow the attached node to read the information as it passes. The repeaters take their power from the ring itself so that they are independent of whether a particular node is powered up or not. Figure 14.5 illustrates the general layout.

There are, however, two main strategies for managing the access to this ring network. These are known as a *token ring*, which is the basis for IBM's local area networks, and the *slotted ring*, developed by Cambridge University and more commonly known as the Cambridge ring.

Token rings

A unique bit pattern called the 'token' continuously circulates the ring while no station requires to send a message. When a repeater station is instructed by its attached node to transmit a message to another node on the ring, the station must wait for the token to pass through its repeater.

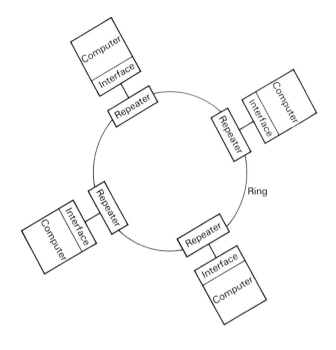

Figure 14.5

When the token is recognised the station alters one of its bits, say from 1 to 0, so that the token is no longer available to any other station. The station then sends its message, which may be of variable length, on to the ring. The message or packet format will include the destination node's address and as the packet passes through each repeater on the ring that station will examine this destination address to see if the packet is for it. If so it will read the message. If not it will ignore it. When the packet arrives back at the sending station, the sender is required to reinstate the token onto the ring so that the next station downstream may use the ring.

Notice that there is no contention as in Ethernet to use the communication medium. The right to use the ring passes in a round-robin fashion from one node to the next in sequence. Hence, if there is a limit to the size of the packet then a guarantee of response time can be given to communication over the ring based on the worst case condition of every node using its right to send a maximum sized packet in turn. This may be important in control situations, such as process control.

Clearly, the system is dependent on the token not being corrupted. If it was (a bit changed, for example) then the ring simply would not operate. To counteract this there are two possible solutions. One is to incorporate a

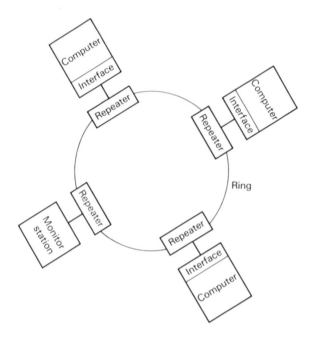

Figure 14.6

special node, called a *monitor* station, into the ring. This is responsible for generating the token, and checking for its presence. It does this by employing a timer which is started whenever the token passes its repeater. The initial value of the timer is chosen to correspond to the expected maximum time between consecutive tokens, whether free or busy. Should a time-out occur, an error has occurred. The monitor station will then reinstate the token, and perform an error logging function.

An alternative to the monitor station is to distribute this function to every station on the ring. Every station will have a time-out period during which it will expect to see a token. There has to be some arbitration mechanism to prevent more than one station putting a token back on the ring.

Slotted rings (Cambridge ring)

The best example of a slotted ring system is the one which originated at the University of Cambridge, although there are now commercial ones available 'off the shelf'. Its topology is very similar to that of the token ring except that it does incorporate a monitor station. Such a ring is illustrated in Figure 14.6.

The monitor station is responsible for placing the slot(s) onto the ring on power up. A slot is essentially a 40-bit mini-packet. The reason why mini-packets are so short (and of fixed length) is that only a relatively few bits can be accommodated round the ring, particularly when there are only a few attached stations. In fact it may be possible only to have one circulating slot, and even then it may be necessary to use a shift register in the monitor station to lengthen the ring artificially.

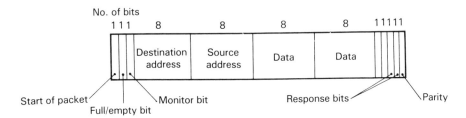

Figure 14.7

Figure 14.7 illustrates the structure of a mini-packet. The full/empty bit signifies whether that slot contains valid data or not. If it is empty, a station can insert two data bytes and the addressing information, mark it as full and send it onto the ring. If it is full a station can merely examine the address field to see if it is a mini-packet being sent to it. When a sending station receives a mini-packet back it is obliged to mark it as empty and send it on, so that again, use of that slot passes in a round-robin fashion from one node to the next in sequence. Since each mini-packet can only contain two bytes of data, the bandwidth of the communication channel is being shared out very fairly over all the nodes.

The response bits in the mini-packet are used to implement low level acknowledgements. On transmission, these bits are set to 11. Receiving stations alter the response bits according to whether they are prepared to accept mini-packets from any source, from one particular source or not at all, as follows:

11 destination absent (e.g. not powered up)
01 mini-packet accepted
10 destination deaf to this source
00 destination busy

Higher level software protocols are required to be built on top of the mini-packet ring service so that the attached nodes can communicate without having to know the details of the ring operation. On top of the mini-packet layer is a 'basic block' protocol which deals with packets of variable length (similar to the Ethernet packet). Above the packet protocol is a 'byte stream' protocol which incorporates flow control by the inclusion of request and acknowledge commands, and sequence numbers in each packet so that lost or repeated packets can be detected. This might incorporate a virtual circuit service or a datagram service (see 14.1.4).

In addition to inserting empty slot(s) on power up, the monitor station is also used to monitor error conditions. If a particular station never marked a packet it had used as empty then the ring would be unusable. The monitor bit in the mini-packet is used by the monitor station to detect and remove such erroneous mini-packets. It is cleared by a transmitting station and set when it passes through the monitor. Any mini-packets reaching the monitor station with the monitor bit already set are marked as empty. Error detection is aided by the use of a parity bit which is set for even parity at each station and checked by the next station down stream. Breaks in the ring can be detected because the first bit in each mini-packet is always a 1, so an unbroken sequence of 0s cannot occur normally.

One drawback with the Cambridge ring is the high overhead of the mini-packet protocol. Only 16 bits out of the 40 carry data. Hence for a ring operating at a transmission speed of, say, 10 MHz, the actual data rate is a maximum of 4 MHz.

However, the fact remains that the big advantage of ring networks over bus networks is their guarantee of a node being able to transmit within a known maximum time, making them more applicable to real time applications, including voice transmission.

14.3 Summary

The issues concerned in the network layer of the ISO reference model have been introduced. With point-to-point networks, these include the principle of switching and the subsequent problems of routing and congestion.

Local area networks, most of which are of the broadcast type, present different problems and the most common types have been described.

This book has traced the structure of a computer system right through from basic logic concepts from which fundamental circuits can be constructed, through the many details of typical structures of a computer and on to sets of connected, communicating computers.

However, do not think that you now know all about computer architecture and communication. Many of the topics included here have only been introduced and in some cases are considerably more complex than appears. You can also be sure that it will not be long before some new ideas and techniques are introduced in order to improve the service a computer system might provide.

14.4 Problems

(1) In a multiple node communications network describe how a packet is routed from its source DTE to its destination DTE. What is the difference between flow control and congestion?

Explain the need for a routing strategy and discuss the advantages and disadvantages of:
  (a) fixed routing;
  (b) centralised adaptive routing;
  (c) distributed adaptive routing.

(2) (a) Explain to which layer(s) of the ISO reference model you would relate LANs, summarising the functions of your chosen layers.
  (b) Compare and contrast Ethernet and Cambridge ring LANs, indicating the strengths and weaknesses of each.

(3) Explain the principle of packet switching and distinguish between the two major types of service provided on a PSDN, namely datagrams and virtual circuits.

(4) Refer to the network shown in Figure 14.2 and assume that node G has just failed. Show how this information propagates through the network and generate the new route table for every node.

(5) Ten thousand airline booking offices are competing for the use of a single slotted *aloha* channel. Each office makes on average 20 requests per hour. A slot is 90 microseconds. What is the average channel load?

(6) Distinguish between a token ring and a slotted ring indicating the advantages and disadvantages of each.

(7) Investigate your local LAN to discover what principle of operation it uses, and the details of its data transfer rate, its error detection mechanisms, and the protocols it uses.

Index

The starred page numbers indicate the main explanatory introduction for those items which are referenced more than once.